IN SEARCH OF JUSTICE IN THAILAND'S DEEP SOUTH

STUDIES IN RELIGION AND CULTURE

John D. Barbour and Gary L. Ebersole, Editors

IN SEARCH OF JUSTICE IN THAILAND'S DEEP SOUTH

Malay Muslim and Thai Buddhist Women's Narratives

Edited by John Clifford Holt

Compiled by Soraya Jamjuree

Translated by Hara Shintaro

University of Virginia Press • *Charlottesville and London*

University of Virginia Press
© 2022 by the Rector and Visitors of the University of Virginia
All rights reserved
Printed in the United States of America on acid-free paper

First published 2022

1 3 5 7 9 8 6 4 2

Library of Congress Cataloging-in-Publication Data

Names: Holt, John, editor. | Jamjuree, Soraya, compiler. | Shintaro, Hara, translator.
Title: In search of justice in Thailand's deep south : Malay Muslim and Thai Buddhist
women's narratives / edited by John Clifford Holt ; compiled by Soraya Jamjuree ;
translated by Hara Shintaro.
Description: Charlottesville : University of Virginia Press, 2022. | Series: Studies in
religion and culture | "The narratives comprising this book were selected among many
others first published in two pocketbooks entitled Voices of Hope and Behind the
Smile"—Preface. | Includes bibliographical references and index.
Identifiers: LCCN 2022026750 (print) | LCCN 2022026751 (ebook) | ISBN 9780813948737
(hardcover) | ISBN 9780813948744 (paperback) | ISBN 9780813948751 (ebook)
Subjects: LCSH: Ethnic conflict—Thailand, Southern. | Political violence—Thailand,
Southern. | Muslim women—Thailand, Southern—Social conditions. | Buddhist
women—Thailand, Southern—Social conditions. | Victims of political violence—
Thailand, Southern. | Insurgency—Thailand, Southern. | Religion and politics—
Thailand, Southern. | Political violence—Religious aspects—Buddhism. | Political
violence—Religious aspects—Islam. | Thailand, Southern—Social conditions. |
Thailand, Southern—Politics and government.
Classification: LCC DS588. S68 I57 2022 (print) | LCC DS588.S68 (ebook) |
DDC 305.6/94309593—dc23/eng/20220714
LC record available at https://lccn.loc.gov/2022026750
LC ebook record available at https://lccn.loc.gov/2022026751

Cover art: Batik fabric created by Asdiana Hasa. (Photo by Soraya Jamjuree)

Dedicated to the memory of all innocent persons
who have lost their lives
in the "Southern Border Conflict" of Thailand's Deep South

CONTENTS

TRANSLATOR'S NOTE

Even though more than seven thousand people have been killed since the latest eruption of sustained violence began in early 2004, the ethno-religious conflict in the southern border provinces of Thailand, or the region more traditionally known within the Muslim community as Patani, is hardly known to the outside world. Apart from some notorious incidents, such as the massacre in the Kru Se Mosque, or the tragic deaths of seventy-eight suspected insurgents who suffocated while being transported from Tak Bai in 2004, or the sporadic occurrence of very significant bombings, incidents related to the insurgency in this region rarely attract serious attention from international media. Not well noticed is the fact that many people continue to be "sacrificed" (read: "killed") in small-scale bombings and shootings, although the intensity of the conflict has abated somewhat for the last several years.

After the inauguration of the peace dialogue process in 2013, the public began to learn much more about the perpetrators of the insurgency. But the nature of the conflict itself between the omnipresent state military forces and the shadowy clandestine underground armed groups, including BRN (Barisan Revolusi Nasional, or the National Revolutionary Front), which is the most influential one, still remains the same. Thailand has experienced two military coups since the outbreak of the conflict, but the fundamental way the government handles the situation has never really changed. Bangkok has attempted to control the unfolding circumstances through local deployments of its military, which enforces draconian special measures including martial law and an emergency decree. These special powers have been imposed on the area of conflict since early 2004, allowing the military to cast a wide net of constraint and to detain suspects arbitrarily. Allegations of torture and the misuse of power have been consistently voiced. The daily reminder of ever-present checkpoints shrouds the region with an oppressive pall.

Under such circumstances, the local population, nearly 80 percent Muslim, have spent their daily lives amid a persistent and menacing fear for their safety. On one side, there are invisible insurgents who seem to be able to stage violent incidents wherever and whenever they choose; on the other side, the omnipresence of the state military that can detain the local population (so far, all the detainees have been Muslims) without any warrant or due cause. People are afraid to speak up, for fear of being either attacked by the insurgents or detained by the state's military. As a result, the safest way, according to the understanding of the local people, is just to shut up, to utter nothing that might cause any further trouble, even if they are severely affected in this conflict by one side or the other.

Unlike in other conflict contexts in which nonstate actors have some control over at least a portion of their liberated areas, in the southern border provinces of Thailand, or Patani, there is not even a single square inch of liberated area. Occupying a piece of land and using it as a stronghold is not the strategy of the insurgents in this region. They have been staging countless small-scale violent attacks for more than a decade by hiding themselves under a shadowy cover.

The only voices often heard in the conflict area are those blatantly delivering the slogans of state propaganda, or opinions in line with them, mixed with sounds of guns and bombs (which are mainly improvised explosive devices, IEDs). Apart from those who have been killed, there are many other kinds of victims, including tens of thousands of those who have been injured and handicapped, several hundred orphans, and those who have lost family members. Apart from this, due to the deployment of draconian special laws, and due to the enervated and often incompetent system of justice,[1] many local Muslims have been arrested, detained, or even imprisoned for almost no cause. Some of them lose their lives during detention, and many of them are tortured. Dozens of people also have been forcibly disappeared since 2004.

Therefore, those victims, no matter if they are victims of violent incidents, victims of injustice, or if they have lost their family members, have been the most challenged in getting their voices heard in this region.

The narratives contained in this book are the very rarely heard voices of those victims, solicited and compiled by Sorya Jamjuree's women's activist network. All but a few of the narratives were recorded or edited by those mentors, who approached the victims and listened to their voices. These mentors mainly consist of young female activists; they are not professional writers. In addition, the focus of some of these writings is on documenting the healing measures of the activities organized by the women's network. Consequently, many of the victims are not able to completely open up. It is difficult to sensitively approach victims of a conflict in a way that encourages them to talk about their own extremely traumatic experiences.

As for the technical aspects of the translation, several factors caused difficulties. For instance, the linguistic differences between Malay and Thai and English presented manifold challenges. Thai has many words that are neutral in terms of gender for children, nephews and nieces, cousins, uncles and aunts, etc. In these stories, there were sometimes few indicators regarding gender. For example, there is no such word in the Thai language for "nephew" or "niece." Moreover, the same word is used to refer to "grand-children." At the same time, if someone says "my *larn*," we cannot be sure if the reference is to the singular or plural. The term *larn* in general means "child" or "sibling." In some cases, I knew the authors personally and contacted them to ask them questions, but in other instances there was no way to know for sure.

The nature of the writing itself also presents challenges to translation. Some authors may have been so overwhelmed by their emotions that their stories primarily concern their feelings rather than conveying information that could be more useful to readers seeking a nuanced view of the various issues in play. Some narratives contain many incomplete sentences or sentences that are too long to be literally translated. Interpreting these texts presented an extra degree of difficulty in translation.

Nevertheless, these factors do not impair the value of this book, which offers one of the very few opportunities to listen to victims' voices attentively. In the following narratives, readers might encounter several euphemistic expressions such as "those who are affected by the conflict" instead of "victims"; "those who have different opinions" instead of "insurgents"; "remedy" instead of "compensation"; "incidents" instead of "massacres," etc. These expressions clearly reflect a deep-rooted hesitancy on the part of victims to give voice to what is actually going on in their minds, or what has happened objectively in real time and space.

Although many books and academic articles have been written on the problems of southern border provinces (or Patani)[2] in English, Malay, and Thai, with some of them touching upon the impact of the conflict, very few have been able to address the victims' personal experiences. Thus, the following narratives offer very rare snapshots of the ongoing conflict of this region, which occurs, ultimately, on a personal level. My hope is that this volume is but the very first step in an effort to ensure that victims' voices are heard and heeded by the outside world.

HARA SHINTARO
Patani, Thailand

Notes

1. Here, again, Duncan McCargo's recent book about judicial incompetence has great salience. He notes that Thailand, despite its population of around 60 million people, has the sixth-largest prison population in the world, the third-highest percentage of its population behind bars, and its conviction rate on charges brought about by Thai authorities is a stunning 95 percent (see his *Fighting for Virtue: Justice and Politics in Thailand* [Ithaca, NY: Cornell University Press, 2020]).—*Editor*

2. Again, but just to amplify, "Patani" with one *t* refers to the entire conflict area of the Deep South of Thailand, which is roughly equivalent to the territory of the Patani Kingdom, or Sultanate, that existed before it was demolished and annexed by the Thai king Rama I in the late eighteenth century. "Pattani" with two *t*'s is used for the name of one of the provinces within this same region and the city that is the administrative center of the province. In general, "Patani" is used in literature written in Malay, whereas in Thai literature, as well as in official Thai documents, "Pattani" is used.

PREFACE

This is a book about victims who sometimes become victors. It is primarily about the lives of mothers, wives, daughters, and victims of their families (mostly fathers, husbands, and sons). It is a book about how lives have been impacted by seventeen years of violent conflict in the southern border provinces of Thailand, a conflict that is centuries old, but one that has accelerated extraordinarily since 2004. Since that time, more than 7,500 lives have been lost and more than 13,000 people have been injured. In addition, the social, economic, and psychological well-being of tens of thousands of people have been seriously impaired by "security cases" advanced by the draconian enforcement of special laws issued by the Thai government, that is, declarations of martial law and an emergency decree.

The narratives comprising this book were selected among many others first published in two pocketbooks entitled *Voices of Hope* and *Behind the Smile*.[1] These booklets were published in the Thai language through efforts of the civil society organization, The Civic Women's Network for Peace in the Southern Border Provinces (hereafter: Civic Women's Network). In this volume, the narratives selected have been translated from Thai into English by Hara Shintaro and then edited and adapted by John Clifford Holt. The publication of this book amplifies these women's voices that, although heard previously in very limited circles, will now be able to be heard by a wider community that is international in scope.

The Civic Women's Network is a civil society organization comprised of female volunteers working for the empowerment of women through providing humanitarian aid, especially assistance and remedies for victims of armed conflict in the southern border provinces of Thailand. Since the eruption of violence in 2004, the Civic Women's Network has worked especially in the field of public communication to provide spaces for the otherwise voiceless women in victims' families to speak out about the difficult challenges they have encountered.

Most of the authors of the narratives contained in this book are also victims of the conflict themselves. They joined the activities of the Civic Women's Network that were designed to empower them to face up squarely to the crises that had impacted their lives. Some of them even transformed themselves from victims to victors, in some instances becoming prominent agents of social change who, in turn, have been eventually rightly acknowledged and acclaimed publicly by Thai society.

The Civic Women's Network has tried to establish a climate of trust. When asked by the Civic Women's Network to tell their own stories publicly, these women did not hesitate to do so, although they had to summon a great deal of courage to transcend their own zones of safety. Many of them chose to tell their own stories very openly, even though at an earlier time they had decided to keep these stories reserved within the quiet privacy of their battered hearts.

This book is special insofar as all of the narrative firsthand accounts document a victim's actual experience. They are fresh, vivid, and interesting in their own rights. Some are dramatic and compelling, reading like a short story or a novella.

Behind the scenes, we faced many challenges in bringing these narratives to publication, and neither was compiling this book an easy task. Nevertheless, I want to stress how these women who had suffered directly or indirectly from violence had to shift from despair and silence to standing up in public, putting tears aside to tell the truth about how they, their families, and their communities have experienced discrimination and injustice. Although for some, tears had somewhat dried because these incidents had happened years ago, the experience of reliving them, of recalling bitter memories in detail, the very memories that they had tried to forget, proved difficult indeed. Narrating their personal experiences meant confronting and coping with pain and deep bitterness once again.

Communicating through writing also proved difficult for some, because writing is a complicated skill, and it is understood by some as work accomplished by intellectuals. For the victims who are ordinary villagers, writing just one paragraph or two to three lines, let alone an entire story, often seemed beyond their abilities, even though these stories were about their own experiences. In addition, in the midst of their writing, the security situation in the Deep South has remained tense, and the atmosphere often teems with terror and suspicion emanating from both sides of the conflict. Remaining silent and saying nothing is often the best strategy for people in the conflict areas to secure their own relative safety, especially for those who have gone through horrific experiences. Thus, their decisions to stand up and tell their stories frankly required courage. Many women, especially those who had been directly affected by "security cases," and thereby often stigmatized by society, requested the use of noms de plume because they still feel unsafe, not prepared to identify themselves in public. But in the end, most of the women decided to use their own real names and present themselves openly to society. They have told their own stories truthfully about how they were treated, how they dealt with consequent burdens, and how they struggled to overcome the deleterious effects of the "incidents" they had experienced. In order to overcome some of challenges presented in the writing process, the Civic Women's Network organized several training sessions. These included efforts at psychological empowerment to enhance self-confidence and affirm competencies, as well as training in the art of narrative writing.

To abet the writing process in particular, the Civic Women's Network also made available trusted mentors. These mentors gave advice on writing (if the women had written their stories independently) or documented the stories (if they could not write at all), and conducted initial rounds of editing before these writings were sent to the editor of the earlier Thai publications, Thitinob Komolnimi, an author and editor with wide knowledge about the southern border provinces, especially with regard to gender issues. For each narrative, we have appended the names of mentors who assisted.

During armed conflicts, conflicting parties are the most powerful actors, holding the power of life and death over the rest of the people in the conflict area. Their loud voices dominate and are suffused throughout the entire region. Other actors are often nameless and voiceless, the victims especially so. Their stories are rarely picked up by the mainstream media, and they only appear among numbers in statistics. Even if their stories are taken up, they are always treated as passive actors with sad stories that call out for sympathy only. But the women whose narratives are collected in this book, despite whatever hardships they have faced, have chosen to send out their messages; they have refused to be silenced. No longer passive, they want to prove that they can stand up as active forces and demand justice.

This book amplifies their muted voices so that their names are not erased from history. These women are agents who have regained self-confidence, asserted their values, recovered their human dignity, and summoned a power that had once vanished when they became victims.

I would like to express my gratitude to organizations that have supported the Civic Women's Network and the local publication of the aforementioned Thai editions, out of which the narratives contained herein have been selected and translated expertly into English by Hara Shintaro. These organizations include the Office of Academic Extension and Services of Prince of Songkla University (Pattani Campus); Oxfam; aid offices of the European Union; and the United Nations Democracy Fund. Funds for the translations comprising the current book in English have been provided through a faculty research fund at the University of Chicago.

SORAYA JAMJUREE
Pattani, Thailand

Note

1. *Voices of Hope: Stories of Women for the Peace Process in the Southern Border Provinces* is a translation of the Thai title เรื่องเล่าของผู้หญิงเพื่อกระบวนการสันติภาพ ภายแดนใต้, edited by Thitinob Komalnimi and published by the Office of Academic Extension and Services, Prince of Songkla University (Pattani Campus) in 2012 (ISBN 978-616-271-086-5). *Behind the Smiles: Stories of Recovering People and Communities in the Southern Border Provinces* is a translation of the Thai title หลัง รอย ยิ้ม : เรื่องเล่าเพื่อพลิกฟื้นตัวตนและชุมชนชายแดนใต้, edited by Thitinob Komalnimi and published by the Office of Academic Extension and Services, Prince of Songkla University (Pattani Campus) in 2016 (ISBN 978-616-271-382-8).

INTRODUCTION

Soraya Jamjuree, who compiled the narratives for this volume, stresses how this book is primarily about resilient women who have rebounded from profound personal tragedies to find their voices, voices that demand justice and peace. As Soraya points out, many of these women have been transformed by bravely coping with the challenges of their travails, enduring grave psychological, social, and economic turmoil while suffering the loss of a husband, father, son, or brother. In his introductory remarks, Hara Shintaro, our expert translator, stresses how rare it is in Thai society for the voices of these women, especially Muslim women's voices, to be heard. Our intention in publishing this book is to amplify their voices. Seventeen of the narratives in this volume have been written by women, while the three written by men are largely about the distress suffered by their wives and families. Fifteen stories are written by Malay Muslims and five by Thai Buddhists, roughly parallel to the percentage of Muslims and Buddhists living in the Deep South.

In this introduction, I will briefly outline important moments of the historical background and identify key issues of the Thai Buddhist/Malay Muslim conflict that are in play today, before proceeding to spotlight how Islam and Buddhism have functioned as refuges and legitimation scenarios, and how these religious orientations have strengthened the capacities for these victimized women to understand their suffering in the face of daunting existential intimidation.

While emphasis is given to the constructive role of religion in the lives of these women, it is also understood that religion is a double-edged sword capable of inspiring the most sublime moments in human culture, as well helping to legitimate some of the most heinous. Buddhism and Islam are not exceptions to this bipolar religious world of possibilities. In the southern border conflict in Thailand, expressions motivated by religious convictions occupy both ends of the spectrum.

Although members of both Buddhist and Muslim communities have inflicted violence on the other, the rise of Buddhist militancy victimizing Muslim communities strikes most Euro-American observers as puzzling. It

Thailand and Thailand's Deep South. (Map created by Samuel Erick Holt)

almost goes without saying that common understandings often articulated in the Euro-American West profile Buddhists as peace-loving, meditative, if not otherworldly seekers of spiritual pursuit. Buddhism has been read as a religion that consummately represents forces of pacifism and gentility. Such a benign and uncritical profile, however, is in part a creation of the Western imagination, derived from selective emphases abstracted from sections of textual Theravada Pali or Mahayana canonical sources first by nineteenth-century European orientalist scholars and then later taken up by Western spiritual seekers who were attracted to this beautifully imagined ideal, especially if they could not find repose within their own religious cultures.[1] Muslims, on the other hand—often branded through Islamophobic renderings engendered initially by centuries of confrontation with Christianity in Europe, and now more recently by the assertions of aggressive radical movements such as al-Qaeda, ISIS, and the Taliban emanating out of Afghanistan and the Middle East, are imagined in almost a polar opposite manner as Buddhists: as uncompromising militants intent on establishing an international reactionary Islamic civilization whose character stands in express juxtaposition to the egalitarian norms of civilized Western society. Such commonly held monolithic depictions of both communities respectively, of course, are very piecemeal at best, and, on the whole, somewhat uninformed. Most people who have lived recently in the Theravada Buddhist–dominated cultural regions of Sri Lanka and Southeast Asia, or have studied the social, cultural, and political history of the region in some depth, know this very well. Not only is the history of the region marked by some notable instances of violent conflict between competing Buddhist kingships or rival religious communities, but in today's world, as in the past, various Buddhists and Muslims might occupy any ideological position (reactionary, conservative, liberal, or revolutionary) across the spectra of religious and political cultures. (While living in Sri Lanka for many years, for instance, I came to see that virtually every political party, from far left to far right, attracted a stable of monastic incumbents who would publicly support their causes.) At the same time, those who have gained a measure of understanding social history in Theravada Buddhist cultural regions also know that, in spite of periodic communal battles, various Buddhist and Muslim communities, more often than not, have lived amicably in concord, rather than in discord, over many centuries, in specific locales. Unfortunately, that some Buddhists are now perpetrators of violence and intolerance, victimizing relatively innocent Muslims living in their midst, has become a depressing aspect of recent political culture in the Buddhist-dominated countries of Sri Lanka, Myanmar, and Thailand. Violent attacks perpetrated by radicalized Muslim insurgents in the Deep South also contribute to an understanding in which Islam and violence are inextricably linked.

Historical and Comparative Contexts

The current, ongoing relatively low-intensity conflict between the Thai Buddhist state and Malay Muslim insurgents in the Deep South of Thailand, known in past centuries as the Muslim enclave of Patani,[2] is but a new chapter in centuries of history reflecting sometimes acrimonious but more often salutary relations between Buddhists and Muslims. Eruptions of sustained violence have been periodic historical events, despite recent efforts from some historically minded revisionists on both sides of the divide to paint the other as a constant threatening menace. Nonetheless, the recent violence between the Thai Buddhist state and Malay Muslim insurgents remains a very serious problem, and although there have been watershed moments of violence between these communities in the centuries past, particularly in the late eighteenth century and the first decade of the twenty-first century, anthropological and historical studies have determined how, in areas where Buddhists and Muslims have regularly shared the land and village life, they have mixed, mated, and often learned from and supported each other over the long term.[3] This social reality is also clearly substantiated in a few of the narratives we've selected, as well as shared lamentations about currently strained relations that have resulted from violent actions from both sides of the divide.

The narratives that we selected also testify that, though violence has been generated from both sides of the Buddhist/Muslim conflict, the actions undertaken by armed forces of the Thai Buddhist state often do not measure up favorably to what might be expected of a government that ostensibly claims to adhere to international standards respecting and protecting civil and human rights.[4] As many of the narratives attest, during the past two decades, the Thai government's military violence and repression, including an unstated and publicly denied policy of torture, have often served as a catalyst for the increased motivation of those Muslims who have been recruited to insurgency. These narratives document instances not only of military and police abuse but also egregious judicial incompetence,[5] especially regarding the long-term detainment of suspected but ultimately proven innocent Muslims.

As in Sri Lanka and Myanmar, where Muslim communities have also been seriously abused recently, one is hard-pressed to find any specifically Theravada Buddhist doctrinal rationale for the violence that the Thai Buddhist state has engaged in against Malay Muslims in the Deep South. However, Buddhist monks and temples have been periodically enlisted to assist the Thai army's mission to control, contain, or eradicate forces deemed inimical to the state.[6] As in Sri Lanka and Myanmar, where militant monks have argued that Muslims pose a sustained and increasingly grave threat to the future well-being of the Buddhist religion, in Thailand the Muslim side of the conflict in the Deep South is often depicted by some representatives of the government, and the largely sycophantic Bangkok Thai media, in terms of "banditry,"[7] as manifesting a lack of respect for the integrity of the Thai state (symbolized by its Thai royalty), or as recalcitrant "guests" (*khaek*) of the nation who can be tolerated as long as they accommodate or respectfully submit to the default positions of hegemonic Thai Buddhist religious and political culture. In Sri Lanka, there is a relevant adage in play also for this Thai instance, one that has been popularly articulated to legitimate the state's military action undertaken during a time of civil war: "the country exists for the sake of the religion." Indeed, there are some devout Buddhist Thais who do, indeed, ascribe to this very position, though only a few others really believe that Malay insurgents pose a severe threat to the general stability of the nation per se. Fear about instability only surfaces regarding the border regions of the Deep South. It needs to be emphasized that many, and probably most in the Malay Muslim community, do not aspire to violent revolution or separatism, or seek to seriously threaten the integrity of the Thai state in general; rather, most simply want to be able to engage in business, legal, educational, or other public or personal matters freely in the Malay language as well as in Thai, to educate their children in their own language, to teach their children about Malay Muslim cultural history in schools, and for the Malay Muslim community to acquire a measure of local autonomy in terms of planning and administrating future local or regional economic development. Far fewer than more would commit to the goal of fighting for political independence culminating in the establishment of a theocratic Muslim state. Likewise, there is very little evidence of sustained links to international jihadist influence in the Deep South among the Malay Muslim populace at large. Those instances of international influence (detailed in a later section of this introduction) are simply not involved in, nor do they seem to be supportive of, armed insurgency. It is not an exaggeration to profile the ethos of the Muslim community in the Deep South as preponderantly traditional and moderate.

For more than the past century, all regions of Thailand, including the Deep South, have been subjected to powerful and defining centripetal and centrifugal forces emanating from and absorbing back into the royal capital in Bangkok, forces that have produced profound centralization and homogenization affects.[8] The ideology, or the normativity of this centralizing dynamic generating Thai homogeneity, is reflected in what became a national shibboleth, "Nation, Religion, King," promoted overtly as public policy by King Vajiravudh (Rama VI; r. 1910–1925), following upon the modernizing and reform efforts of his father, King Chulalongkorn (Rama V; r. 1868–1910), and his grandfather, King Mongkut (Rama IV; r. 1851–1868) in the mid- to late nineteenth and early twentieth centuries, an inchoate rationale postulated to establish a fundamental national discourse about "Thainess." More specifically, the elements of this "Thainess" consist of these three corresponding basic elements: the Buddhist religion (its realization and preservation as exemplified by the Thammayut order of monks first established by Mongkut); Buddhist kingship of the Bangkok-based Chakri dynasty (that commands respect for its elite religio-political embodiment of "Thainess"); and the Thai nation (especially as it has become linguistically bounded by "standard" Bangkok-inflected Central Thai language). More practically, "Thainess" has also meant subordinating regional identities and economies to the overriding and dominant economic interests of the capital. Integrating into the homogeneity of this "Thainess," therefore, has been an exceedingly difficult, if not seemingly unwanted impossible task, definitely not a normative aspiration for most people of the Deep South who are predominantly Muslim (80 percent), speak Malay, and still kindle memories of political and economic autonomy during earlier times in their centuries-long history of living in Patani. Their own religio-cultural mosaic is structurally and substantially at odds with contemporary renderings of "Thainess" as constituted by "Nation, Religion, King." The narratives in this volume illustrate the challenges faced especially by Malay Muslim women stemming ultimately from the ideological entrenchment of "Thainess." Their narratives force us to seriously rethink the consequence of its persistent deployment by the state. The impact on Thai Buddhists in the Deep South is one of emphasizing "otherness" from the Malay Muslim community.

Not only are there fundamental structural problems involved for a prescriptive integration of Malay Muslims into the homogeneity of "Thainess," but the Deep South region shares a predicament with other regions of Thailand as well. While the centrifugal forces of "Thainess" are basically cultural in nature, the centripetal forces are economic. That is, some regions of Thailand, especially the north (Lanna), the east (Isan), as well as the Deep South (Patani), contribute a higher share to the country's gross domestic product (GDP) than whatever share they receive back from the government in terms of economic or infrastructural development. Thailand remains one of the most centralized—or better, "centralizing"—nation-states in the world today. The economic gap between the wealthy elite classes of Bangkok and the rural or peripheral populations on the country's margins is one of the most pronounced in the world. Bangkok remains increasingly empowered by its position of being the hegemonic pivot of the contemporary Thai political *mandala*.[9] What is different about the new contemporary center of the Thai

mandala, however, is that during the Ayutthaya and Sukhothai historic periods from the thirteenth through the mid-eighteenth century, tribute and
patronage were expected as a matter of course, as a sign of recognition of the
kingdom's authority or ultimate political preeminence, but tribute did not
involve intense centralized control bureaucratically enforced over a tightly
"boundaried" nation. Local rulers were allowed discretion to manage affairs
as long as they paid some form of acceptable tribute and did not challenge
the eminence of Bangkok. Before the twentieth century, distinctive cultural
and linguistic regions were not integrated autocratically into a consolidated
governmental bureaucracy created to cultivate cultural homogeneity and the
continued economic and political ascendancy of Bangkok. The contemporary *mandala,* which now arguably is a function of continued class lever-
aging, has widened the gap economically and politically between the center
and the peripheries, at the same time pushing its program of "Thainess" to
ensure loyalty to the state.[10] Rather than understanding "Thainess" exclusively in religious, linguistic, and other cultural terms, it is possible to assert
that its real material significance plays out more clearly if the intentions of
the center of the *mandala* are understood as matters of "semi-colonialism" or
"crypto-colonialism."[11]

While Thailand, Sri Lanka, and Myanmar have each experienced intercommunal conflicts between their Theravada Buddhist majorities and Muslim minorities in the recent past, aspects of these conflicts go back many
generations, or even centuries.[12] Patani's rivalry with the Thai Buddhist
kingdom of Ayutthaya can be traced to at least the sixteenth century CE or
even earlier, after Patani's populace had become predominantly Muslim, and
it had begun to emerge as a successful midlevel entrepôt of international
trade, with a port city of increasing commercial efflorescence in subsequent
centuries that conducted an international array of business exchanges with
Portuguese, Dutch, Chinese, and Japanese entrepreneurs.[13] Patani town
thrived as a small cosmopolitan city while at the same time developed
religiously into a venue for serious Islamic scholarly study. After a long-
established political tradition in the seventeenth and eighteenth centuries
of paying tribute as a rival but subordinate power to the imperial Thai in
Ayutthaya, following low-level intensity antagonisms in the mid-eighteenth
century, and about twenty years following Patani's fateful collusion with the
Burmese to sack Ayutthaya in the 1760s, Thai forces under the first Bangkok
Chakri king, Rama I, in turn, descended upon Patani with a wrathful ven-
geance, destroyed the *raja*'s palace, decimated his court, burned the town
down completely, cut down all of its trees, obliterated its agricultural and
transportation infrastructures (canals and bridges), enslaved many people
before bringing them back to Bangkok, and caused most of the remaining

indigenous population to flee. Perhaps only 10 percent of the local Muslim population remained in the aftermath. Patani's *raja* and the *orankaya* (the wealthy commercial establishment) never recovered from this spectacular devastation,[14] and the venue for ensuing strategic conversations about recovering a measure of Patani's autonomy shifted away from the *raja*, nobility, other courtiers, and successful business leaders to the Muslim *ulama* (religious scholars) thereafter.[15] After that watershed occasion of Patani's spectacular loss, Islam became the ideological frame, or definitive discourse, for framing the history of Patani and its continuing conflict with Siamese Buddhist assertions of hegemony.[16] Perhaps this shift to a more religious understanding was also a concomitant development parallel to Bangkok's own developing self-understanding. For, as Tomas Larsson has stated concisely: "The overarching ideological framework within which a 'secular' Thai state emerged in the 19th and 20th centuries reflects a fundamentally 'Buddhist' world view."[17] If this is indeed the case, it means that to understand the current conflict, it is necessary to consider the profundity of religion's function as it informs the rationalized ideologies of both sides of the conflict. Or, to follow Duncan McCargo on this matter, the Buddhist and Muslim political ideologies claiming ascendance in the Deep South became a contest between competing legitimation scenarios rooted in religious discourse.

For example, with regard to the legacy of Malay Muslim ideology deriving from the religious works of Patani-born Sheik Daud al-Fatani, writing in Mecca after fleeing the destruction of Patani in 1785, the themes of loss and recovery are accentuated. While the Neo-Sufism of his thought stresses a yearning for a sustained intimate presence with the divine, Sheik Daud also stressed a concomitant realization of what Allah has deemed consistent with His will, a will to be accomplished in the behavior of His devoted followers. It is in this realization of doing Allah's will that redemption, spiritual and political, lies. In religious terms, it is also deemed key to recovering intimacy with the divine. It is in Sheik Daud al-Fatani's works that we find quintessential expressions of loss and a yearning for the homeland, a thirst for a lost intimacy. This spiritual-political aspiration, of course, is consonant with the inspiration held by many Muslims in the Deep South today, but it also is congruent with the political aims of some insurgents and their sympathizers: the contemporary recovery of a lost autonomy for their homeland.[18]

What we learn from Sheik Daud al-Fatani and his disciples is that this loss and yearning is not recent, although it seems to have become increasingly desperate in the 2000s after the Thai government provided the matchsticks that set off a new round of insurgent fire (developments to be addressed shortly after a brief reprise of antecedent events).

The devastation of Patani in 1785 was not only catastrophic politically; it also resulted in a paradigm shift in terms of how Islam would be understood in relation to a "national" quest or recovery. Sheik Daud al-Fatani's emphasis on recovery from loss, coupled with fidelity to Allah's will, gained increasing traction among Patani Muslims as the degree of vassalage to Bangkok simultaneously intensified during the nineteenth century, an intensification resulting in a lessening of Malay Muslim self-determination. This trajectory of exerting more control was driven, in part, by growing Siamese worries about the threatening spread of European colonial power in Cambodia and Laos (the French) and in Myanmar and Malaya (the British), a threat that effectively surrounded Siam. Brewing consternation of the Siamese culminated in more or less forced agreements with the French regarding a hard border along the Mekong River in the late 1890s, and then a period-defining Anglo-Siamese Agreement in 1909, which resulted in the formal political incorporation of Patani into Siam, an arrangement that was emphatically (and disingenuously) legitimated at the time by Prince Damrong Rajanubhab, a persuasive royal adviser to King Chulalongkhorn, who is quoted as saying: "Pattani has belonged to the Thai since time immemorial,"[19] an unfortunate and inaccurate claim with a legacy still seen within conservative political quarters in Bangkok. In any case, Bangkok's approach to the Deep South in the twentieth century vacillated between encouraging assimilation, sometimes in heavy-handed fashion by outlawing the use of Malay language, the wearing of traditional clothing, and even the practice of Islamic law,[20] and providing degrees of accommodation (e.g., the Patronage of Islam Act in 1945) as Thai governments, particularly after the disestablishment of absolute monarchy in 1932, swung between more autocratic and less democratically oriented regimes to more liberal and ideologically inclusive governments. It is within the context of one of the more authoritarian regimes in the late 1940s and early 1950s that the fate of the critically important historic figure of Haji Sulong was determined.

Haji Sulong may not be well known in Thailand outside of the Deep South, but he is regarded by many in Patani as a martyr and harbinger of the later struggles of resistance to the Thai Buddhist state. Born in 1895, Sulong, in addition to being from a prominent Patani family, proved to be something of an intellectual and religious child prodigy by the time he was twelve, insofar as he was selected to go on the Hajj pilgrimage to Mecca, an esteemed honor for religious aspirants in the Patani community. Following his participation in the rites of pilgrimage in Mecca, he met and began to study with Sheik Wan Ahmad bin Muhammad Zain al-Fatani, a renowned scholar in the diasporic Patani community in Mecca who was also a follower of the legendary Egyptian modernist, the highly influential and controversial Muhammad Abduh. This was an era during which the issue of Islam's compatibility with the sweeping social, economic, and political changes occurring in many parts of the world was ardently contested and debated in Middle Eastern Muslim circles, one that culminated, in part, with the establishment of the progressive Turkish government of Kemal Ataturk following the demise of the Ottoman Empire in 1919. On the other hand, it was also a time of the further ascendancy of the ultraconservative Wahhabi movement in the Saudi Arabian peninsula, a development that would affect Haji Sulong's own future in Mecca. Haji Sulong would spend twenty years in Mecca, where he also studied and was deeply influenced by the extensive nineteenth-century writings of Sheik Daud al-Fatani, who was seen locally in Mecca at that time as the theological godfather of the Patani diaspora dating back to the late eighteenth century. Eventually, Haji Sulong gained a prestigious academic appointment of his own, specializing in Islamic jurisprudence at an important Mecca mosque, a mosque that also functioned as an important resource for Muslim pilgrims from Indonesia, Malaysia, and Patani, as well as for aspiring scholars coming from the Malay world for higher studies in Mecca.

As opposed to the Wahhabis, Haji Sulong took the view that the practice of Islam could be reconciled with modern values such as equality, rationality, civil rights, and democracy. His stance was also staunchly anticolonial. He did not see these modern values as intrinsic only to European or American political thought. But after the conclusion of World War I, the Wahhabis, supported by the House of Saud, began to seize control of the ritual venues and performances of Mecca's pilgrimage circuit, and Haji Sulong belatedly was forced to join many others of the now long-standing Patani diasporic community in Mecca in finding a new venue to teach and study. He chose to return to Patani. The consequences were prodigious.

Upon return to Patani, Haji Sulong began a tour of the Deep South, preaching his progressive values and, after a visit to Bangkok where he secured the support of then prime minister Phahol and future prime minister Pridi Phanomyong, built a new school and mosque where his values could be institutionalized and further inculcated. Unfortunately, a change in political leadership in Bangkok in which the fascist military leader Phibun came to power ultimately led to the closing of his school and mosque, as Haji Sulong became warily regarded in Bangkok's newly ensconced reactionary quarters. During World War II, Haji Sulong aligned himself with an underground movement that worked against the Japanese-allied Phibun government. In the immediate postwar years when Pridi came back into power, Haji Sulong and his aspirations for the Muslim community were apparently again regarded more positively and constructively. In fact, in 1947, Pridi sent a government investigatory team to Patani to tease out the possibilities of greater autonomy for the Muslim region. About a year earlier, King Ananda

(Rama VIII), had donated twenty thousand baht in support of Haji Sulong's school and mosque, at that time a generous endowment. With hopes raised, Haji Sulong was chosen as the leader of the Malay community to meet this investigative team, and he greeted them with a seven-point proposal:

1. A Muslim governor should be appointed over the four southern provinces;
2. Malay should be the language of instruction in all schools through grade 7;
3. taxes collected in the four southern provinces should be expended there;
4. 85 percent of local government officials should be Malays;
5. both Malay and Thai should be recognized as languages of government;
6. a provincial Islamic committee should adjudicate religious matters for Muslims; and
7. the Muslim judicial system should be kept separate from the government's courts.

(It is remarkable that Haji Sulong's practical proposals remain at the core of unrealized aspirations for many Patani Muslims today, some seventy-five years later.) Sometime after the investigative team returned to Bangkok, the government eventually demurred, a sign of the deep-seated reluctance on the part of conservative influential Thai Buddhist politicos to embrace any other conception of Thailand than its status as an absolutely unitary Thai Buddhist state. Frustrated, Haji Sulong began agitations throughout the Deep South in which he declared that if his program was accepted, he would also promote Haji Mahayiddin, a son of the last sultan of Patani, to be governor of the four provinces (including Songkla) of the Deep South. This proposal raised the stakes further. Meanwhile, the independence movement to the south of Thailand in Malaysia was gathering steam, and some influential officials in Bangkok misread Sulong's movement in Patani as a branch of the Malaysian independence movement. In late 1947, a military coup overthrew Pridi's reformist government, and a crackdown against potential dissidents ensued. Haji Sulong was arrested on charges of sedition and spent four years in a Bangkok prison. When he was finally released, it was on condition that he refrain from teaching and engaging in political activity. Months later, he was summoned to appear at a police station in Songkla for questioning. He, his fifteen-year-old son, and two colleagues were never seen again.[21]

Haji Sulong remains something of a household name in the Deep South of Thailand today. He is regarded by many as an exemplary martyr for their cause, and as the primogenitor of the movement for greater autonomy by some others. His preeminent stature in the eyes of Malay Muslims in the Deep South is also evident in that fact that he has also been absorbed into the lore of the separatist insurgent movement. But what is more salient about Haji Sulong's career is that he couched his progressive, modernist agenda for greater autonomy within the context of the Thai state. His seven-point program was not a clarion call for a separate political independence but more a matter of measured self-governance: that is, devolved degrees of power, self-determination, and confirmation of a recognized distinctive religio-political identity for Malay Muslims. Seventy-five years later, the seven measures that Haji Sulong called for remain unaddressed, though they are still regarded by most thoughtful Muslims in Patani as core aspirations. Correspondingly, Haji Sulong's seven measures would still be regarded by many Thai Buddhist people today as affronts to "Thainess" and a challenge to the unity of the nation, an indication that these "guests" are not really interested in being genuinely Thai.

The "post–Haji Sulong era" of resistance has been characterized by a dynamic of competing factions. One important faction was the movement continued by Haji Sulong's son, Den Tohmeena, who dominated, to some extent through his Wadah political faction, Pattani politics for three decades, seeking to work within the constraints of successive Thai governments to secure more autonomy and resources for the economic development of the south. Den served as a member of parliament, a senator, and as a deputy cabinet minister in various governments, in the process trying to establish a bridge between the influential *imam* (Muslim clerics) of the rural Deep South amid traditionalist Muslims (sometimes referred to as the *khana kao*) and the changing, wobbling dispositions of Thai governments in Bangkok. Despite his moderate positions, he was still suspected by some security and military leaders in the Thaksin government (2001–6) as being one of the leaders of the separatist movement.[22] By this time, the militant movement for separatism had become more radicalized in ideology, aims, and methods. Indeed, it is likely that Den was also seen by some of the leaders of the separatist movement, whether they be from the National Patani Liberation Front (BNPP), the Patani United Liberation Organization (PULO), or the National Revolution Front (BRN), as part of an elitist segment of Patani political leadership that had been co-opted by Bangkok governments to maintain the status quo.[23] Moreover, Den was viewed by conservative reform-minded and fundamentalist Salafist followers of the dynamic preacher Ismael Lufti Chapakia, who had founded his own school of Muslim theology in Yala, as resistant to the new reforms of stricter practice and doctrinal purity (sometimes referred to as *khana mai*) that viewed the syncretistic character of traditional local Patani Islam as heretical and in need of reform.[24] It is this direction of Islamist thought that has gained increasing traction within some important circles of the intellectual Muslim community in Patani, along with concomitant influence from the South Asian–based Tablighi Jama'at. Although it is debatable, Lufti also claimed to be the ideological successor of the teachings of Sheik Daud al-Fatani, owing to his emphasis on adhering to Allah's will that is made clear in derivative *shariah* Muslim law based on the exemplary *sunnah* of Muhammad and the early generations of his followers. What is further of note in this context is that Lufti's followers are generally not outspoken supporters, and likely not supporters at all, of the militant separatist insurgents, despite sometimes being accused of being Wahhabis in another guise, a label they reject, this despite holding views very similar to the Wahhabi in relation to the need to reform traditionalist (*khana kao*) Islam. Duncan McCargo has pointed out astutely that "whereas in the wider Islamic world 'Wahhabi' ideology was often constructed as the handmaiden of political violence, in Patani the opposite arguably held true."[25]

Srawut Aree and Christopher Joll have provided a creditable view of the transformations and influences on Patani Islam since the 1960s that complicates the binary differences between so-called *khana kao* (traditionalist) and *khana mai* (reformist) Islam typified by Lufti and the Tablighi.[26] They have described, following other scholarly assessments, how Lufti's more Saudi-inspired, conceptually and culturally Arabic-based movement is at once reformist (critical of traditional Muslim education that tolerates heretical "magical" practices), modernist (insofar as it supports private Islamic schools that also teach secular subjects), and fundamentalist (since it advocates a rather strict adherence to the *sunnah* [behavioral and customary example] of the Prophet based largely on the Qu'ran and *hadith,* the primary sources for *shariah* conceptions of Islamic ritual and personal law). Lufti's movement can hardly be described as a liberal reform, in that it continues to support many restrictions on women, their attire (he supports wearing of the *niqab*), their vocational aspirations (a woman's place is strictly nonpublic), and creative innovations in cultural expression (particularly in literature and art). Despite disavowing a connection to the Wahhabi, Lufti's brand of reformist Islam is socially and culturally puritanical in orientation. His stance vis-à-vis insurgency is decidedly oppositional, and he has accepted positions as an advisor to the Chularajamontri, the government-appointed "spiritual leader" of Muslims in Thailand; was a participant in the National Reconciliation Commission in 2007; and was appointed to the Senate following the 2006 military coup while, however, advocating government recognition of Malay Muslim identity. It is clear that he operates within a Thai national framework.

Aree and Joll also profile the successful emergence in Patani of the South Asian–based reform-minded Tablighi Jama'at, particularly the background and career of Loh India, who has remained steadfastly apolitical in relation to the current conflict but is also consistently critical of traditionalist practices. The Tablighi has understood its role as bridging the gap between "global" and "local" traditionalist Islams. It has stressed the importance of *ijitihad,* that sometimes interpretations of Islamic principles have to be decided on the basis of rational, independent analysis when faced with ambiguities in relation to its application. Loh India also predicated the importance of *qiyas,* or the need to think analogically in relation to *sunnah* whenever necessary. It is not surprising, then, that Tablighi missionary efforts have garnered the attention and support of conservative but educated businessmen, university teachers and students, and others seeking to reconcile the religious practices of Islam with modernity.

What is clear from this brief summary of the two most successful international influences on Patani Islam is that neither overtly supports insurgency; rather, each seeks to coexist within the Thai state as constructively as possible while remaining firmly committed to conservative renderings of Islam. An important takeaway from Aree and Joll's review is their conclusion that the importance of Middle Eastern or Arab-based influence has been overstated in the past, and that the influence of the South Asian–based Tablighi Jama'at has been underplayed. That is, due to various factors, including the oppressively political, there is a growing number of Patani Muslims who have understood their religious quests as apolitical on the one hand but resistant to being co-opted by the Thai government for political purposes on the other. What this more nuanced overview also tells us is that any facile comparisons to ethno-religious conflicts involving Muslims in other parts of the world beyond this Theravada Buddhist–dominated region of Sri Lanka and Southeast Asia would likely obscure, rather than clarify, the idiosyncratic religio-political dynamics under consideration here. However, the discussion about the relation of what it means to be Malay and what it means to be Muslim continues. Some would argue that to be Malay means to be Muslim, much in the same way that many Sinhalas, Burmese, Arakanese, Mon, Thai, Khmer, or Lao would argue that to be one of them means being Buddhist. Others would argue that the two are separate issues, that Islam transcends any forging of specific religio-political identities. Both positions have their fervent advocates, but among traditional Muslims the former position is normative.

Where do the Malay Muslim women's narratives of this volume fit within this scenario of competing visions of what normatively should be the Muslim path? The previous scenario notwithstanding, the answer is within the 70 to 90 percent of the Muslim demography in the Deep South who continue as *khana kao* (traditionalist). With reference to the earlier discussion, Haji Sulong's continuing significance to them lies in the fact that he became a martyr who has epitomized their cause, and therefore remains an emblematic, or a metaphoric, means to understand the deleterious reasons for the loss of their fathers, husbands, brothers, and sons. As such, it is also within this orbit of Muslims that insurgents have drawn their support, and it is also within this same orbit that most of the suspects, innocent or complicit, taken into custody or killed by Thai security forces are drawn. Ironically, it also this mass that has mixed with local Thai Buddhists and forged, at times, close ties.

A discussion of the internal dynamics of Muslim religious demography and politics in Patani does not exactly bring us very close to an explanation for the upsurge in violence that occurred in the early 2000s. Reasons for the increase in violent incidents can be understood, instead, by cataloguing some of the miscalculated, ham-fisted mistakes committed by a provocative Thai Buddhist government and its undisciplined military. In the same way that an extraordinary government blunder gave rise to the legendary Haji Sulong's celebrated martyrdom, so the killing of many Muslim men, many of them villagers not directly involved in violent insurgency, has inadvertently stoked the ranks of the militant insurgents as well. In hindsight, the populist Shinawatra Thaksin government elected by a landslide vote in 2001, chiefly owing to its popularity in Isan (northeast Thailand), was ill-prepared to handle the increasingly contentious climate of the Deep South when it came to power. Perhaps one of its biggest mistakes was abolishing the Southern Border Provinces Administrative Centre. According to Duncan McCargo, "Radical 'separatist' elements began waging a guerrilla war against the Thai state in the 1960s: fighting was most virulent during the late 1970s and early 1980s. . . . By 1980, as many as a thousand insurgents were carrying out regular attacks in the south and had even staged bombings in Bangkok. But the Prem Tinsulanond governments (1980–88) successfully reined in the violence, granting amnesty to former militants and setting up new security and government arrangements in the area coordinated by the Southern Border Provinces Administrative Centre (SBPAC)."[27]

The SBPAC gained a measure of confidence from a considerable section of the Patani's Muslim populace, who regarded its administration as at least open to addressing the common problems of unemployment and poverty, as much as it had also been assigned to cooperate with security forces to suppress the insurgency.[28] Development programs were launched, sometimes brokered by the military, which, to this day, maintains a great many business interests in the Deep South, not all of them licit. As McCargo notes in a continuation of the same passage noted above, "The Prem-era policies were broadly effective in muting the violence for about two decades." But one of Thaksin's basic moves as prime minister following his landslide victory in

2001 was to abolish the SBPAC and turn security matters over exclusively to the state police. (In his early career, Thaksin had been an officer in the state police and believed in the efficacy of their charge.) This change in administration signaled a shift from a previous policy driven largely by economic concerns to one dominated by security concerns. Thaksin would later regret this move.

During the early 1990s, organized Patani fisherfolk had joined with farmers from Isan to mount periodic large-scale demonstrations in Bangkok against government development plans that were deemed deleterious to their future well-being. While sometimes raucous, these demonstrations were peaceful on the whole and tolerated by the government. But from December 2001 through January 2004, periodic attacks by insurgents on police stations in Narathiwat, Yala, and Pattani left more than a score of policemen and several civilians dead. In January 2004, the insurgents raised the stakes by storming a weapons depot near Narathiwat and making off with a significant cache of weapons killing four soldiers in the process,[29] much to the embarrassment and consternation of the government. Thaksin responded angrily by openly criticizing the incompetence of the military and then declared martial law, and with that came a sense of ominous foreboding. The Thai army would now be deployed throughout the Deep South and eventually balloon in numbers and budget to become essentially the occupying force it is today of at least sixty thousand soldiers, replete with ubiquitous checkpoints deployed throughout the three provinces. McCargo has detailed how the Thai army was summarily unprepared for its task of maintaining martial law in 2004, that many of its recruits were very young, poorly trained cadres from Isan who had no political, cultural, or social understanding of the mounting vortex of violence into which they had been thrown.[30] Eventually, more highly trained troops would be brought into the mix. But the recipe for disaster known as Tak Bai had already been baked. Months later, a large Malay protest against the arrests of many suspected insurgents alleged to have been involved in the events surrounding the heist of weapons took place in Tak Bai. The military handled it in a historically disgraceful fashion. At first, when demonstrators refused to disperse, soldiers began firing into the crowd and attacking with rifle butts. At least twenty died on the spot, including fourteen from being bludgeoned to death. Scores of others were injured as well. But this was not the worst of it. In the words of McCargo:

> Tak Bai saw the reputation of the [a]rmy at an all-time low. The gratuitous deaths of seventy-eight protestors at the hands of the army were inexcusable. The victims had been put into the back of trucks, face down with their hands tied behind their backs, stacked as many as five high, and

spent several hours on the road to the Inkhayut army base in Pattani. Most trucks contained between sixty and eighty men; one contained ninety men, twenty-three of whom died. Most of those killed had apparently suffocated, though relatives and community leaders insist that many of the corpses contained bullet holes.[31]

While Tak Bai sank the army's reputation to "an all-time low," a massacre at Pattani's famous Kru Se Mosque six months earlier than the Tak Bai debacle has become an almost equally infamous landmark in the memory of Patani's Muslims. On April 28, 2004, hundreds of impressionable youths, drawn largely from *pondoks* (traditional Muslim schools) and led by charismatic *ustadz* (teachers) who claimed to possess magical powers that they conferred on their student warriors, simultaneously attacked dozens of police stations in the three provinces. Most of them, armed with little more than machetes, were no match for the police and the military. There were 105 youths killed compared to just five police and army personnel. But it was what happened at the cursed Kru Se Mosque[32] in Pattani town that became the focus of attention by the media in the aftermath, and like Tak Bai, a memory difficult to erase; and again, a severe blow to the reputation of the Thai military in the eyes of Patani Muslims. Kru Se subsequently became something of a monument. Mira Manickam has reconstructed what happened at Kru Se in the following way:

> It was a grizzly scene to imagine. The men arrived at the mosque the night before the incident, telling the imam that they were coming to meditate. Then, at 4:30 a.m., a small group of them left to attack the police checkpoint next door, a tiny target not much larger than a roadside noodle stall. Here, they stabbed two officers to death. In a scuffle that followed, four militants were shot before they retreated to the mosque. By 6:00 a.m., anti-riot troops arrived and blockaded the mosque, and spent the next eight hours in a spat of firefights with the militants inside, who refused to surrender. . . . At 2:00 p.m., despite orders from the deputy prime minister of the country to refrain from further attacks on the mosque, the commanding general ordered his troops to storm the mosque and shoot to kill. Thirty-one militants died that day at Kru Se.[33]

I have highlighted Tak Bai and Kru Se because these terrible moments became metaphoric in the minds of many Patani Muslims, including several of the women whose narratives are presented in this volume, women who lost husbands on those days. In the manner in which these "incidents" are remembered, both events flag profiles of a government unwilling to confront

Kru Se Mosque, Pattani. (Photo by John Holt)

its detractors in a restrained and constructive manner, instead choosing the route of brutality, including the desecration of a holy shrine, to emphasize its determination to maintain control. For some, the army had attacked Islam. It is not surprising that the aftermath witnessed insurgent attacks on Buddhist *wats*.

To be sure, many attacks by militant insurgents gained in frequency during the months and years ahead. They continue today, although the Covid-19 pandemic helped to mitigate their frequency. In addition to roadside bombs targeting military, police, and village security volunteers, scores of government schools and their teachers have been targeted by the militants, and, as noted above, some Buddhist temples have also come under fire. Two bomb attacks on the C. S. Pattani Hotel (a major venue for various types of meetings or conventions held by government constituencies), the first injuring its Chinese Christian owner who happened to be a senator in the government and an enthusiastic supporter of Thai royalty, and a bomb attack on the nearby Big C department store, further reflect the intended symbolism of many insurgent attacks: the Thai Buddhist establishment of the state and its business affiliates.

If Tak Bai and Kru Se are landmarks in the collective memory of Patani

Muslims, the May 2006, kidnapping and the subsequent death of Khru Chul-ing Pongkhanmoon, a young Thai Buddhist woman from northern Chiang Rai who had volunteered to teach in the government school in Narathiwat's Kuching Rupa village, has been etched deeply in the minds of Thai Bud-dhists. Following her attack, Chuling survived for eight months in a coma before she died, and recriminations were launched against both the military and attendant villagers for not responding to her peril more expeditiously and perhaps saving her life. The attackers, apparently unarmed late teenaged boys, fled before the army could arrive and before villagers finally began to respond to her jeopardy. The aftermath of Chuling's death also led to an es-calation on both sides, insofar as a program of arming Buddhist villagers was put into effect as a result. In addition to the distribution of weapons to villagers, seventy-five army personnel were ordained into the *sangha* to serve as an armed protectorate of Buddhist *wats* thought to be endangered by the militants. Buddhism had been directly implicated, both as a target and as a force in the conflict.[34] On the Buddhist side, the tragic death of a young dedicated teacher fortified the support of hard-liners in the government and throughout the nation. Her victimhood came to symbolize the ungrateful demeanor of recalcitrant "guests."

The narratives we present in what follows reflect how specific events of violence in the past, especially the deaths of seventy-eight arrested suspects allegedly involved in the Tak Bai "incident," or the massacre of thirty-two "insurgents" at the Kru Se Mosque in Pattani, both in 2004 by security forces, or the kidnapping and assault by Malay Muslim insurgents leading to the eventual death of the young Thai Buddhist female school teacher, Chuling Pongkhanmoon from Chiang Rai, remain landmarks in the minds of many Muslims and Buddhists in the Deep South. The heartbreak resulting from these unnecessary and cruel deaths redounds even today. These symbolic moments of brutal suppression on the one hand, and of savage insurgency on the other, continue to catalyze the feeling of unjust violence in the Deep South and generate a "never forget" mind-set of militancy and revenge among some on both sides of the conflict. These are scars in time that are not easily erased.

Comparing the Thai to the Sri Lankan and Myanmar Contexts of Buddhist-Muslim Conflict

In comparison to Thailand, there have been virtually no Islamic-inspired aspirations asserted for autonomy or political independence in Sri Lanka and Myanmar, the other two Theravada Buddhist–dominated nations that are also currently experiencing Buddhist/Muslim ethno-religious conflicts.

Moreover, the histories and natures of conflict in all three of these countries vary considerably in important ways. Yet, a study of the rise of Buddhist militancy aimed at Muslims in Sri Lanka and Myanmar reveals a similar reactionary pattern of militant Buddhist ideology, a fear stoked by disinformation and conspiracy theories, abetted by an incompetent policing on the part of Facebook, that the minority Muslims within each country have designs to take over the political economies of both. Indeed, the ideology of the monastic-led Bodu Bala Sena (Army of Buddhist Power) in Sri Lanka and the monastic Ma Ba Tha (an acronym for the "Society to Protect the Religion") movement in Myanmar are remarkably similar in both tone and substantive ideology. In both contexts, Muslims have been scapegoated by Buddhist monks and their lay supporters for precisely the same reasons, despite the fact that the two Muslim communities in these respective countries are also very different in nature. In the Sri Lankan and Burmese national contexts, Muslims have been accused of insurgent and seditious activities generated with support from abroad; of engaging in unfair business practices to the detriment of Buddhist competitors; of failing to practice birth control and thereby proliferating their populations, which eventually will surpass those of the Buddhists; of conspiring to appropriate Buddhist-held temple lands; and of attempting to convert Buddhists to Islam, especially women; among other largely unfounded accusations disseminated through various and relatively unregulated social media platforms. Instances of Muslim men sexually harassing Buddhist women have been invented, then exaggerated, and repeatedly emphasized time and again. Alleged attacks on Buddhist monks have also been spotlighted and embellished to illustrate in microcosm the perceived Muslim threat to Buddhism. To my knowledge, although Thai Buddhist monks have not organized into self-identified organizations specifically aimed at protecting Buddhism against the alleged dangers generated by the Muslim community in Thailand, or have not articulated a xenophobia with the same force and scope as their Sinhala and Burmese counterparts, some of the same types of claims advanced against Malay Muslims in the Deep South have been leveled by some fringe extremist Buddhist nationalists in Thailand.[35]

The insurgency since 2004 mounted by alienated ethnic Malay Muslims continues to be repressed by Thai government security forces in Pattani, Yala, and Narathiwat. As of this writing, there are still at least sixty thousand Thai military troops deployed in the Deep South, and checkpoints manned by these troops are everywhere, creating an ambiance of siege and unease. Again, as of this writing in early 2022, the violence inflicted from both sides of the divide has claimed the lives of at least 7,500 people since the early 2000s.[36] While the situation in the Deep South has cooled a bit at this time, at least in terms of the number of violent deaths occurring during the past three years, the root problems of the conflict have yet to be engaged successfully by negotiators representing the Thai government and the insurgents. The base question to be addressed diplomatically in the sporadic yet ongoing negotiations remains what I have indicated earlier, but repeat for emphasis here: how does an ethno-religious community that identifies itself primarily in terms of language, religion, and history (Malay, Islam, and a distant historical memory of political and cultural autonomy) accommodate within a nation that defines itself by appealing to "Thainess," that is, a national identity that has been constructed essentially by appeals of identification to the central Thai language, Theravada Buddhist religion, and almost a thousand years of political independence marked summarily by lineages of Thai Buddhist dynastic kingship? This fundamental structural problem, the question of how a minority people can fully belong within a state that has insisted, for more than a century now, on religious, cultural, and linguistic homogenization, is the fundamental issue at hand.[37] In Myanmar, "Burmanization" has functioned in a somewhat similar manner since the 1960s and remains a primary issue in the present for the many minority and indigenous peoples who are struggling to find a place of belonging in the union. In Sri Lanka, the state's attempts at formal recognition of language (Sinhala) and religion (Buddhism) have also been provocative issues contributing to the political divisions vexing the country's attempts to sustain a democracy responsible to all of its various ethnic and religious constituencies: Hindu, Christian, and Muslim.

In Thailand, on the Buddhist side of the problem, there is an unsettled future regarding the question of whether the Thai demographic can eventually summon a political will, or establish a more democratically responsive state power, to embrace a more pluralistic conception of their society or national political culture, so that regional and ethnic tensions, of which the problem of Malay Muslims in the Deep South is the most acute, might abate. As in Myanmar among the Bamars, and in Sri Lanka among the Sinhalas, there has been a long-standing assumption that Buddhist religious culture is the standard basis for the country and that other minority people need to either integrate into or conform to this religio-cultural-political default position.

More practically, what remains is the question, can any efforts at decentralization and devolution of power gain any traction in the future? Retrospectively, we can understand that this was precisely Haji Sulong's agenda. Although there have been recent demonstrations orchestrated by Thai high school and university students calling for significant constitutional reforms to further enable (or recover) democratic enfranchisement, including the controversial suggestion that the state's relation to the monarchy needs reform, there is little sign that a conception of pluralism, multiculturalism, or devolution can be translated into public policy in the near future, especially given the fact that the current government remains in the grip of army generals and staunch royalists. The link between religion and the state, embodied by the symbolism of Buddhist kingship and the state's formal administration of the Buddhist *sangha,* an administrative feature of Myanmar as well but not of Sri Lanka, is still thoroughly entrenched and embraced, enthusiastically so, by a powerful constituency of the Thai Buddhist demographic.

Thai Buddhist people outside the Deep South often display very little in the way of understanding empathetically the perspective and aspirations of the minority Malay Muslim population. Few have even traveled to this remote part of the country. Despite this problem of not being well understood, the situations faced by Muslims in Thailand (and in Sri Lanka) are not nearly so dire as what the Rohingyas Muslims of Myanmar have confronted, especially insofar as the Muslims in Thailand and Sri Lanka are formally recognized as citizens of these countries, whereas citizenship remains a highly contested issue for Rohingyas in Myanmar.

Thailand remains "the most Buddhist" of all Theravada-dominated countries, with 90 to 95 percent of its citizens regarding themselves as Buddhist in religious identity. A formula for peaceful coexistence with Malay Muslims, who constitute only 2 to 3 percent of the national population but 80 percent of the population in the Deep South, continues to seem a distant reality, one that will take many years of goodwill at the negotiation table to accomplish, and then a good effort aimed at selling an agreement to the rank-and-file on both sides. It will also need a rethinking of what "Thainess" can mean. Will it continue, for instance, to mean Buddhism exclusively as the religion within the threefold shibboleth, which is the manner in which it is understood by the vast majority of the Thai demographic? There are signs in Thailand's political past, as it has ricocheted between a military-royalist autocratic state and times when it has posed as an aspiring democracy, that a differently inflected understanding of "Thainess" seems possible to generate. For instance, in 1945, as mentioned earlier, when facing increasing unrest in the Deep South at the conclusion of World War II, the Thai government passed the Patronage of Islam Act, which specified that Islam could be recognized as religion in the "Nation, Religion, King" formula. What this belies is the possibility that a more inclusive understanding of "Thainess" lies dormant in the body politic, that there are segments of the supermajority who are open to supporting, rather than erasing, the distinctive social, cultural, and religious identities of erstwhile Muslim Thai citizens.

What is unique about the Muslim situation in the Deep South of Thailand, when compared to Myanmar and Sri Lanka, is that the border provinces of Pattani, Narathiwat, and Yala have very developed educational infrastructures, including traditional Muslim primary- and secondary-level institutions per se that run parallel to government schools and hybrid private Islamic schools. The region, as well, has a well-regarded university, the Prince of Songkla University in Pattani. In addition, there are many Muslim and non-Muslim NGOs hard at work to help ameliorate the immediate problem on the ground,[38] an abundance of goodwill being exercised by many to see this thorny moment in history through. Unlike the context facing the Rohingya in Myanmar, Malay Muslims are not derided for choosing how they want to be known collectively. In addition, many Malay Muslim families can move back and forth across the Malaysian border for educational reasons, job opportunities, or prospective marriages. The border is not regarded as a barrier. Indeed, the relatively open border often functions as something of a safety valve. To some extent, there is a brain drain of some Muslim youth leaving Patani for Malaysia either for education or work. Unlike the Rohingya of Myanmar and the Muslims of Sri Lanka, Malay Muslims continue to have other options besides the homeland into which they have been born. Importantly, there is also a formal political discussion taking place between Malay Muslim representatives of the insurgents and the Thai state, with Malaysia as an observer. That opportunity to engage the state formally in negotiations seems a far distant and unlikely hope for the Rohingya of Myanmar. The Rohingya have yet to begin to find a concerted or unified voice of representation; nor have they been given an opportunity for political representation and negotiation.

In concluding this part of the introduction, as I noted earlier but will emphasize once more: what is common between the Thai context and the Sri Lankan and Burmese contexts is that many people in the majoritarian Buddhist communities of each identify their countries as *essentially Buddhist.* Consequently, democracy, when it is functioning (e.g., when Thailand and Myanmar are not controlled by military juntas or their proxies), has often come to mean a hegemonic majoritarianism in practice. This identification of Buddhist national identity with the state has been institutionalized in different ways within each country, but the problem of belonging remains fundamentally the same for minority peoples in each of these countries respectively.

Contemporary Context and Significance of Religion and Education

While the preceding discussion has been germane to understanding the historical and political context of ethno-religious conflict in Thailand's Deep

South in general and comparatively in relation to Myanmar and Sri Lanka, the issues I have raised are somewhat abstract realities in the lives of many people on the ground. Many of the issues just described focus on generalities of the problem as it can be understood conceptually on regional, national, or international levels. But to deploy a well-worn adage and to risk cliché, "all politics are local," and so is the brutal reality of intercommunal violence in Thailand's Deep South. In the accounts that form the substance of this book, we are confronted with personal historical memories of the recent past, in particular the sordid violence associated with Tak Bai, Kru Se, and Chuling Pongkhanmoon in the mid-2000s, scarring moments that continue to mobilize passions on both sides of the ethno-religious divide even today, many years after they have occurred. But perhaps even more important, from these autobiographical reflections we gain an understanding of the human costs of violence, and how the humanity of those who have suffered has been tested, questioned, altered, transformed, or sustained. What is remarkable about these narratives is that they are now being publicly articulated by women, especially Muslim women, who rank at the bottom of Thailand's national social hierarchy that remains publicly male-dominated and Buddhist-oriented. These are voices of the subordinated, similar to what an earlier generation of historians of South Asia referred to as a "subaltern voice." Here, the heavy hand of colonialism to which they have responded is not European or American, but the by-product of a colonial "Thainess," the cultivation of which remains a guiding principle of national policy priorities by conservative royalist Thai governments.

There can be no discounting the significance of Islam in the lives of many individuals who have been dramatically affected by the violence in the Deep South. It may not be inaccurate to characterize their religiosity as a "religion of the oppressed."[39] In narrative after narrative, Muslim victims, or members of their families, interpret their misfortunes as a "test" from Allah, a manifestation of His divine will being imposed on their lives in a manner that demands a resolutely faithful response. This is clearly seen in oaths taken to exercise patience, forbearance, and trust in Allah who is understood as a powerfully transcendent god who does not betray His faithful adherents. Supplications and prayers for Allah's intercessions frequently follow as expressions of this faith, expressive of an understanding that Allah's will is fundamentally concerned with their individual lives, and it is a will that has to be accepted, no matter how difficult to endure.[40] What one observes is not the inhibition of agency but rather an expression of *hope*. It is trust in Allah's personal plan for their lives that is discernible in so many of the narratives. And it is obedience to His will that is sought.

It is also, I think, imperative to note what is *not* found in appeals to discerning Allah's will. There is *not* an attempt to enlist or cajole Allah's power for immediate political purposes or for revenge, to call down His perceived magisterial sovereignty to immediately punish those who have caused grave suffering. In this, we observe a central Islamic theological principle: that sometimes the meaning of life's events is inscrutable in the immediate context, but that does not mean that because the results are mysterious that they are devoid of ultimate meaning. In observing how some of these women have been dramatically transformed by means of expressing their irrepressible wills to seek justice, we observe how challenge has elicited the strengths that have fostered their personal transformations. In Soraya Jamjuree's words, they have been transformed "from victims to victors." In their perspectives, this may have been the real purpose of Allah's plan for their lives: to seek justice where it has proved elusive. And in this, they see that the realization of justice is constitutive of Allah's will for the world.

Of the Buddhists on the other side, one observes a functional parallel to Muslim understandings of theodicy. The Buddhist theodicy of suffering appeals to karma as an explanation for misfortune, and the hope implied by the reality of *anicca,* the inexorable and persistent dynamic of phenomenal change. In affirming the inevitability of change, that suffering (*dukkha*) arises and passes away like all phenomena within *samsara,* hope is inspired for the possibility of a different future. What both the Buddhist and Muslim instances of suffering's explanation illustrate is the verity of Duncan McCargo's general assertion cited earlier that religion has become the frame of reference for understanding the existential and current political plight of conflict in the Deep South.

A few of these narratives also reveal, as noted earlier, how Buddhists and Muslims have shared aspects of their religious cultures with one another, and that before the tensions of the conflict became more and more intense following the upsurge of violence in the mid- 2000s, many villages had enjoyed a history of amity and concord, an amity and concord that has now been seriously ruptured. In the first instance, shared religious practice or influence can be seen in Muslims talking about earning merit based on the morality of their actions, of Muslim's transferring merit to their departed kin, or of Muslims engaging in a "calming ritual" functioning in a similar fashion to Buddhist meditation. Here we see the impact of living with Buddhists for whom karma is not only the main currency of suffering's explanation but also the currency that is deployed to assist the departed in making the transition to the "other world." While Muslims, of course, do not subscribe to Buddhist rebirth theory, they do link moral cultivation to prospects for life beyond. In the second instance, signs of convivial or genial social relations previously enjoyed between Buddhists and Muslims are signaled by interreligious marriages, of Buddhist lawyers defending Muslim defendants in court, of Muslim insurgents on the run taking refuge in the houses of Buddhist families, and of Muslim women activists working with Thai Buddhist officials to help ameliorate the destitute circumstances of victimized Muslim women.[41]

Beyond these instances of mutual influence and cooperation, Buddhists away from the nation's capital, along with Muslims of the Deep South, share a problem in counterbalancing the power of a Bangkok-centric political economy. In this vein, it is interesting to note how many Patani Muslims have expressed support for the young students in Bangkok who for months in late 2020 and throughout 2021 protested by demanding change from the autocratic government that has perpetuated the policies of the military junta that ruled Thailand repressively from 2014 until 2019. Of course, the vast majority of this student constituency are nominal Buddhists, but many Patani Muslims admire them and share in the rationales for their public protests.

All of these instances, whether indicating how practices of one tradition are borrowed or influenced from another, or how Buddhists and Muslims have worked together practically in common pursuits, flag a legacy that for long periods of time in the Deep South, Buddhists and Muslims have lived and worked together in common. Hence, the tragedy of alienation in the present weighs heavily.

Having said that, there are powerful national Buddhist forces that are represented in the Deep South, forces that function in ways somewhat similar to reform-minded Muslims who see traditionalist Islam as heretical. These are not just limited to the Buddhist *wats* and their monastic incumbents who have allied with the military. The aggressive Dhammakaya movement from Bangkok has also entered the scene in recent years and pushes a unique form of Buddhism that claims an exclusive truth, a stance that does not encourage mutual affectation between communities. Dhammakaya has a national policy of rehabilitating abandoned temples as a means of spreading its brand of Buddhist practice. Publicly, it aligns firmly with Thai military exploits in the Deep South. Their presence seems to serve the purposes of those who do not necessarily see social rapprochement between the communities as desirable. While their presence does not surface in any of the stories we present, their impact has been palpable in a number of localities where Buddhists form a significant presence. To highlight this signals that, to some limited extent, the conflict that comprises the context for these narratives remains something of a question of competing religious nationalisms. I hesitate to frame the problematic context entirely in this fashion, in part owing to what is known about the nature of the variegated Muslim and Buddhist communities in Patani. And, to emphasize once again, the existential circumstances confronted and endured by both Buddhists and Muslims in their narratives cannot be

reduced to matters of political expediency. The personal dimensions re-
vealed in these narratives relate more squarely to how violence and injustice
per se, regardless of their deep-seated causes, are the immediate issues at
hand. They are the foreground and not the background of the problem.

Beyond the factor of religion, these stories also signal the deep value
attached to education in the Malay Muslim community and the apparent
recognition of this value by the Thai state as well. Earlier, I mentioned the
presence of an extensive educational system in the Deep South that ranges
from primary through the university level of education. The Deep South
may be one of the more impoverished regions economically in Thailand, but
it is not the least educated. In narrative after narrative, we read about great
personal sacrifices being made by Malay Muslim and Thai Buddhist women
for the educational welfare of their children. The education of children, religious and secular, often becomes the primary financial preoccupation of
those left with the responsibility of caring for children whose parents can no
longer provide. We read about sacrifice after sacrifice being made to ensure
that children can progress with their educations. Moreover, initiatives undertaken by agencies of the Thai state, or by private NGOs, to assist in the provi-
sion of scholarships for children bereft of immediate parental care due to the
armed conflict, reflect a recognition of education as a religio-cultural value
that is especially infused throughout the Malay Muslim community. That the
Thai Buddhist state has sometimes stepped up to assist in this manner also
testifies to a Thai recognition of this Malay Muslim value and signals a positive constructive remedy. The Thai state—or at least the personnel working
within certain ministries—deserves credit in this regard.[42]

These narratives also provide some insight into the routines and demands
of education within the settings of both *pondoks* (schools dedicated only to
Islamic religious education) and "private Islamic schools" (which combine
Islamic religious education with secular subjects of study). Again, attempts
by the state to support Islamic private schools further signal state recognition of the importance of education's value among the Deep South Malay
Muslim community, though often supported in the hope that it will lead to
integration in Thai society at large and break down insularity. It is also a sign
of the wariness that state officials feel for traditional *pondoks,* in that these
traditional schools organized around a single teacher are often thought to be
breeding grounds for potential insurgents. They may be. On a different note,
there are moments in these narratives when the influences and dedication of
Muslim teachers on their students become apparent in disparate ways: from
inspiring students to gain knowledge per se as a way to secure well-being in
their futures, to other instances of persuading students to take up the cause
of fighting for their community's future collective well-being, even if this

requires a commitment to *jihad*. As with Buddhist monks, Muslim teachers and clerics also inhabit the full spectrum of political perspectives.

As each author recounts her experience, it also becomes clear how frustrating the struggle for justice within the Thai legal system can often become. Plagued by uncertainty or by the knowledge that one's husband, son, father, or brother is innocent of charges leveled against him, it can take years for cases to be finally adjudicated. Meanwhile, the accused, those who have been incarcerated justly or unjustly, are more often than not denied bail summarily and repeatedly, and so are forced to languish in jails or prisons under extremely harsh conditions for inordinate periods of time. Without provisions for adequate legal assistance beyond their means, families are powerless to engage a process that seems designed to prolong a result, so that arrest has become, ipso facto, an extended punishment before an adjudicated resolution can be reached finally after a long period of time. Arrest has become, practically, a weapon to punish under martial law. Moreover, the Thai legal system appears to be one where the charged party is often presumed guilty until proven innocent rather than innocent until proven guilty, despite the fact that formally this is not supposed to be the case. The number of innocent people caught up in broadly cast nets of often unwarranted suspicion resulting in arbitrary arrest and detention is unknown, but these stories would seem to indicate that the numbers are far higher than they could be if sweeping, ham-fisted security measures were to be replaced with due diligence, carefully executed. The sheer incompetence and wanton power of the state's security apparatus have victimized not only those who have been detained without even an explanation of the charges brought against them, but consequently have victimized their families as well, insofar as their financial lives are often ruined, and the intimacy of family dynamics irrevocably distorted or destroyed. It is obvious that torture and intimidation of victims who are innocent leads to the further alienation of the families of targeted people. Navigating the state and legal processes to gain justice for their kin has bankrupted the lives of so many women and fed the fires of insurgency in many cases as a result.

The unique plight of Malay Muslim women in a highly gendered society deserves further comment to help readers understand the experiences the women have narrated. It would not be an exaggeration to say that the primary role of traditionalist Muslim women in Patani is to take care of and nurture others in their families. Their husbands, often married not by personal choice but by a convention (*kha sinsot*) somewhat akin to dowry, are often absent throughout the day, working or socializing while their wives are at home managing the family affairs dominated by childcare. Birth control measures are rarely in play, so it is not unusual for a young teenaged bride to give birth to many children until she is in her forties, a situation that brings with it very early-morning rises and late-night reposes, and increasing economic pressure. In families that live in multigenerational units, some women do work at rubber-tapping, or selling food, or engaging in sewing as a cottage labor, etc., but many others simply do not have the time or energy to pursue money. That has been traditionally the chief responsibility of the men of the house. When men are absented from this type of setup, it places an enormous burden on surviving spouses to somehow find the means to replace the income formerly provided by working spouses. If the role of traditional Malay Muslim women is to care for others in the family, when the husband or father is absented, who is left to care for them?

It is a woman's perspective and emotional drama that we are drawn into while reading these stories. There is one particularly important aspect of this perspective that does not find a prominent place in these narratives, but I raise it nonetheless because I am persuaded that it has simply gone unsaid. During one of my extended conversations with Soraya Jamjuree, she related to me a brief exchange that she had engaged in publicly with a Thai army general who had agreed to meet with her and other women activists. The general was discussing prospects for future negotiations between "Party A" (the Thai government) and "Party B" (the Malay insurgents). When he was finished, Soraya inquired of him how he thought negotiations would proceed if "Party C's" views were considered. For Soraya and other activists, "Party C" consists of the women of the Deep South. Many feel that this conflict is fundamentally not of their own making, though women have suffered so much on its account. The conflict has been nothing short of being the creation of Thai Buddhist and Malay Muslim men. Shouldn't women be allowed an intervention to recover their lost intimacies?

JOHN CLIFFORD HOLT
Chicago, Illinois, and Harpswell, Maine (USA)

Notes

1. Here, I am referring to Euro-American seekers such as, among many others, Henry Steele Olcott from the United States, William Colvin (U Dhammaloka) from Ireland, as well as some academically oriented scholars including T. W. Rhys Davids and I. B. Horner from Britain, who played pivotal roles in the establishment of the Pali Text Society in London, and Suzanne Karpeles from France, who became the librarian of Cambodia's Royal Library and led efforts to initiate the Institut Bouddhique in Phnom Penh. For a study of Olcott, see Stephen Prothero, *The White Buddhist: The Asian Odyssey of Henry Steele Olcott* (Bloomington: Indiana University Press, 1996); for U Dhammaloka, see Alicia Turner et al., *The Irish Buddhist: The Forgotten Monk*

Who Faced Down the British Empire (New York: Oxford University Press, 2020); for T. W. Rhys Davids, see L. A. Wickremeratne, *The Genesis of an Orientalist: Thomas Wilhelm Rhys Davids in Sri Lanka* (Delhi: Vedic Books, 1984); for Suzanne Karpeles, see Penny Edwards, *Cambodge: The Cultivation of a Nation* (Honolulu: University of Hawai'i Press, 2007), passim. For an overview of "Buddhist modernism," the eventual consequence of the benign Western gaze, see David McMahan, *The Making of Buddhist Modernism* (New York: Oxford University Press, 2008).

2. "Patani" is the historical name and how Malay Muslim reference the regions now encompassed by the Thai provinces of Pattani, Narathiwat, and Yala. See both maps. "Pattani" is the official Thai government name for the town that is the principal administrative seat of the province given the same name.

3. See especially two articles by Alexander Horstmann, "Ethnohistorical Perspectives on Buddhist-Muslim Relations and Coexistence in Southern Thailand: From Shared Cosmos to the Emergence of Hatred?," *SOJOURN: Journal of Social Issues in Southeast Asia* 19 (2004): 76–99, and "Living Together: The Transformation of Multi-Religious Coexistence in Southern Thailand," *Journal of Southeast Asian Studies* 41 (2011): 487–510. An excellent Ph.D. dissertation in anthropology at the University of Wisconsin in 2009 by Michiko Tsuneda, "Navigating Life on the Border: Gender, Migration, and Identity in Malay Muslim Communities in in Southern Thailand," highlights how Buddhists and Muslims have lived, until recently, in relative harmony, attending each other's life-cycle rites and exchanging moments of due respect on a regular basis. More recently, see also Ryoko Nishii, "A Corpse Necessitates Disentangled Relationships: Boundary Transgression and Boundary-Making in a Buddhist-Muslim Village in Southern Thailand," in *Buddhist-Muslim Relations in a Theravada World,* ed. Iselin Frydenlund and Michael Jerryson (Singapore: Palgrave Macmillan, 2020), 169–95.

4. Before the World Conference on Human Rights was convened in 1993, several Asian nations, including Thailand, signed the "Bangkok Declaration" reaffirming their commitment to the United Nations Charter and the Universal Declaration of Human Rights of 1948.

5. See especially Duncan McCargo's recent book *Fighting for Virtue* (2020) for an exposé and critical assessment of the Thai judiciary and its politicized machinations. McCargo points out that 95 percent of the cases brought about by Thai authorities result in convictions and that Thailand boasts one of the highest percentages of prisoners per population in the world.

6. In particular, see Michael Jerryson, *Buddhist Fury: Religion and Violence in Southern Thailand* (New York: Oxford University Press, 2011), a study that provides specific details of instances regarding a nexus of relations between elements of the Buddhist *sangha,* the government, and the Thai military to repress insurgency or to protect against it.

7. "Banditry" was the term used by Prime Minister Thaksin Shinawatra during his term in 2001–6 to characterize the rise of Malay Muslim insurgency, particularly after the Kru Se and Tak Bae "incidents" of 2004 (more on the significance of those watershed events later in this introduction). The term has largely stuck in the minds of many

urban Thai Buddhists when asked about the causes of the insurgency in the Deep South.

8. See especially the excellent collection of essays edited by Volker Grabowsky, *Regions and National Integration in Thailand 1892–1992* (Wiesbaden, Germany: Harrassowitz, 1995.)

9. Here I am quite consciously invoking the traditional Thai political paradigm of *mandala* as it was described and analyzed in S. J. Tambiah, *World Conqueror, World Renouncer* (Cambridge: Cambridge University Press, 1976). By referring to Bangkok as the center of the *mandala*, I mean to emphasize its continued legacy as a premodern axis and core of economic power in the country.

10. See Jim Glassman's essay "Class, Race and Uneven Development in Thailand," in *Routledge Handbook of Contemporary Thailand*, ed. Pavin Chachavapongpun (London: Routledge, 2019), which highlights how Thai nationalism and the formation of a racialized class structure in Thailand (first apparent under absolute monarchy before 1932) is a contributing vestigial cause to persistent underdevelopment in especially Isan (the northeast) and in the Muslim Deep South.

11. See especially Glassman, "Class," 30.

12. For historical accounts of the conflicts in Sri Lanka and Myanmar, see John Clifford Holt, ed., *Buddhist Extremists and Muslim Minorities: Religious Conflict in Contemporary Sri Lanka* (New York: Oxford University Press, 2016), and *Myanmar's Buddhist-Muslim Crisis: Rohingya, Arakanese and Burmese Narratives of Siege and Fear* (Honolulu: University of Hawai'i Press, 2019). See also Iselin Frydenlund and Michael Jerryson, eds., *Buddhist-Muslim Relations in a Theravada World* (Singapore: Palgrave Macmillan, 2020).

13. There remains an influential and economically robust Chinese business community in the Deep South to this day that consciously traces its origins to these very early times.

14. The wanton, malevolent, and utter destruction of potentially rival kingdoms was a potent political methodology deployed by the early Chakri dynasty forty years later against the Lao in Vientiane as well (see my *Spirits of the Place: Buddhism and Lao Religious Culture* [Honolulu: University of Hawai'i Press, 2009], 72–75). Descriptions of the devastation that occurred in Laos are similar to what one reads about in Patani.

15. For a full and excellent detailed account of the social, economic, and political history of Patani from its inception through the nineteenth century CE, see Francis Bradley, *Forging Islamic Power and Place* (Honolulu: University of Hawai'i Press, 2015), chapters 2 and 3. Bradley's book also chronicles the career of the Patani-born Sheik Daud al-Fatani in Mecca and the lasting legacy of his influence on Muslim theology and jurisprudence for what is now the Deep South of Thailand, Malaysia, and Indonesia, especially how his protégés were instrumental in establishing *pondoks* (traditional Muslim schools) throughout the Malay world. Sheik Daud al-Fatani published more than fifty books on Islamic theology focused on his understanding of neo-Sufism and Islamic jurisprudence (the Shafi-i school). He also translated more than fifty tracts from Arabic into Malay, thereby making significant extracts of Islamic thought accessible to Muslims in Southeast Asia. His own works are sometimes laced with

reflections on Patani's loss and a yearning for his people's recovery through adherence to Islamic practice. Bradley argues persuasively that his influence was paradigmatic for the emergence of a Muslim worldview that informs current aspirations for the recovery of autonomy.

16. This crucial shift is emphasized by Duncan McCargo, *Tearing Apart the Land: Islam and Legitimacy in Southern Thailand* (Singapore: National University of Singapore Press, 2009), 183–89.

17. Tomas Larsson, "Secularisation, Secularism, and the State," in *Routledge Handbook of Contemporary Thailand,* ed. Pavin Chachavalpongpun (London: Routledge, 2019), 279.

18. The ethos of this legacy has been explored incisively and empathetically by Muhammad Arafat bin Mohamad, first in his "Memories of Martyrdom and Landscapes of Fear: Fear and Resistance among the Malays of Southern Thailand" (master's thesis, Department of Southeast Asian Studies, National University of Singapore, 2007), and in his "Be-longing: Fatanis in Makkah and Jawi" (Ph.D diss., Department of Anthropology, Harvard University, 2013).

19. Cited in Norbert Ropers, "The Deep South of Thailand: Neither War nor Peace," in *Healing under Fire: The Case of Southern Thailand,* ed. Virasakdi Chongsuvivatwong, Louisa Chan Boegli, and Supat Hasuwannakit (Bangkok: The Deep South Relief and Reconciliation Foundation and the Rugiagli Initiative, 2014), 17–18.

20. Tomas Larsson, "Secularisation," 281.

21. The preceding paragraphs outlining the life and career of Haji Sulong are largely drawn from James Ockey, "Individual Imaginings: The Religio-Nationalist Pilgrimages of Haji Sulong Abdulkadir al-Fatani," *Journal of Southeast Asian Studies* 42 (2011): 89–119.

22. Duncan McCargo, *Mapping National Anxieties: Thailand's Southern Conflict* (Copenhagen: NIAS Press, 2012), 54.

23. A detailed and precise analysis of how Den staked out his positions in relation to traditionalist and "new school" Islam is provided expertly by McCargo, *Mapping,* 51–65.

24. Here we see some inconsistency between Haji Sulong, a modernist, and his son Den. Den was/is a shrewd, pragmatic, and astute political player who during his career consistently appealed to traditionalists for political support while arguing for the integrity of Malay Muslim identity within a pluralist conception of "Thainess."

25. McCargo, *Tearing the Land Apart,* 28.

26. The collaborative work of these two scholars has yielded an incisive assessment of the cumulative impact of international forms of Islam on the contemporary Muslim populace in Patani (see Srawat Aree and Christopher M. Joll, "The Religious Geography of Thailand's Malay Southern Provinces: Revisiting the Impact of South Asian and Middle Eastern Transnational Islamic Movements," *Sojourn: Journal of Social Issues in Southeast Asia* 35 [2020]: 343–63).

27. McCargo, *Tearing the Land Apart,* 2.

28. See especially Matt Wheeler, "People's Patron or Patronizing People? The Southern Border Provinces Administrative Centre in Perspective," *Contemporary Southeast Asia* 32 (2010): 208–33.

29. The haul amounted to 330 M16 rifles, two machine guns, seven rocket-propelled grenade launchers, and twenty pistols (see Mira Lee Manickam, *Just Enough: A Journey into Thailand's Troubled South* [Chiang Mai: Silkworm, 2013], 16).

30. McCargo, *Tearing the Land Apart*, 98–115.

31. McCargo, *Tearing the Land Apart*, 110–11.

32. Kru Se Mosque has never been completed because, as its legend avers, it was cursed by a young woman from China, Lim Kun Yew, who had made her way to Patani to convince her brother, the architect of the mosque, to return to China with her to marry in order that their family might prosper. Her brother refused, having converted to Islam. Lim Kun Yew, in the name of filial piety, cursed the mosque that it should never be completed and then committed suicide rather than return to China without her brother. Every year, her sainthood is commemorated en masse by the Chinese community, including many who come on pilgrimage from Malaysia. A watery shrine to her spirit is located just off the shore in the nearby Bay of Pattani. (I owe this account and a visit to the shrine to Hara Shintaro.)

33. Manickam, *Just Enough*, 58–59.

34. Michael Jerryson, *Buddhist Fury*, is the most detailed account of how the *sangha* became further implicated in the years that followed.

35. For a résumé of similar assertions by Buddhist nationalists pertaining to the Malay Muslims of the Deep South, see the chapter entitled "Buddhist Fears," in McCargo, *Mapping National Anxieties* 16–44; see also the extended relevant discussion by Jerryson, *Buddhist Fury*, 50–142.

36. For accurate statistics regarding the number of violent incidents and deaths recorded over the past sixteen years, see https://deepsouthwatch.org/th.

37. For an excellent study on how Malay Muslims have contended with "Thainess" in their daily lives, see Marte Nielson, *Negotiating Thainess: Religious and National Identities in Thailand's Southern Conflict* (Lund, Sweden: Centre for Theology and Religious Studies, Lund University, 2012).

38. The future capabilities of NGOs and CSOs to operate effectively in the Deep South are currently being threatened by a new law that requires that any financial support from foreign sources (read aid from USAID, other charitable agencies in the United States, the United Kingdom, the European Union, Japan, or even funding from the United Nations, etc.) must be channeled through the Thai government and approved for "appropriate use" by the Thai Ministry of the Interior. Aid must be seen as commensurate with the government's development plans, its "twenty-year agenda" (see https://www.thaienquirer.com/26557/new-government-legislation-could-spell-the -end-for-local-and-foreign-ngos-working-in-thailand/).

39. By invoking this phrase, I do not mean to suggest the types of messianic movements described by Vittorio Lantenari and Lisa Sergio in their classic study *The Religions of the Oppressed: A Study of Modern Messianic Cults* (New York: Knopf, 1963).

40. This profile of trust and faith in Allah is so powerful that sometimes one wonders about the extent to which this unwavering fidelity to transcendent power doesn't inhibit, to some extent, the agency of those trying to cope with such deleterious existential circumstances.

41. Parenthetically, I can note how a Muslim female doctor who has served as the Thai government's director of mental health in the Pattani District spoke to me at length about how, after some initial confusion upon her arrival on the scene in the aftermath of extreme violence, she and her team (consisting almost entirely of Muslims) were almost always warmly welcomed and deeply appreciated in Buddhist villages where the trauma of violence had recently occurred, while people were trying to cope with shock and emotional despair.

42. In some of my own interviews with Malay Muslim activists and intellectuals, comments have been made about inconsistent responses by the Thai government to the consequences of violence in the Deep South. Some ministries have made concerted efforts to address the needs of people seriously affected by violence, whereas other ministries seem to work only in lockstep with Thai military objectives.

IN SEARCH OF JUSTICE IN
THAILAND'S DEEP SOUTH

This Land Is for You

ROSHIDA DAO' WITH ROHANI CHUENARA

About forty years ago, I remember that my father was still with my family. He was a headmaster of an Islamic religious school. He taught religious subjects in a *pondok* called Al-Islamyyah, located in Talamkuerawat Village, Klong Yai Subdistrict, Yaring District, Pattani Province. I still clearly remember the scenes of that time. My father taught religious subjects in the prayer hall of the school to students from various generations, including youths, middle-aged men, and elderly people. Some students boarded in the school, while others came to the school from their houses. Most of his students were villagers from nearby. Apart from the principles of Islamic belief and religious practices, my father also taught about the plight of Patani Malays during that time. He said: "Patani Malays have been suppressed. We have our own Islamic law, but we cannot deploy it."

After the historical big demonstration in front of the Patani Provincial Hall in 1975, my family's life began to change. At that time, I was seven years old. State security officers frequently visited my father. The purpose of these visits was not to establish an amicable relationship but to find a way to throw him into jail. These circumstances finally drove my father to leave his house, in order to escape from the cruelty of the state security officers. He had to leave his *pondok* school unattended, his children fatherless, and his wife having to work hard to raise children alone, even though he had not died yet and had enough strength to raise children and send them to schools to have sufficient education.

My father had five children with my mother. I'm the second child; the youngest child was still very small at that time, just about five months old. Before leaving his house, my father came to every one of his children to kiss each one of us. While holding the youngest child in his arms, he said gently: "Behave yourself, and don't quarrel with each other. I have to go to work."

Almost forty years have passed since that day, and my father never came home again. My father left the *pondok* school and his family, which caused my mother great difficulties. She had to find any kind of job available. She did not complain about any job she had to do, as long as it was ethically

1

acceptable. She always said, "I will take up any kind of job in order to educate my children."

Nevertheless, I still had opportunities to visit my father in the forests with my mother. I always found a lot of rubber bands around the place where my father was, because every day villagers delivered food to my father and approximately twenty of his friends in the forest. The food delivered by villagers was so plentiful that they hardly could finish what had been provided.

Whenever my mother came home from work, she was utterly exhausted. After she fell asleep, driven both by affection and anxiety, I always put my hand on her chest to make sure that her heart was still beating. The thing I was most afraid of at that moment was that my mother also would leave us like my father.

When my mother sent me to a kindergarten, I was already eight years old. I was the tallest in the class, and my classmates always teased me, asking why I had just entered the kindergarten, whereas boys and girls of the same age were all in the first year of primary school. When I told my mother what my friends had said, she explained: "I couldn't send you to kindergarten like the others because you didn't have a birth certificate. It took a long time to get it. So you entered the kindergarten later than your friends of the same age." But luckily my achievement in the school was good, and my friends liked me and played with me well.

When I was in primary school, my mother's health began to deteriorate. Sometimes she was not capable of working. And so we had to go to school without pocket money, but my mother prepared lunch for us. As far as I could remember, the amount of money I could bring to school never exceeded five baht.

One day a teacher told us to think over the following questions: "Why can some people have good educations, and become teachers after they graduate? Where does the money to study come from?" I remembered these questions and mentioned them to my mother.

My mother gave me a political reply: "They are Siamese. They govern our country. So they have a lot of money. We are Malays, who are governed and suppressed by them. All we can do is just work. Even if we have an advanced education, we still have to serve them."

After I graduated from primary school, I wanted to extend my study to secondary school, but my mother said: "You don't have to study academic subjects. Studying religious subjects will be enough, because I have no money." But I was determined to study, and I tried to earn money myself. At that time, a villager hired me to package sweets. I earned twenty to thirty baht a day, which I spent as pocket money in school.

For my lower secondary education (from Form 1 to 3), I was in Prasarnwitthaya School, located in Phongsata Village, Yarang District, Pattani Province. I enjoyed my school life a lot, but I was sorry for my mother too, because she had to borrow money from other villagers for her children's schooling. My mother was always exhausted, but she never complained, because at the bottom of her heart, she wanted that all her children to have a good education. After I completed my lower secondary education, I wanted to continue my study, and I told my mother so. When I finished speaking, I saw tears falling on her cheek while she was nodding. Then I applied for Thamvitya Mulniti School in Yala Province. For this secondary education (from Form 4 to 6), I needed more money for expenses. Sometimes I had to fast because the amount of money I had was not enough to buy food. I only could afford the base fee to and from school, which I still remember was four baht. During four years of my upper secondary education, I only had two sets of school uniforms.

After I completed my upper secondary education, I thought it was no longer necessary to learn academic subjects. So I only extended my study in religious subjects until I finished the third year of *thanawi* curriculum, or Class 10 of the religious curriculum. When I was in the final year, I did practice teaching in a *tadika* school in order to evaluate how much I had learned. At that time, I had to buy miscellaneous things, and my mother had to borrow more money. I felt really sorry for her, but she kept her feelings inside. My mother asked one of her friends to lend us one thousand baht. Instead of lending, she gifted the money to us.

After I finished my third year of *thanawi,* I didn't want to stay without doing anything. So I went to Malaysia to study Islam with my father. (After he could no longer stay home, he had escaped to Malaysia and set up a *pondok* school there.) My father arranged for me to marry one of his favorite students in the school. His name was Sakariya Yuso, one of the victims who died in the Kru Se Mosque on 28 April 2004.

Originally, my husband studied in a traditional *pondok* school in Patani, but when he heard the news that my father, who had earned a wide reputation as a charismatic religious teacher, had moved to Malaysia and opened a *pondok* school there, he also moved to Malaysia to study with him.

After our wedding ceremony, my husband and I came back to our homeland. Even though life in Malaysia was safe and comfortable, it still could not compete with our homeland. We had no property, but we both had knowledge.

After we came back, we set up a small hut to live in it. Gradually there came children from nearby to study religion and the way of reciting the Qur'an. Our life at that time was tough. We did not have permanent jobs. At one time farming was our main occupation, working in paddy fields. However, we never left our books. We read books all the time, especially books about society. Later my husband got a teaching job in a school nearby.

My family's life was happy, and we had five children, two boys and three girls. Apart from teaching, whenever he had spare time, my husband was engaged in farming, working in paddy fields, and planting fruit trees. He also did some part-time jobs such as cutting grasses and raising seedlings, or catching fish in the marshes. It can be said that he did everything he liked to do, regardless of the difficulty of these jobs. The only thing he cared about was that none of the jobs he did violated Islamic principles.

The income for an *ustaz* (male religious teacher) at that time was not stable. When money was short for the school budget, his salary was not paid. When the school had only a small amount of money, only half of the salary was paid. But driven by his love of teaching and providing knowledge, no matter if he got his salary or not, he performed his duty as a teacher without complaining and being disheartened. He thought that a knowledgeable person had a duty to disseminate knowledge to a society in which the importance of religious affairs was increasingly neglected.

Therefore, the main source of family income at that time was not his salary as an *ustaz* but the miscellaneous odd jobs we did in our spare our time. Even though our income was small, we managed to control our spending. We were anything but extravagant, buying only what was urgently needed. If things were not really necessary, we bought them later.

I still remember one day when villagers came to ask a favor from my husband—to teach the way of reciting the Qur'an and Islam from textbooks written in Jawi script called *kitab*s in the evenings. He agreed to teach them every night except Fridays. He devoted his life to teaching and reading. In the daytime he taught in the school. In the evenings he taught the Qur'an and *kitab*s. He also opened a special class for *nahu saraf* [Arabic grammar]. All of this teaching left him no time for farming. He spent a lot of time reading, searching for reference books, opening up Arab-Malay dictionaries, or seeking advice from Muslim intellectuals.

Our life went on smoothly. We lived simply, not attaching any importance to acquiring property. My husband once said: "Our knowledge that we have acquired is our priceless property. No one can plunder or steal it from us. Most importantly, our knowledge can bring us property."

In 2003 I gave birth to my youngest child in the Pattani Hospital. This was the first time I had gone into labor in a hospital. All of the older children had been born in my house with the help of a midwife. I preferred giving birth to my children in my own house because a woman helped with the labor, and she believed in Islam like us. When I had pain, she could come to my house to massage me and encourage me according to Islamic ways. She always told me to be patient, to remember Allah at all times and firmly to believe in Him. When I was in labor she always smiled to encourage me, patiently waiting for the coming of a new baby. When a baby arrived, she would immediately recite *doa'* [supplication] in the baby's ear.

The reason I chose to give birth to my child in a hospital this time was because I felt incapable of doing so in my house. When I first had labor pains, I felt exhausted, probably because of my age and because this was the fifth child. So I decided to give birth to it in the hospital. In the hospital, my husband and I got to know the owner of the Fitri Palas Gold Shop. We had good conversations and became good friends, visiting each other afterward.

The date 28 April 2004 is a dreadful one for Patani Malays and everyone in the world. On the day of that incident, the innocent lives of those who were demanding justice from the Thai state, which had governed them for a long time, were brutally terminated by the cruel hands of those who have power in our country. My beloved husband was one of the victims.

The security officers ruthlessly used heavy firearms to attack the Kru Se Mosque without heeding any humanitarian principles. They used all kinds of weapons, and the amount of money spent to kill innocent people had to have been enormous. They never thought that the money spent to kill those who had been demanding justice from the state would lead to an endless devastation in our country.

My husband left our home in the evening of Wednesday, 27 April. While I was feeding my youngest child, who was about one year old, my husband told me that he would go to a mosque near our home for the *maghrib* prayer [the prayer after sunset]. I waited for his return all through the night. Finally, I dozed, waking up for the *subuh* prayer [the prayer at dawn], but he hadn't come home yet.

At about eight o'clock on the new day, Thursday, 28 April 2004, there were news reports from various TV channels about a group of terrorists gathered inside the Kru Se Mosque. It was said that they had used the mosque as a shield. The reporters alleged that those who were inside the mosque were terrorists, "southern bandits," or security disruptors. These news reports really broke my heart. At that time, I didn't know at all that my husband was inside the mosque too, because I thought he was still sleeping inside the mosque near my house where he went to perform *maghrib* prayer last night.

While listening to the news reports, I wondered who the "southern bandits" would turn out to be and whether or not my husband was inside the mosque as well. Why hadn't my husband come home yet? Is he one of the people branded as "southern bandits?" I was so confused that I had to turn off the television. I sat down without saying anything, looking at things like his clothes still hanging on the clothesline, his textbooks, and his pens and pencils on the desk. I also noticed his shoes were still on the stairs. Then my children became petulant and began to cry because they were hungry. I went to the kitchen and cooked rice and fried eggs to feed them. I couldn't eat anything myself. So, I laid down, hugging my small one, while my thoughts scattered in every direction.

Finally, something completely unexpected happened. The village headman came to my house and told me to search for my husband's identity card to be brought to the district office. When I handed over my husband's identity card, the village headman said, "Your husband may have already died in the Kru Se Mosque and his body brought to the Ingkhayuth Military Fort." I was taken aback, not knowing what to do. I sat down on the spot and recited a prayer for the dead. My older children understood what had happened. They said nothing and asked no questions.

In the evening, somebody told us to pick up the body from the Ingkhayuth Military Fort for the funeral according to religious principle. I couldn't eat anything that day. Things related to the funeral were dealt with by relatives. After they claimed the body, they came back in the late evening. Relatives came to pick us up so we could stay in a house near the graveyard. Neighbors and his students came in great number to join the procession of carrying his body to the grave, which had been already prepared.

The *imam* asked me whether my husband had ordered anything before he left our home. I honestly answered that he had ordered nothing because he hadn't thought that he would die, and there had been no sign whatsoever that he was departing from his children, his wife, and his students, whom he had always loved and taken care of.

We didn't wash the body of my husband because in Islamic law it is stated that the body of those who died in an encounter with *kafir*, or infidels, mustn't be washed, and it should be buried with the clothes being worn at the moment of his death. It is prohibited to dress the body with any other clothing.

For a week after his death, my appetite was gone. My small child got irritable because she couldn't drink enough milk from my breast. I had to buy powdered milk to feed her. The older children also had no appetite. They grieved for their beloved father because he had died in such an abrupt way. What's more, their father's life had come to an end at the cruel hand of the country's security forces. I still could hear his reminder to the children: "You study hard, my children, so that you don't have to be their slaves. We had our own dignity, but it has been stolen by these others."

The news of the mass killing in the Kru Se Mosque caused the entire world to pay attention to Thailand. The question was raised as to why people in the southern border provinces had to stand up against the state. Since

Patani was first invaded by the Thai until this very day, the struggle has never stopped. No matter how many times the government has changed, the unrest still continues.

Surely, one of the many negative impacts of the death of my husband for me, his wife, his children, his students, and those who knew him was that journalists referred to those who were involved in the Kru Se Mosque massacre as "southern bandits." Those we knew who had heard the news of my husband's death expressed their condolences, saying that the journalists were not careful enough in choosing their words. They unanimously said that it was the government that should be called a bunch of terrorists because of the damage they had inflicted.

My husband's young students were too scared to visit my home because the security officers were always watching those who came to see us. They might be seen as having had a close tie with my husband.

Not long after the "Kru Se Mosque *incident*," the security officers detained some young fellows in the village acting on the authority now prescribed by the special laws [martial law]. They were asked about my late husband's character, whether or not he had been a commander of "security disruption incidents," and if he had recruited the local youths to follow his path. Every one answered that he had been a good man with good religious knowledge.

After my husband's death, all the burden of raising my children fell upon me. The amount of money donated by villagers was decreasing. My children had to go to school every day. The government, at that time, didn't care about the lives of those who were left behind. They couldn't care less about the lives of the bereft families, letting those who had been affected by the incident fend for themselves.

Ajarn Soraya Jamjuree was the first person to come to visit our home. I still remember that when she came to my house it was already late in the evening. She asked about where the daily cost of living for my family came from. I said I sold foods and sweets to the students of the Islamiyah School. The average daily income was around 100 to 150 baht. But I had no source of income during weekends and school holidays. Before Ajarn Soraya left our home, she took three one-hundred-baht banknotes from her wallet to give to me, saying that the money was to buy sweets for my children. She also said she would come again.

Not long time after that, she called to tell me that some well-intended person from Bangkok would come and visit me. At first I was confused, imagining that the person might be a spy sent to search out my family or might be coming to threaten the family members of those who had been killed in the Kru Se Mosque. I got scared when I was told the person was a senator in the government.

The senator did come to our house as had been arranged. I was stunned because I hadn't thought that he would really come to visit us, given that the situation at that time in the region was really tense. Soldiers and police officers were everywhere, and so were countless military checkpoints on the roads. Villagers had to be cautious when they went out because they were afraid of stray bullets from the guns deployed by security officers. These soldiers with guns were ready to pull the trigger anytime they suspected the villagers of being bandits; there were no safeguards, and all powers were vested in their hands. Even if they shot villagers mistakenly, there would be no problem because the government had budgeted money to be paid to victims' families as "remedy money."

The senator I mentioned before was Sophorn Suphaphong. He was a humble person of good behavior who spoke very politely. He sat down on the floor of my house, which was not very clean. He came with some students from Prince of Songkla University. At first, he asked casual questions that were easy to answer. We had a good chat including a lot of laughter. Apparently, he was not the kind of person who regarded himself more highly than others and who would condescend to us. He was kind to my children too. He didn't stay long because he had to visit other families as well. Before leaving, he encouraged my children and told them, "Study hard so that you can be like your father." From his speech, it was clear that he didn't regard my husband as a bandit.

I was very impressed by this senator. How could he understand us to this extent? I thought if he had been a Muslim, he could have reached out to more people. Or, had he been the leader of this country, he would be able to establish peace and order. On that day he gave us ten thousand baht to be used for the schooling of my children and other necessities, so that I wouldn't have to borrow money from anybody.

After he went back to Bangkok, driven by his sympathy for those who had been affected by the "incident" like us, he visited us again. On this occasion he said: "You look happier now. Last time I saw you, you looked listless."

My children were always talking about him. They asked why he was so nice. They thought he must be a Muslim. I told them that his behavior followed the ethics of our Prophet. On his second visit, he gave us some more money to encourage us, to be used for the education of the children. And he continued to provide us with financial support because he saw that most of those families who were affected were poor and had many children. In order to help those who were in difficulty, he offered five scholarships of five hundred baht every three months for my children. Our life and financial status improved a lot, and we could save money in the bank. When we had no job to do or during school holidays, we could rely on this money.

In 2008 Sophorn stopped providing money because he thought those who had been affected by the incident had already overcome the crisis. They could fend for themselves as the children had already grown up. But before that time, the government was led by Thaksin Shinawatra. He had made an arrangement in the Pattani Province so that the children of those who had been affected by the "incident" could receive scholarships and sent Graduate Volunteers to keep data on those of us affected. Finally, my children were granted scholarships, which continue to this day.

In any case, even though the government gave us hundreds of thousands of baht as remedy money, in regard to the "Kru Se Mosque 'incident,'" I still see the government in a negative way, because no justice has been delivered to those who sacrificed their lives. The remedy efforts should not merely be giving money or bringing family members to Mecca. The real remedy would come from finding out the facts about what our people really wanted and punishing those who were responsible for the "incident" according to the law.

If I am asked whether or not I am grateful to those who paid tens of thousands of baht to the families of those who were killed in the "incident," I don't know how to answer, because all these things were done by "them" for their own political purposes, after they had received pressure from all over the world, especially from Muslim countries. And so, I say, "Justice has not yet come to us."

Whose Security Is This?

ROPIAH SAMAE AND PATEEMOH YUSOH

The night before Idilfitri (Eid al-Fitr)[1] of 2003, I hurried to the house of my elder brother on the opposite side of the road. I shouted, asking him to open the door. At that moment, my brother was sewing white skullcaps called *kapiyoh* to send to Saudi Arabia, to be sold during the period of the upcoming *hajj* pilgrimage. My brother opened the door and let me in. I saw hundreds of finished skullcaps in a pile tied together with strings. My sister-in-law was also sewing skullcaps with her hands.

My brother asked if I already had gotten a new dress to be worn on Eid. I said "no" in a feeble and spiritless voice. The dress I had ordered from my friend wasn't finished yet. My brother said if I had already bought cloth, I could give it to him so that he would be able to sew a suitable dress with it, with embroidery of beautiful flowers on it. Extremely glad to hear this, I hurried to my home to pick up the cloth and handed it to my brother.

However, my brother was concerned about the order of skullcaps that he had to finish. He said, if he could finish the order, they would come and pick up the skullcaps the next day. I was disappointed to hear that because I thought he might not have the time to sew my dress before the advent of Eid. So, I went home and cried secretly, because on the day of Eid everyone would have a new dress, both adults and children.

At dawn of the next day, on the day of Eid, Yasir, a son of my brother, brought my dress for Eid, which his father had just finished sewing. It was a long gray dress in Pakistani style with embroidery of wildflowers with light-green pistils. The neck of the dress was decorated with white spirals, the same pattern of decoration used for skullcaps.

I tried on the dress. It fit me perfectly, even though my brother hadn't measured my body before sewing. At that time, I felt that this was the most beautiful Pakistani-style dress in the world. After that, whenever I had to go

1. A Muslim festival to celebrate the end of the fasting month during Ramadan. Id Al-Fitr is on the first day of Shawwal, the next lunar month of Islam after Ramadan.— *Translator*

out, I wore this dress and proudly told my friends that my brother had made the dress embroidered with flowers.

After the day of the "incident," however, I stopped wearing the dress and kept it inside the case of the long pillow that I embraced so that I would remember and see him, my brother, in my dream.

The date of the Kru Se Mosque "incident" was 28 April 2004. I remember the date well to this day. The incident is still stapled to my eyes and my heart. On that day I was in Sabayoi District, Songkhla Province. I went out for rubber-tapping with my husband around five o'clock after the *subuh* [*fajr*] prayer. We finished rubber-tapping at around seven o'clock, and we sat down in a hut inside the rubber estate. I heard the sound of a motorbike approaching, ridden by my brother-in-law.

He walked to our place in an alarmed way, telling me that my family had called him to tell us that my brother had been shot. I was shocked, and I asked in great confusion, "Where was he shot?" My brother-in-law said he wasn't sure, because on that day there were many violent incidents in several places, especially at the junction of Ban Niang and the Kru Se Mosque. My brother-in-law said he saw the news on TV.

I was overwhelmed at hearing of these incidents. What was going on? How were these "incidents" connected to my brother? I tried to console myself by believing that he might just have gotten hit by stray bullets, and that he must be safe.

I went home immediately. When I arrived at the junction of Ban Niang, I saw a lot of people standing on the road near the place where there were bloodstains. After seeing this, I sped up my car so that I could get home as soon as possible. When I finally arrived at my house in Ban Som Village, Khuannoree Subdistrict, the village was completely silent, as if it had been abandoned. When I entered my house, there was nobody inside. Someone told me that my family had gone out to find my brother, together with the relatives of villagers who had disappeared after these violent "incidents" had occurred. The only thing I could do was to wait alone inside the house, enshrouded in utter confusion about what had happened.

While waiting for my family's return and hearing the details about the "incidents," I tried to follow the news from TV and radio. The announcer mentioned the names of those who were injured in the "incidents," and one of the names was "Abdulroni Cheloh," my brother. He was injured in the "incident" that had occurred in Maelan District, Pattani Province. The announcer said that their relatives would be able to visit those who had been injured in the Ingkhayutthaborihan Military Base on the following Wednesday, five days later.

On Wednesday my family and I hurried to the Ingkhayutthaborihan Military Base, but we were disappointed because when we arrived, we were told by a soldier that my brother wasn't there. We didn't accept that. During that time there were plenty of journalists, so I asked them to help us to find my brother. Noticing that my family and I wouldn't go home, the soldiers let us get into a military vehicle, on the condition that we wouldn't tell the journalists that, in fact, my brother was there.

The military vehicle driven by a soldier brought us around the military base and finally arrived at the military hospital inside the base, which was not far from the entrance gate. When I got out of the vehicle, I felt scared, not having strength to accept what was going to happen. So, I let my mother, sister-in-law, nieces and nephews (the children of my brother)[2] go inside the ward to see him first. I waited outside and had a chance to talk with a soldier. He said they had kept one of the insurgent leaders here, one who was very religious and never left his prayer. I asked which one. He pointed at my brother, saying that "the one who is going through haemodialysis."

I was taken aback. From the soldiers' point of view, those who prayed would be immediately regarded as terrorists. I could only make up my mind to find out what had really happened.

I entered the ward to see my brother after the others. I saw him chained to the iron bed with handcuffs. On his chest there were gauze bandages to stop bleeding. His face was very pale. There was a trace of a stitch on his chest. I hugged my brother with anxiety. I asked, "What happened?" He replied, "A guy called Roya invited me to send someone who wanted to clear the forest." Then he began to cry.

I couldn't help feeling sorry for my brother. He asked when he would be able to go home. I tried to soothe him, telling him to wait until his condition improved. He was worried that they might send him anywhere, even though he hadn't done anything wrong. He asked me to help him, but I didn't know what to do because I had no idea about what had happened and what could happen. The only thing in my mind was utter confusion.

Before I went out of the ward, a police officer told me to find a lawyer. He said the lawyer must be a good one. If not, he said, my brother would surely be thrown into prison. What he had told me caused a severe headache. I was even more stressed than before. So, I tried to compose myself to find a way through.

The first thing I could think of was to find someone who understood [the

2. In Thai, both a niece and a nephew are called as "laan." A reader cannot tell if the term refers to either a niece or nephew, or even to both. The lack of the plural indicator in Thai nouns also causes problem in the translation. In this article, the term is translated to refer to both nieces and nephews (in plural). — *Translator*

circumstances] and was close to us. I visited the village headman to ask for advice, but his reaction disappointed me even more. He said: "Your brother's case is connected to the security of the state. There's hardly any chance that he'll be released."

At that time, I had absolutely no idea how to help my brother. The only thing I could do was to visit and soothe him. Later, my brother was sent to the Pattani Central Prison. My family and I began to become determined to fight for my beloved brother.

I started to find a lawyer who would help us deal with my brother's case. My stepfather introduced me to a volunteer lawyer. He worked out of sincerity without charging any fee. I wanted him to help us, but he was reluctant to do so. So I consulted him and tried to bail my brother out by using a title deed of a piece of land belonging to a relative. However, we were disappointed again when the court refused to grant him bail. We tried to apply for bail again but were refused by the next court too. While my brother was detained, my family and I had to make a very concerted effort to find a way to help him. Probably no one could understand what kind of hardship villagers like us had to endure. We had had no idea about the judicial system, and we had never appeared in court before either. But we had to stand up and engage in a business that is difficult for ordinary villagers.

Finally, the day for which we had waited such a long time arrived. On that day the court delivered its verdict. But the verdict made all of us powerless. The court sentenced him to death. We immediately appealed. My brother denied all of the charges, but the sentence delivered by the court of appeal was the same: capital punishment.

My family and I didn't give up in our efforts to prove my brother's innocence. We appealed to the Supreme Court. During that period of time, someone told me that if my brother confessed, he would get a less severe punishment, from the death penalty to life imprisonment. But my brother was firm in his innocence. He denied every charge against him in every court. While waiting for the verdict from the Supreme Court, my family and I were extremely stressed about the impending verdict from the Supreme Court. It would decide life or death for my brother. Finally, the Supreme Court sentenced him to life imprisonment. We felt relieved, because life imprisonment was still better than the death penalty.

Even after the final sentence had been delivered and his case was closed, the question that has always haunted my family has never been answered. Why must such things happen to my brother, despite the fact that he is a man of good nature, helping others all the time, honest, never thinking or speaking ill of others? Why must it be my brother? He and his family lived and worked in Saudi Arabia for nearly twenty years. During that period, he had never come back to visit our family in Thailand. He lived in Thailand for just a few years before the "incident" happened. How was it possible for him to become a sympathizer of the insurgents in such a short time?

Why did he wear a *telok belanga* [a Malay-style shirt] on that day? It was different from how the other people who were involved in the "incident" had dressed themselves on that day. They all wore their black suits used to stage violence. And why had he never agreed to confess to all the accusations against him in order to prove his innocence, even though acknowledging the accusations would have meant his survival and the denial his death?

The unrest in the southern border provinces has affected many people. Whenever violence occurs, the life and properties of the local people are inevitably affected. As a consequence, these events cause a lot of pain, hatred, and stress. These violent occurrences can affect anybody, but people might be affected in different ways, either as a father, a mother, a child, a husband, a wife, a brother, a relative, or a friend.

Many government agencies and local organizations offer help and remedies for those who are affected by the unrest in the southern border provinces, especially to children and women who have lost their beloved fathers, husbands, or brothers. They are provided with help from both the government and private sections.

However, they have neglected or forgotten yet another type of people who are also affected by the unrest. These people haven't lost their beloved family members, but they have lost *freedom*. They are defendants in security cases who will be detained until the cases finish. The problems that happened to my family are no different from what happens to a child who has lost his or her father, a wife who has lost her husband, or a sister who has lost her elder brother. But what is the reason that people like us have never been provided with any remedy when such a burden falls on sisters, wives, and mothers? This burden is really difficult and exhausting to bear, causing us feel to feel hopelessness. But we will never withdraw, because we must sustain the lives of our children, nieces, and nephews. We also have to support their educations as well.

If a family member is detained in the Ingkhayutthaborihan Military Base and brought to court, we always feel stigmatized. Even when we brought our nieces and nephews to the court, one of the officers there said: "Don't bring them inside. It's not good to let the children see their father who is a terrorist." I tried to take it in a positive way. The officer might think that it would be better not to let children see a terrorist out of his goodwill. However, the term "terrorist" used for the children's father was something we didn't wish to hear, and I won't forget this insult for the rest of my life.

During the first four years, we had no idea about the law and the judicial system. We needed legal aid and explanations about my brother's case. We only knew that it was a security case. But what is security? What kind of legal processes did we have to go through? The thing I most worry about is the future and education of our children, especially boys, because there is a serious problem of drug abuse in this region.

So far, there has been no one who speaks up and tells the public that this is one of the consequences of the unrest. Probably some government agencies think that helping families like us is a matter of helping the families of terrorists. But according to the law, a defendant is still innocent until proven guilty. But if there is no one to come to offer a hand to help us and hundreds of other families who experience the same fate as us, the number of local people who fight against and hate the state will only increase. There will be more children who are deprived of opportunities for education, lacking affection from their family, not attending school, or becoming drug addicts due to the lack of a breadwinner in the family. Even though the government is trying to reduce the number of children who are out of the school system or drug addicted, there is little chance for these efforts to be successful.

There are still more than five hundred defendants in pending security cases. This means that almost five hundred families in the southern border provinces, including the four districts of Songkhla Province, have to go through hardship. Every government agency organization should think again and revise [their policies] and reduce their prejudice in order to stop violence.

Justice Should Be Fought For

Yaena Salaemae with Soraya Jamjuree and Suraiya Wani

My struggle for justice in the three southern border provinces began when I was orphaned. My mother died when I was two years old. My father left our house one month after my mother's death. I have ten siblings. Four of them were from the same parents, whereas with six others I share either mother or father. My auntie, my mother's elder sister, received us, and two elder brothers from a different father also took care of us too. They sent every one of us to school, but we only could finish the fourth grade of primary school. My younger brothers' father had died when they were still small. My father left us after my mother had died.

I started my schooling when I was eight years old and finished fourth grade when I was fourteen years old. I went to Ban Sala Mai School, Sala Mai Subdistrict, Tak Bai District, Narathiwat Province. It was about 3 kilometers from my house to the school. We had to walk to the school because there was no car at that time. I had never worn shoes because my family couldn't afford to buy them. A pair of shoes cost fifteen baht, but I had never bought a pair of shoes until I finished my primary education due to the poverty of my family. At times I didn't take any money with me to school because I had no money to take. Sometimes I took fifty satang and brought a lunch from home. From first grade to fourth grade, I was always a top student. When the teachers examined our notebooks, they always examined mine first in order to identify an example. Ever since I began school, I was conscious of justice. If teachers had beaten students for no good reason, I didn't accept such behavior, and I told other students that they shouldn't accept it either.

After I finished my primary education in Ban Sala Mai School, I went to Muno Pondok School, Sungai Golok District, Narathiwat Province. I studied there for three years, both religious and academic subjects. The *pondok* school had three classes for academic subjects, and ten classes for religious subjects. I could only study there for three years without graduating because there was no money for me to continue. When I was in the *pondok* school, the amount of money I could spent in one month was one hundred baht. I had to be very frugal, buying only things that were really necessary. I only spent three baht per day because I only had one hundred baht per month. In the morning I had to wake up early to cook rice so that I didn't have to buy cooked rice. Every morning I paid fifty satang for fish. I got a lot of fish, and I could eat them all day. I brought everything from my house, including rice and cooking oil. I made the cooking oil by myself from coconuts so I didn't have to buy it from markets.

When I was in Muno Pondok School, the trip from my home to the school was difficult because at that time there wasn't a motor road to Sungai Golok. I had to take a long boat going down the Bangnara River to Sathorn Island. Then I had to take another boat going up Golok River to the *pondok* school. The *pondok* was a boarding school, so I studied and lived there. I went home only twice a year because the trip to and from home was difficult. I was a good student in the *pondok* school too. At that time my dream was to have higher education. But it was impossible. I was called back to my home because my auntie didn't have enough money for my schooling.

I came back to my home in Carok, Phraiwan Subdistrict, Tak Bai District, Narathiwat Province, and studied in Sala Mai Pondok School that was near my home. I had to walk to school again. My family didn't have a car. I studied *kitab* [learning of religion by using Malay] and Quran for one year in the *pondok*. I didn't have to spend a lot of money like when I had studied academic subjects. We studied two *kitabs*[1] for a year. After that, when I was seventeen years old, I got married. My husband's name was Mayuso Malong.

Seven months after our marriage, I got pregnant. Our life was tough, and both of us had to work to earn a living. My husband worked in a rice refinery in Malaysia two times every year. Every time he went to Malaysia, he had to be there for forty to sixty days, and he brought back five to six thousand baht. We were happy to have that significant amount of money. We saved money to buy a piece of land for paddy fields. At that time, we only had two children.

My husband's education was only until fourth grade like me. His family was poor. He had his father and mother, whereas I didn't have father and mother. Even though my father was still alive, he left our home one month after my mother's death. I didn't seen him again until I was seventeen years old. I was about to get married, and I had tried to find him. Finally, I found him in Pattani, as he lived in Palas, Panare District. At that time, he already had three children from his new wife. It's been fifteen years now since he passed away.

When I got married, we still stayed with my auntie because we didn't have

---

1. *Kitab* is a textbook on Islam written by an *ulama,* written in Malay by using Jawi script.—*Translator*

enough money to build a house. We worked until we had four children, and at that time we could afford to build our own house.

My first job after my marriage was sewing headscarves for a big Chinese merchant in Narathiwat. He sold these headscarves in weekly markets. He gave us cloth and needles to be sewn into headscarves. At first, he ordered us to sew fifty scarves. I finished the job in one week, and he paid ten baht per each scarf. Later these scarves sold well, and the merchant ordered me to sew thousands of scarves. I couldn't do that alone, so I hired villagers from the same village. I paid eight baht for each scarf and took two baht for profit. Finally, I could save money that came to five hundred thousand baht. This was the money that was used to build a house near my auntie's.

While I sewed headscarves for the merchant, I got to know retailers in markets in Tak Bai and Rantau Panjang, Malaysia. I became the owner of my own business, hiring hundreds of people. I sent headscarves to small retailers in markets in Tak Bai, Sungai Golok, and to Malaysia for ten years.

When I made headscarves I endured a lot. I had hardly enough time to sleep because I had to meet deadlines for the orders. Sometimes I got an order for thousands of headscarves. On such occasions I had a big profit of 1,500 to 2,000 baht; that was a large amount of money at that time.

When I had seven children, I rented out a shop in the Taba Market [a border market in Tak Bai] so that I could sell headscarves every day, both for retailing and wholesaling. I did this business for ten years, but I still had difficulty in finding enough money for my children's education.

After our capital ran out, we closed our shop in the market and sold it. With that money, I bought a sewing machine, and I began to accept orders for headscarves in my home. The income was very good. I could earn 1,000 to 1,200 baht per day. I worked without sleeping for three years, to the extent that my skin became white because I had no time to go out and to be exposed to the sunlight. I didn't even have enough time to go to markets. My husband helped me by doing whatever he could do, such as making holes in the headscarves to make patterns, cutting unnecessary threads out of headscarves, etc. When I didn't sleep, he didn't sleep.

At around that time, my husband's younger sister passed away. We had to take care of her three children. After that I got pregnant with our eighth child, the last one, who is fifteen years old now. In addition, I had to raise two more children of one of my siblings. Their parents lived in Malaysia, so we had to take care of them. Their father was a suspect in a security case. So, altogether we had thirteen children to care for, and five of them are still in school. Although this burden is heavy, I must endure so that everyone can get an education.

The villagers in my village, Ban Charo, were farmers. Most of the youths from the village went to school and studied until they finish their educations. Women worked as seamstresses, and men worked in construction sites. Almost all the villagers were Muslims. There were only two Buddhist families.

I was highly regarded by the villagers. When there were events like Maulid [celebration of the Prophet's birthday], festivals of a *tadika* school or a mosque, villagers always asked for my advice and invited me to be the leader. I used the knowledge I obtained from my primary education of four years for the benefit of the community. I had never done anything wrong in my community. I didn't go outside the village and stayed there until the Tak Bai "incident" happened in 2004.

Before the Tak Bai "incident," I was very ill and couldn't walk because I had worked too hard. One week before the "incident," I had recovered enough to go to markets. I had been ill for two months, and I was soaked in tears all the time. I couldn't help thinking about what would happen if something happened to me. How could the children under my care survive? Could they finish their educations? For the two months I was ill, I always prayed so that Allah would heal me so I could start working again to take care of my children. Sometimes I performed *salat al-hajjah* [prayer of need], and sometimes I thought it could be a challenge from Allah to test my endurance.

After the Tak Bai incident happened on 25 October 2004 [during the month of Ramadan], Muhammad Maruwasi Malong, one of our sons, was involved in a case involving the demonstration in Tak Bai. He was accused of being one of the ringleaders of the demonstration. The security officers also added another accusation: hiding weapons.

From the day of the incident, I had stopped sewing because I had to follow my son's case. My relatives had to face charges related to the demonstration too. Altogether fifty-eight people were charged. I began to think a lot because I had to find a way to bail out my son, though it would cost 250,000 baht for bail. Our lawyer suggested that we gather the title deeds of our relatives' lands, which were valued about 1.5 million baht, and so we used these deeds to bail out my sons and my relatives in the village, altogether six people. We suggested that others do the same thing, and finally we were able to bail out all fifty-eight people.

When we were fighting our cases in the court, I played the role of a liaison between the lawyers from the Lawyers Council from Bangkok and defendants of the Tak Bai cases. The head of the lawyer team at that time was Ratsada Manuratsada. He gathered more than thirty local lawyers from Songkhla, Pattani, Yala, and Narathiwat to conduct our cases without charging us any fee for their help. These cases needed a lot of lawyers. We didn't know these lawyers before.

At that time, I felt I was in a real difficulty. When the lawyers wanted to contact defendants or their families, some of them didn't have a phone. So I had to go to their houses. Some of them lived in a place far from my village, such as Koh Sathorn or Bang Khun Thorng. I didn't know where they lived, but I had to try until I finally could find their houses.

I often went to court, at first two or three times a week. Then it became once a month, then once in every two months. Altogether I went to court fifty-two times in two years until finally the cases were withdrawn. I went to every session of my son's case and was the only woman in the courtroom. The other women were children or wives of the defendants waiting outside, not daring to go inside. One day a judge asked me if I was a defendant. I stood up and replied: "No, sir. I'm a mother of a defendant. I worry that my son might give wrong answers, as he is not very good at speaking Thai."

The judge made a suggestion: "In that case, you'd better be a liaison. We can work more conveniently."

Lawyer Ratsada [Manuratsada] told the judge, "Yes, she's already acting as the liaison to help us in contacting the relations of fifty-eight defendants."

Sometimes I had to be a translator in the courtroom too. The judge recommended something to the defendants. After the session, the judge told me to translate what he had said to the defendants. At that time, I wasn't good at speaking Thai, but I could understand what I heard.

In fact, after the incident in Tak Bai, I became the liaison between security officers and those who were charged, and between the defendants and the lawyers. Not long after the incident, security officers tried to see the defendants by visiting them, and on some occasions they brought a basket filled with gifts. However, the defendants, out of fear, didn't want to see the officers. My son didn't want to see security officers either. I had to tell the officers to try to understand how the defendants would feel about the security officers. I also explained to the officers that those who were charged were not terrorists. They had done nothing wrong. Some of them had just gone to the scene to see the demonstration or had gone to the market, and some others were arrested in an intersection on their way home from their work. I asked the officers not to disturb them because they were going to go to court to be judged. During the period of two years, the officers no longer disturbed us, and no defendant escaped. They attended court every time according to the appointments.

The lawyers always asked me to organize a meeting with the defendants before going to the court or submitting letters to ask for justice from government agencies. In some cases, I had to perform the task of an interpreter, because the lawyers from other places didn't speak Malay, while most of the defendants didn't speak Thai very well. When the lawyers had postponed the date to go to court, they would call me, and then I had to tell the defendants about that.

At first, I contacted the defendants without using a phone because I didn't have one. I went to their houses. Later my eldest son gave me his phone after seeing my difficulty in contacting them. After that, I appointed one leader for each *tambon* [subdistrict]. I felt it was a faster and more convenient way of coordinating than when I had had to go to their houses. It was really difficult because I couldn't ride a motorbike, and so it was inconvenient to go anywhere.

When I helped the defendants, I didn't know what position I occupied. I was not a *kamnan,* a village headman or a head of the Tambon Administrative Organisation (TAO). But why did I have to take up this task? Although I didn't have any position or money, I was ready to sacrifice everything to help my son and fifty-eight others who were charged. In some cases, I had to use my own money for transport or for meals for those defendants who couldn't afford a meal. Apart from the Lawyers Council, there were many other organizations with which I had to make a contact and cooperate, such as the National Human Rights Commission, the Young Muslim Association of Thailand, women's groups that worked for remedies, and the state officers too.

Before the charges were withdrawn, I had to work closely with the National Human Rights Commission and its members like Russee Kotlanawin and Phongcharat Ruairam, and the women's group. We organized meetings with the defendants, including meetings with Commander Wiroj Buacharoon, the commander of ISOC Region 4 at that time, and Lieutenant General Udomchai Thammasaroraj, the present commander, who had worked closely with Commander Wiroj.

We organized forums to listen to the problems faced by and opinions of the defendants and those who were affected by security cases, so that those who were concerned could find ways to help them. I and all the defendants wanted the charges against them to be withdrawn. If the cases were not dismissed, the villagers would face more hardship because it would take many years before the cases could be finally concluded. During the past two years, only three witnesses for the security officers' side were examined in the court, but they had almost two thousand witnesses in total. Imagine how long it would take to examine all of them. At that time, one of the defendants had already died after he had been shot. Another defendant was seriously ill.

Remedy programs for those women who had been affected by the Tak Bai "incident" were organized by the women's group led by Soraya Jamjuree and students from Prince of Songkla University, Pattani Campus, and Nari

Charoenphiriya from the Centre for Peace Study and Development, Mahidol University. They contacted me so that I could invite the families affected by the Tak Bai incident, including the families of those who had died during the incident, to join public forums to exchange ideas. This was the starting point for me to join the women's group that was working for remedy efforts. Finally, this developed into the Network of Civic Women for Peace in Southern Border Provinces.

I didn't only assist those who had been charged with involvement in the Tak Bai "incident" but also assisted with [the families of] those who had died or were injured in the incident. Later this group filed a civil case to call for compensation from the state. I helped to coordinate between the victims, the lawyers, and the National Human Rights Commission.

There were a lot of big challenges while the case was in the court. At one time I told a soldier who came to the court as a witness for the plaintiff: "Do you know how much difficulty we have to face? For the last two years, every time when we had to come to the court, we had to stop our work. Some of us work in Malaysia. On the day of the court's appointment, some have to come home to go to the court. They have never complained. But you complain only because you have to come to the court today. I only want to have this case finished as soon as possible."

At last, the justice we had demanded was delivered to us on 8 November 2006. I, my son, and the others who were involved in the case went to the court to listen to the verdict. The public prosecutor had withdrawn the Tak Bai cases. We were very glad because everyone could go home and work to earn a living as usual. The years of going to court were over, and we no longer had to worry about our case. I saw the news, and other people in the country were glad too. According to the news report, the attorney general was of the opinion that pursuing these cases wouldn't be beneficial for the public. On top of that there were too many witnesses to be questioned. Therefore, the case had been withdrawn.

However, this good news and the happiness of living an ordinary life didn't stay with us for a long time. It was less than a year. . . .

On 10 October 2007, I attended a funeral of a relative in Rueso District. I was inside a pickup truck when I came back, and I heard a shouting voice from a boy from my neighborhood. The car stopped.

"Uncle has died!" said Abidi, the boy.

I didn't believe what he had said and asked him, "Which uncle?"

"Your husband."

"What happened to him?"

"He was shot like my father." Abidi's father had been shot dead in the previous year.

"*La ilaha illallah*" [There is no god but Allah]. This was the first sentence that came out of my mouth.

We arrived at the scene at twelve past ten. Uncle, or Bae Soh, my husband, was shot dead at twelve past five. I sat on the pillion of the motorbike of the boy who had told the news at the place where my husband had died. It was at a grocery shop on the corner of the alley leading to my house. Bae Soh had worked as a motorbike taxi driver for five years, and it was the place where he regularly waited for his passengers. When I arrived there, there were only a few people. My children arrived after me, and they cried emotionally. I didn't cry. I tapped their backs instead, telling them: "Don't cry. If your tear touches your father's body, he will suffer."

In the late afternoon, the body of Bae Soh was buried in the cemetery of our Badokmati Village. I tried to brace myself by believing that he now rested in peace. Even before this incident, we had thought that we had to be very patient. A lot of relatives and villagers visited us in the house. However, there were some people whom I didn't allow to come into my house. These were soldiers and police officers. I didn't know what he was thinking, but one of the soldiers told me: "The perpetrator . . . you know these days many people dress themselves like soldiers."

"You don't have to talk a lot. Let the perpetrator be punished for his sin."

Before Bae Soh died, on one evening of Ramadan, before he performed his *maghrib* prayer [the prayer after the sunset], he turned around to face me and said, "I'm worried, you know."

"What you are worried about?," I asked my husband.

"The thing you are doing. It's not a small thing. It's bigger than you can manage." he answered.

At that moment I didn't take it seriously. Bae Soh said this with a usual facial expression. After that, he performed his prayer. After the prayer, I continued to talk with him.

"What we should do when Allah has given us this task to perform? There are many other people who have better education than me, but they don't help us even a bit. Yes, what I'm doing is more than my ability, but I must do that." After I finished my speech, my husband said nothing more.

On that evening, I didn't know that these were the last words from my husband to express his concern about what I was doing at that time. But the task of calling for justice in this region was a task entrusted by Allah to me. So I had to continue.

I could accept Bae Soh's death as *takdir* [destiny] of Allah and that it had been the time for him to leave us. We had no power to call him back. But at the same time, I couldn't help thinking about who had killed him. Why did he have to die? He was a polite man, not talkative, and had no dispute with anyone. Was it because of my work of helping those who had been affected? Was that a part of the reason for his death? This is the question that has remained in my heart all the time.

Forty days after my husband died, a group of forty wives of those who had been detained from Kutong Village, Rangae District, Narathiwat Province, came to me to ask for help. I contacted organizations working for human rights. One week after that, all of them were released. This was the first time I helped villagers after my husband died.

After that I didn't stop helping those who had been affected. If anything happened, they came to me, including those who were from outside the region. Later more and more people knew me, and they called me to ask for help with various problems. For instance, when security officers detained villagers as suspects, they asked me to contact the officers to inquire into the whereabouts of the suspects and when the families could visit them. If somebody was shot dead, the wife or the mother of the deceased made a phone call to me. I explained what needed to be done and who to contact in order to get "remedy money." Some families didn't get "remedy money" because all of the parties had not duly signed documents to testify that the case was due to the unrest. Instead, a death would be seen as caused by a personal dispute. In such cases, I tried to contact deputies in the district offices, soldiers, or the police so that they would investigate the case again. In some cases, a mother or a sister of the suspect was also detained and tortured. They also came to me for a help. In those instances, I had to contact high-ranking officers to investigate the allegations to solve the problem.

I visited victims many times, both Buddhists and Muslims, with the women's group to remedy them psychologically. When there were scholarships from some organizations for orphans, I acted as a coordinator.

On 12 August 2011, there was a riot in Narathiwat Prison. I was one of the mediators called upon to negotiate a quelling of the riot. I was glad to be of some help to stop this riot. It was not only in the Narathiwat Prison riot, but I also mediated in other cases too, such as a blockade or cordoning off of a villager's house, or the blockade of Islam Burapha School. In some occasions I, together with the Civic Women's Network, met the commander of ISOC Region 4, General Udomchai and other officers, to tell of the problems faced by those who were affected so that they would be able to help them later. This commander also helped us a lot. When I received a serious complaint that couldn't be dealt with by low-ranking officers, I often called him directly to consult him and to ask for help.

The Civic Women's Network conducted a radio program, and we appeared in a TV series called *Voices of Women from the Southern Border Provinces* during the last Ramadan. I thought this was effective because after I had appeared in these programs many people called me. The victims were glad that there was a program that could motivate them. I was glad that I could tell other women the story of our struggle so that these stories would inspire them to stand up like me.

The task of helping people with difficulties obtain justice was something I wanted to do, and I had never expected that Allah would grant me rewards. I received the Human Rights Defender Prize from the National Human Rights Commission; the Brave Civilian Prize from the Sanya Thammasak Institute; the Fighter Prize from a TV program called *Khon Khon Khon* in 2009; and on 8 March 2012, I got the Exemplary Woman Award in the field of human rights protection from the Ministry of Social Development and Human Security.

Before I got to this point, I had had to go through a lot of obstacles. When I was working as a liaison between the state officers and the local people eight years ago, my house was searched almost ten times. I wasn't worried because I thought I hadn't done anything wrong. I was always innocent. I felt friendly with the officers who searched my house. Sometimes I thought it was a test from Allah, and on other occasions, I understood that the officers might think I was a terrorist because I was performing this task. I had to be very patient. Although I was summoned twice under the emergency decree to be interrogated, I never reported because I knew that I had never done anything wrong. What's more, I was an elderly woman. What was the use of summoning me?

In any case, after I helped to quell the riot in Narathiwat Prison as one of the mediators, the security officers no longer disturbed me because they understood that I worked sincerely to help the villagers facing difficulties, on whichever side they belonged. In some cases, the assistance I provided was beneficial for the state officers, and they often came to express their gratitude to me.

In May 2012, I became a member of the subcommittee for the remedy of those who were affected from the Tak Bai incident. The government gave remedy money, as much as 7.5 million baht. I was glad that the government didn't forget about them. Police Colonel Thawee Sodsorng, the secretary general of the Southern Border Provinces Administrative Centre, or SBPAC, unit that was in charge of taking care of the remedy effort, worked hard and was very seriously devoted to his work. I felt that the remedy effort had become much fairer. When my husband died, I received only one hundred thousand baht, but since then the remedy committee increased the amount of the remedy money for those like me who had been affected by violent incidents to be as much as the remedy money given for government officers, that is, five hundred thousand baht. The state paid more remedy money to those who were affected by the state officers in "incidents" such as Tak Bai, Kru Se Mosque, or in Sabayoi, in order to show more responsibility. The remedy money didn't affect the rights of the victims or their families to sue those who were responsible for damage and file a criminal case against them.

The position of a member of the subcommittee for remedy was my very first official position. I felt I should be more responsible. I often had to attend meetings held in the SBPAC in Yala. I had to contact hundreds of people who had been affected by the Tak Bai "incident" to tell them about receiving remedy money. There were lots of challenges and obstacles, but I never gave up, regarding them as tests from Allah, as He had tested me in the past.

The happiest moment for me was when I could perform my pilgrimage in Mecca, Saudi Arabia, between 19 September and 6 November 2012, in a program sponsored by the SBPAC together with more than two hundred people who had been affected.

"Oh Allah, return peace and happiness to the southern border provinces! I'm afraid one day I will be no longer able to take the task and responsibility from Allah, because the burden is so heavy." This was my prayer to Allah in front of Baitullah [Kaaba] during my pilgrimage.

My hope is to see justice and peace in the southern border provinces. The purpose of my struggle is not to win, but I struggle for justice. I want people to live happily, helping each other. There shouldn't be suspicion between the local people and the state officers. If any problem happens, we should meet face-to-face and talk.

A Mother's Hope

Masta Cheuma with Suraiya Wani

One of my sons was killed in the Tak Bai "incident." My daughter-in-law was shot dead, and one more son disappeared. How I can live after this? If I could cut up my belly, I would want to show you how I feel inside.

My fifth child, "Dek[1] Yee," or Muhammad Sabree Abukhari, was only fourteen years old. He was my beloved one and left me forever in the fasting month [Ramadan], on 25 October 2004, on the day of the demonstration in front of the Tak Bai Police Station.

On that day I didn't know that Dek Yee went to join the demonstration because he didn't stay with me in my house in Khoksina Village, Kaluwo Subdistrict, Muang District, Narathiwat Province; he stayed with his relative in Nakuwing, a village in Sala Mai Subdistrict, Tak Bai District, Narathiwat Province. The next day someone made a phone call to tell me that he hadn't come home during the previous night. I asked my husband to go to find him but to no avail. So, I was quite sure that he must be in the Ingkhayutthaborihan Military Base in Pattani Province.

In the morning of 29 October 2004, we arrive at the military base at around six o'clock. At first, we couldn't find my son. We went to a tent where they kept the bodies of the victims, but we didn't find him there either, because we couldn't recognize Dek Yee's face. The faces of the all victims were very swollen. I called a relative who lived with Dek Yee. Finally, he could recognize Dek Yee because of a necklace made of beads that Dek Yee had woven in the morning of the day of the "incident," before he had left the house. After we found his body, we hurried to our home and buried him.

I finally received an amount of "remedy money" as a person who had been affected by the "Tak Bai Incident" from SBPAC [Southern Border Provinces Administration Centre] on 17 August 2012 [eight years after the "incident"].

I couldn't help thinking about him. When he was six years old, his favorite

---

1. The term *dek* is originally from the local Malay word *adek*, which means younger siblings. The local people pronounce it in a short form as *dek*, which can be used both for men and women. — *Translator*

dish was Phad Phed Gai [spicy dry chicken curry)] cooked with dried chilies, not with fresh chilies as usual, because it would taste sweeter. Dek Yee was a lovely and playful boy. One day when I was so engrossed in weaving baskets made of climbing fern, I forgot to prepare a meal for my family. In the evening of that day, Dek Yee prepared the meal by himself and invited me to have dinner by saying, "Madam, the dinner is ready." His loveliness made me smile. I always prepared meals for my children, but this was the only day when he prepared a meal for me.

I have seven children, six boys and one girl. The first three children are boys, Rosueki, Abdulloh, and Lawee. The fourth one is a girl, Nuseela. The fifth one is Muhammadsabree, the sixth one is Asron, and the last one is Faisol. Everyone listened to me and we had a happy life. When my children were still small, my husband went to Malaysia to work as a contract laborer in construction sites in Malaysia.

Many years ago, I had a part-time job of making bags from dried climbing ferns, which I wasn't engaged in very seriously. Before starting, my auntie, who was a teacher, invited me to learn this skill. After I finished making some bags, I sent them to my auntie's house, and then she sent them to Lady Charungchit Theekhara, who followed and attended the queen when Her Majesty visited Narathiwat. Later I had a chance to have a royal audience with my sons. She was a nice person. She invited my son to work for her. So my eldest son got a job as a diamond-cutter in a palace in Bangkok.

Five years after Dek Yee left us, on the morning of 12 December 2009, I got a phone call from Rohaning, wife of my second son, Loh [Abdulloh]. "Has Loh come back to your house?," asked my daughter-in-law.

"No," I replied.

As soon as Rohani heard my answer, she hung up. I didn't think that anything wrong had happened to Loh. On the next day I got another phone call from a friend of my daughter-in-law. I was told that Loh had disappeared, with his bicycle left on the roadside. I was surprised, and I thought my son had disappeared like Somchai Neelapaijit, a lawyer who had been forcibly abducted in March 2004. The next morning, my daughter-in-law and I, together with other villagers, tried to find Loh near the place where he had left his bicycle and in other places too. We thought we might find him. But on the second day of searching, a soldier from the nearby military post told my daughter-in-law to stop searching for him.

"You don't have to search him. You will never find him. They would not leave him near here."

"Why would he say things like that?" My mind began to suffer.

My son Loh, or Abdulloh Abukhari, lived in his wife's house in Buechaeng Village, [Bongo Subdistrict, Range District, Narathiwat Province,] after they got married. He was a contract laborer in construction. He had two children, one boy and one girl. He was a nice fellow, always helping others. After he was charged for the raid on the Pileng Army Camp [in Pileng Subdistrict, Cho Ai Rong District, Narathiwat Province] on 4 January 2004, a lawyer named Somchai Neelapaijit helped him in his case. Later, Loh became one of the important witnesses for Somchai Neelapaijit, the former president of Muslim Lawyers Association, in the torture case brought by him after the raid of an arsenal. Later still, on 12 March 2004, Somchai also disappeared.

After that, Witthaya, a lawyer and friend of Somchai, provided Loh with legal help in his case, because Loh hadn't been involved in the "incident" [raid]. Eventually, Col. Piyawat Kingket, director general of Department of Special Investigation (DSI), invited Loh to work for him. Loh was allocated the task of protecting the witnesses in Somchai's case before finally he himself disappeared.[2]

On the day Loh was arrested, soldiers and police officers came to our house. Loh wasn't frightened by these officers, and he could talk with them in a friendly way because he hadn't done anything wrong. The officers arrested him and brought him to the Khaotanyong Police Station in Muang District, Narathiwat Province. Then he was sent to the Bangkok Remand Prison. Loh said it was better than the police station because in the police station he had been tortured, slapped, and given electric shocks.

After my son disappeared, I made a police report and asked for help from Gen. Piyawat Kingket. He said he had reminded Loh not to go home. I also asked for help from Angkhana Neelapaijit, wife of Somchai Neelapaijit, and many other people.

I was waiting for any news about my son. One day I got a phone call from an important person, and he promised to help us. However, after two years there had been no progress whatsoever. I thought of Somchai Neelapaijit, who had helped us to pursue justice. But in the end, he was abducted and forcibly disappeared too. I was really sorry, and grateful to Somchai, who had

---

2. Abdulloh Abukhari was charged with involvement in the raid of the Pileng Military Camp in Cho Ai Rong District, Narathiwat Province, but the charge was dropped by the court. The Department of Special Investigation (DSI) treated him as a witness for the torture case brought by Somchai Neelapaijit, as he (Abdulloh) had been tortured to confess his involvement in the raid of the military camp. Abdulloh's disappearance caused great criticism against the slow and inefficient judicial system, and the protection of the witness by DSI. DSI alleged that Abdulloh did not follow the agreement for the protection of witnesses, because he went home during Hari Raya (Eid) period (Source: Isra News Agency, Association of Southern Journalists, 1 September 2011 [1]). — *Translator*

helped us. I only could pray to ask Allah, Subhanahu Wa Taala [Praise for Allah], to reward him for what he had done.

I was very upset after my son had disappeared. Some nights I couldn't sleep. Whenever there was a clattering sound around my house, these sounds always disturbed my sleep. I picked up a flashlight and held it tightly. During some nights, I had to visit my brother's house and stay there until I felt sleepy. At that time, I got no sound sleep at all. I had no appetite, but I always felt full. My children had to persuade me to eat something.

Two years later, I had to encounter another nightmare on 29 August 2011 at around six o'clock in the evening, during the fasting month of Ramadan.[3] A friend of my daughter-in-law called me and said that Rohani had passed away. I turned around and saw my niece and nephew. While crying, I told them: "Don't cry, OK? Your mum has passed away." Hearing what I had just said, they cried.

Two days before that, I had gone to Rohani's house to fetch my niece and nephew. In three days, we were to celebrate Rayo Poso [Aidil Fitri, Eid al-Fitr]. Rohani said that at dusk she often thought of Loh.

"Why do you still think of him when you have just gotten married again?," I asked.

"During the fasting month, Loh liked to eat *khao yam* [a kind of local dish of cooked rice, fresh vegetable, fish sauce, etc. mixed together]," Rohani said.

On that day Rohani talked abnormally, so much so that I wondered why. She had never talked like this before, and she went on to apologize to me. I also cried over what Rohani had said then.

Rohani was shot dead in the evening of Monday on her way home, after she had picked up her motorbike in a workshop. When I saw her body, it had been disfigured and appeared as if she wasn't a woman.

For me, when I compare the fate of my children, between the one who died and the other one who disappeared, I feel more sorry for the one who disappeared. For my son [Dek Yee] who died, we know for sure that he is no longer with us, and we could arrange for the burial of his body. But for my son who disappeared [Loh], we don't know if he is still alive or not. Even if he is already dead, we still cannot arrange a funeral for him. If he is still alive somewhere but cannot come home because somebody is detaining

---

3. Ramadan for the local people in the southern border provinces, called the month for *poso'*, is the ninth month in the Islamic lunar calendar. It is a month for performing religious duties. Muslims all over the world fast by refraining from eating and drinking, as well as curbing negative emotions from sunrise until sunset (บรรจง นกา ซัน สารานุกรมอิสลาม ฉบับเยาวชนและผู้เริ่มสนใจ, กรุงเทพฯ : อัล อะมีน 2542, หน้า 136).—*Translator*

him or for other reasons, then it will be good if only I can hear some news of him.

Whenever I see a picture of my son and daughter-in-law in front of my dressing table, I often cannot help but cry. I have missed my son who disappeared. I miss my daughter-in- law less because I saw her body. My feeling is that my son is still alive, as if he's working somewhere and just doesn't come back.

Some villagers have been sympathetic to me. Others might see that I already feel better. But they don't know how much worry there is in my heart. After these tragedies, for a while I cried alone in my house. I would feel better if I joined in activities organized outside, but anxiety in my heart was still with me. My husband allowed me to join these activities without complaining about that.

Today I feel stronger because I have gone through such horrible experiences. Allah wants to test us, and He wants to know how much I can endure. I have patience, and I submit everything to Allah. Even when I have to face security officers, I feel differently now. In the past, I was so afraid to face them.

The only help I want to ask from the state is to help me to find my disappeared son and to provide scholarships for his two children. They are still small, studying in a primary school. Sometimes I cry when I see their faces because I can't help feeling sorry for them. If someone asks them, "Where are your father and mother?," they always answer, "Our father was arrested, and our mother was shot dead."

Transition of Fear

BUNGA GANTANG (PSEUDONYM) WITH ASRA RATTHAKARAN

Just one incident happened on that day that made our village notorious all over the country, but it took nine years before we finally dared to talk about our stories to "outsiders."

After the incident [involving the Thai Buddhist female teacher Chuling "Pongkhanmoon"], Kuching Lepah village was teeming with soldiers, police officers, and enormous dogs. The doors of each house were tightly closed. No outsider ventured to come to our village. The villagers had difficulties leaving the village because the soldiers and the police officers were everywhere.

Some households had nothing to eat. Shops in the village didn't dare to open. Those merchants who used to come to the village every day to sell fish and vegetables in their pickup trucks stopped coming here. In our village there was hardly anything to eat.

A woman in the village had labor pains. Out of fear of the soldiers, no one dared to bring her to the hospital. Finally, she gave birth to her baby helped by a midwife. Luckily that business went smoothly.

Before the "incident," Kuching Lepah Village, Rangae District, Narathiwat Province, was a quiet place. My husband was hired to work in a rubber plantation. I was a hired seamstress. Our income was enough to make ends meet. We also worked in paddy fields. In the harvest season, villagers helped each other winnowing rice. Both sides of the road are covered with paddy put on blue vinyl sheets to be dried there. After the harvest season, we also planted cow peas, cucumbers, lemon grass, and cassavas. In the canals, we could catch eels, mudfish, and tilapia, which would bring us some extra income. I was a health volunteer in the village too. Our family was happy at that time.

On 19 May 2006, "the incident" occurred in which female teacher Chuling was taken as a hostage. There was a call from the mosque loudspeaker asking for villagers to gather together. I went out following the call. We neither took the teacher nor harmed her. I only came to join the villagers on the grounds in front of the mosque.

Not long after that our village was surrounded by soldiers, police officers, and administrative government officers. They said some outsiders were hiding inside the village.

Then . . . in June, the police came to see the village headman and summoned me to the Rangae Police Station for two days. I asked, "Why do I have to go?"

His reply surprised me: "An arrest warrant was issued by the Narathiwat Provincial Court."

"What offense did I commit?" The police told me to come to the police station for further investigation. He said it would be over in two days.

I asked my husband's opinion about what I should do. Our children were still very small. My husband said: "You better go. We did nothing wrong. You can come back soon. I will take care of the kids."

On my arrival at the police station, a police officer said, "You must sleep here." On that day there were altogether eight women from our village who were summoned. We asked, "In which room will we sleep?" The police replied: "You will be brought to cells. Which of the cells do you like, the big one or the small one?" The reply made us speechless because of the fear of not knowing where to be brought. Every one of us cried loudly all night.

Two days later, the police brought us to the Narathiwat Provincial Court and then to the prison. We still couldn't go home. We didn't stop crying, during our conversations and even in our prayers, because every one of us had a family and children to care for. I myself had two small children.

After thirty-one days in prison, the court granted bail. After that I fought my case for five years. It was tough for me and my husband to go to the court so frequently. While fighting the case, we had one more daughter in October 2008. In 2011, the court of first instance delivered the verdict to imprison me for six years for the accusation of illegal detention.

On 10 March 2011, the day of the judgment, I returned to the square world again. My husband appealed and asked permission for bail five times, all to no avail. The court didn't approve the request for fear that I might escape. At that time, it was tough for him because he had to take care of our three children on his own. In the fasting month [Ramadan], my husband said I would be able to come home. I waited for permission from the court to grant bail, but in vain. In September, I decided to withdraw my appeal and asked the prison officer: "Please end my case. I need the red card [the document that states that the case is finished]. I don't want to fight my case any longer." After that I submitted my request to the court.

My friends and I who had been charged in the same case thought that if we didn't fight the case and agreed to end the case, we might be granted amnesty and would be able to get out sooner.

On 13 September 2011 I got the red card. It meant that the case was ultimately closed.

"Since I was put in here, I miss you and my children all the time. Why do I have this feeling about what has to happen to me? The only thing I can do here is wait for your visit. When will you be coming? Sometimes I'm sorry for you because it must be a trouble for you. I'm really sorry. Since the first day in this place, I feel sorry every day and miss you, the one who I love most. As a person in this square world, all I can do is wait and accept my fate."

"I really want to go home. I want to stay with my family." This is the feeling I recorded while I was in the square world.

[*The next part is a story that was told by the husband.*]

I was really disappointed with what had happened. At that time, life was tough for me because I had to play the role of both father and mother at the same time. Sometimes I cried alone, exhausted from household chores and my jobs to earn a living. But I had to face this fate and visit my wife every day, except on holidays.

In the first year of my wife's imprisonment, I had to take care of my three children on my own, without help from anybody, because I thought my wife would soon be granted bail. I asked for the permission many times, all in vain.

In the second year, I asked my parents to take care of my three children, although they were already quite aged. At that time life was really difficult, because I had to work in several places. I always thought that I must be strong and patient. I always prayed to Allah so that we would be able to go through this test.

[*The narrative resumes here.*]

"You don't have to worry about me. I want you to be strong, taking care of our children." This is what I said to my husband almost every time he visited me.

On that day, he was very pale, surely from the lack of sleep. I was worried that he might faint. I later learned that his friends had to bring him to hospital because of high blood pressure.

Our distress could be reduced if we could help others.

Two weeks after I was imprisoned, an officer from the local health center visited me. Then the prison ward learned that I had been a health volunteer of the village. The warden appointed me as a health volunteer to take care of female prisoners in the prison. I performed my tasks such as weighing them and checking their blood pressure. Those prisoners who had chronic diseases got an OPD card. Every new prisoner was asked questions such as what kind of chronic disease they had or what case they had been charged with.

I also looked after aged prisoners who had diabetes or high blood pressure. Taking care of pregnant prisoners was one of my tasks too. While I was in prison, I attended twelve pregnant prisoners. When labor was close, I had to tell the wards to prepare nappies, towels, baby's clothes, gloves, stockings, masks, milk bottles, soap, baby powder, a bed, washing soap, and so on.

Sometimes there were prisoners who lost consciousness or had an attack of asthma. I had to help them with inhalers. If the condition was serious, I had to tell the wardens to bring them to the hospital. If someone caught a cold or flu, I took care of it myself. I told them to take medicine in front of the wardens. Someone might have a labor pain. I looked after them by massaging, trying to relax them. If the water broke, I told the warders to bring them to hospital. I also took care of HIV-infected prisoners. I told them to take antivirus medicine regularly.

As a health volunteer in prison, I was always busy and occupied with my tasks, such as distributing medicines and taking care of patients. Some prisoners even got TB. I had to feed them their food because they were so weak. I took care of some of them to the last moment of their life before they died inside the prison.

Every morning I had to report to the wardens about how many patients there were and their conditions. The wardens handed me medicines to be distributed to the sick prisoners. I had to make sure that they would ingest medicines in the morning, at noon, and in the evening.

Taking care of pregnant prisoners could lift my morale, making me realize our own value. I felt like their baby was my own niece or nephew. While I was in prison, I attended twelve small babies. They could be with us for less than one month. The relatives of the prisoners would come to take care of the babies outside the prison because the prison didn't allow us to take care of a baby inside. Nevertheless, it was exciting for us to hold and hug a baby, change their nappies, bathe them, etc. It was a small happiness that could reduce our distress of always missing our families.

Muslims pray five times a day to remember God. We only could pray together once a day during daytime in the multipurpose building that had no wall. The rest of the prayers were to be performed in the cells.

Female prisoners collectively requested that we needed a prayer room. After that, the Southern Border Provinces Administrative Centre (SBPAC) came to give us prayer clothes, the Qur'an, dates, and new clothes to be worn on Hari Raya, and extended the multipurpose building to be made into a prayer room for female prisoners. The floor was covered with mosaic tiles, with a low fence, and the building was painted. It looked beautiful. I became the *imam* of prayers for female prisoners too. Even though we only could perform our prayer one time a day in that place, we felt really good.

In the prison, there was a competition in reciting the Qur'an. Outsiders came as judges. I got the first prize.

Life in this square world? There were good and bad things. In the evenings we had to sleep squeezing in with each other. If someone woke up and went to toilet, when she came back there would be no space for her to sleep.

My motivation was my husband, who visited me every day. I got amnesty when I still had three years, seven months, six days of imprisonment remaining in my sentence. My sentence was suspended after I had been in prison for two years, ten months. On 10 January 2014, I got back my freedom.

A fear in my heart didn't fade away easily. After I got out of prison, I had to adjust myself in many ways. Understanding myself was not as difficult as making others understand me. Not long after that, the Civic Women's Network for Peace in the Southern Border Provinces came to visit me. I was glad because I thought no one would come to take care of me.

After that, the Duaijai Group invited me to join a meeting in Narathiwat with my child. While we discussed our vocational problems, children played together. The Research Coordination Centre for Those Who Are Affected by Violent Incidents in the Southern Border Provinces gave us three thousand baht for vocational purposes. I gave it to my child to sell hamburgers. The sales were good. After that I got an extra two thousand baht. I bought a cauldron to cook rice noodle. I started my business in January 2014. At first it wasn't successful, but it has improved now, especially when people go rubber-tapping.

The International Committee of the Red Cross (ICRC) was another organization that provided assistance to me. The organization visited prisoners from security cases and also foreign prisoners from Malaysia, Burma, Laos, and so on. In February 2014, I received thirty thousand baht to open a small grocery shop in the village. They also taught me about how to keep accounts to run a business.

Many organizations came to encourage us, and I felt strong enough to stand up again to continue my struggle. Every morning I woke up before my children. I went out to work in a rubber plantation to do rubber-tapping of one hundred trees, and I got fifty baht per day. After finishing that, I sent my children to school. Then I opened my grocery shop and sold rice noodles. I began to have hope in my life, and I wanted to learn more. Whenever I was invited by the Civic Women's Network to join activities, I didn't hesitate to join them, because if I stayed home, I would feel lonely, locking myself up in fear and suspicion. Going outside the village made me realize that other people also had to face difficulties. It was not only me. These activities were a remedy for my heart, because I got encouragement from others.

After training for a public forum, I felt brave enough to face the soldiers. It was different from the initial period after I was released. I had to report to the local police station and the district office every month. At that time, I felt really scared. But after this training, I dared to face this fear and go over the top of a wall in my heart to express my thoughts.

When joining a seminar with state officers present, at first I felt so frightened that sometimes I shivered. But when I saw that they dressed in civilian attire at the request of the Civic Women's Network, I felt less scared and more relaxed. I dared to talk and open up. The more I talked, the more I wanted to talk. I dared to express my thoughts, and I didn't feel suspected anymore. After the forum, there were several changes in my village. Suspicion against the officers gradually disappeared. The soldiers didn't come to have a meeting every Friday. The frequency of their meetings was reduced to once a month. But I still felt uneasy. Why is it that the officers didn't trust our village . . . although almost ten years had passed since the "incident"?

I also joined a training for radio programs that was exciting. It was incredible. . . . I could talk in the media. At first, I didn't dare to speak, or only could speak a little. The trainers instructed me to prepare agendas to talk in the program. It was lucky that we had a chance to talk about our experience to outsiders so that they would understand that our village was not like what they might think.

What's more, those women who had been affected by violent "incidents" in Kuching Lepah Village got an additional job by setting up a vocational group called "KL Muslimah Group" to produce herbed fish crackers. We were helped by Phoming Wanita Group, a vocational group from Phoming Village, Panare District, Pattani Province. They taught us how to make herbed fish crackers. The cracker was delicious and sold well.

"Kuching Fish Cracker" was our media to outsiders to tell them that Kuching Lepah Village was not like what the society thought. Some people might be scared, but if they come to our village, especially in the fruit seasons, they can taste fruits from our village such as rambutans, durians, and longkongs. We will welcome you.

Thank God, because our village could stand up again.

The Time Has Come for Me to Stand Up

Nada (Pseudonym) with Arida Awaekachi

Everything started in 2008. I was only sixteen years old. An unexpected "incident" happened. My brother-in-law, my elder sister's husband, died. Then, in 2010, my sister and mother were shot in the rubber plantation by bullets without any explanation as to why.

My brother-in-law was going to have his second child. At that time, my sister was seven months pregnant. The "incident" made my nephew a fatherless child when he was only one year old. But that was not the worst that befell our family because after this horrible thing happened to my brother-in-law, we also almost lost other family members three days later.

On the day of the "incident" in which my brother-in-law died, the police told our family that we had to make a report in the police station. Three days later, when all the chaotic circumstances calmed down, we made an appointment with the village headman, who would accompany us to see the police. We asked him if, as a favor, he would drive us in his car to the police station. On that day the weather was hotter than usual. After we had finished our business, before going home, we dropped in at a market in Tanyongmas, Rangae District, Narathiwat Province. After buying things in the market, we went home.

On our way to go back to the village, when we came to Pase Village, suddenly a pickup truck cut in front of our car. The village headman immediately stopped his car. When he tried to drive his car back, the mysterious car collided with our car violently. Then two men inside the car fired bullets repeatedly at our car, intending to kill everyone inside. After the sound of the bullets stopped, the gang immediately drove away from the site. We were left inside the car, stricken by the horror of the "incident." The village headman died on the spot. My sister and I narrowly escaped the bullets. It was only three days after my brother-in-law had died.

Three years later (February 2010), my mother and sister went out to tap rubber in the very early morning as on previous days. My father was about to follow them. We heard the sound of many bullets being fired. My father felt that a horrible "incident" must have happened. He came back and called me with a pale face, apparently stricken by horror. At that time, I was preparing to go to school. My brother was in a *pondok* school [he wasn't in the house—*Translator*], so I called some villagers to accompany me. As soon as I got there, I saw my mother and sister lying dead in a pool of blood. They had left us.

At that moment, I was shocked, not knowing what to do with what was happening before my eyes. The villagers helped to bring their bodies to the hospital. Both of them suffered two bullets in their critical organs. My heart was occupied with a question, "What kind of wrongs have they committed to be killed in such a way?" I asked police officers, but the answers they gave were confused. Someone said, "Your mother was a terrorist," and some others said, "They were escaping to Malaysia," or, "They were killed as a consequence of a land dispute." All of these explanations were utterly irrational. If they had really been escaping wrongdoing, they would have left our village a long time ago.

Shortly after the "incident," there were a lot of rumors. Every word of these rumors hurt us. These rumors had nothing to do with the facts. No one came to ask us about what the truth was. They only concocted rumors. If my mother had been really rich, why did she have to tap rubber? My mother and sister worked hard to earn a living, to send their children to school like many other parents. Whatever the perception of outsiders might be, our family firmly believed that these unworthy accusations were not true.

In retrospect, the loveliest time in my life was when I was in school. In 2004, when I was thirteen years old, I made up my mind not to study academic subjects in my lower secondary education. I chose to study religious subjects only, and I wanted to study until the twelfth class, or at the same level for a diploma in religious studies. At that time, my friends would choose to study in universities and colleges.

I studied in a *pondok* religious school favored by Malay Muslims in the southern border provinces. Most of the students had to help themselves in their lives. We also could learn how to cook and how to manage our time. The timetable of a *pondok* was very different from that of ordinary schools. We woke up very early in the morning in order to perform the prayer before the sunrise. At five o'clock in the morning, the students gathered together to study *kitab* [religious textbooks about Islam]. After that, everyone went back to dormitories to take a shower, eat breakfast, and prepare for the day's classes. This was the daily routine repeated day after day.

[As a *pondok* is a boarding school] I had to stay in the precinct of the school like many other students. I only went home once every month and stayed in my home for two days. By staying in the dormitory, I made a lot of friends. Fridays were school holidays. We asked for permission from the *ustaz* [religious teachers] to go to the nearby market to buy fish and vegetables. We bought things by splitting the costs among us. On holidays we had to clean up the school, and we also played like other students. Sometimes we went to a friend's house. In the fruit seasons, she might invite us to come to her home, and to the orchard to pick fruit to eat there. There was no electricity in her house. They used candles in the evenings. Although her house was very far, we liked visiting her house because there was a waterfall inside the village, and it was the place where we played every time when we came to her house. My school days were the happiest time in my life. There were lots of activities with my friends, like visiting their houses and breaking fast together [during the fasting months].

Even though I could stay at my home for only two days each month, I had to do household chores, including preparing meals for the family. I also had to go for rubber-tapping with my family when it didn't rain. The rubber estate where my mother was hired was not far from our house. My younger brother and I accompanied my mother to the estate to practice rubber-tapping so that we would be able to earn money in the future. Even though we had to work hard, we were happy. Sometimes my mother harvested vegetables in our farm, such as peppers, eggplants, cucumbers, and asparagus beans. We prepared meals and ate them on the hill where we tapped rubber. It was enough for our family, because we could live together and were genuinely happily.

Although I couldn't stay with my family for a long time while I was in school, I was always motivated by my mother, who taught me to be strong, patient in facing difficulties, and to be a good person.

After the horrible incidents happened to us, my life changed. I decided to stop my schooling and take up the burdens of my family when I was nineteen years old. Learning *kitabs* and other activities of youth gradually disappeared from my life. I felt downhearted that I had to take care of two orphaned nephews. If I had continued my study, there would have been nobody to take care of them. My younger brother also decided to stop his schooling.

One day an *ustaz* came to my house to see my father. He asked if my brother and I would come back to school. He suggested that for the time being we could commute to school instead of boarding in the dormitory as we had to take up the burden of taking care of our family.

At first, my father and I were worried about money. There were lots of expenses in my house. But my grandmother and father told me that they would take care of that matter. I was concerned about who would take care of our nephew, feeding him milk, and preparing meals for the family. My grandfather was very aged, and my father had to go out to work. But finally, I accepted the offer on that day to return to school.

Everything had changed. I had to wake up earlier every morning, boiling water to make milk and preparing the breakfast before I went to school. After coming home from school, I had to take care of my nephews and do other household chores. On holidays my brother and I had to accompany my father for tapping rubber. In the past I had been just a helper of my father, but now I had to do rubber-tapping seriously.

At that time in my family there were men, children, and elderly people, that is, father, my two younger brothers, grandparents on my mother's side, and two small nephews. I was the only daughter who had to take up the burden from my mother and sister, who had passed away. There were lots of problems, and I was often very stressed. But I didn't know upon whom I could rely. There used to be my mother and sister who could listen to me. But now I had to keep my feelings inside. My nephews were still very small. I was afraid that I didn't take care of them well enough. Sometimes on Hari Raya[1] holidays, I saw they were absent-minded. All other children dressed themselves with new clothes and ornaments, but my nephews were different from the others. The saddest thing was that they had no parents to take their hands like other children. As a consequence, they were not as happy as they would have been. When there was a meeting of the parents in the school, or on Father's Day or Mother's Day, I had to go to their school as a guardian. I was afraid that I didn't perform my duties well enough, not knowing to what extent I could respond to my nephews' feelings.

During that time, my nephews grew up and were old enough to be schooled in a prekindergarten. After waking up, I ironed their uniforms and fed them before I showered them and dressed them in their school uniforms. At first, I hid myself to see if they could get on well with other children. Apparently, they could mingle with their friends, and so I didn't have to observe them. I only had to pick them up after schooltime was over. When I saw other families that had every family member, I felt sad. I asked God why He hadn't taken my life together with that of my mother. If so, I wouldn't have to feel as painful and lonely as I did. But I was innocent, to the extent that I didn't understand that my mother and sister had to leave us because it was the time for them. This was a test, and I had to face it with patience.

My dream was that, after finishing my study, I would return to my village as a religious teacher so that the future of the children in the village would be

1. Hari Raya is a religious holiday of Islam. In one year, there are two days of Hari Raya: the first day of the first month of the Islamic calendar or after the fasting month; and the tenth day of the eleventh month of the Islamic lunar calendar. — *Translator*

better. I felt like many of my friends who also wanted to go back to their own communities to be a religious teacher.

It was now difficult to make that dream come true. My younger brother and I had to stop our schooling again because our family couldn't afford to send both of us to school. My family's cost of living was increasing, and we had to cut down some of our expenses, and our school fees were the first choice. The second-heaviest burden was the cost of buying powdered milk for the orphaned nephews. Sometimes we were lucky that there was a civil society organization that gave us powdered milk for my nephews. We could save a lot for our expenses. But I can't remember the name of the organization. After that we were also sometimes helped by other organizations and still are to this day.

The horrible "incidents" that had happened to my family had disheartened me. I thought it was impossible to face all these things. But after I got support from outside organizations and encouragement from people in the community, my sense of loss gradually abated and was replaced by positive feelings. People in the community always asked about our circumstances. They didn't discard us. Otherwise our family would have felt lonely. Sometimes they also give things to us, much or little, depending on their abilities, such as food, clothes, and money. For my nephews, sometimes villagers gave sweets. On festival occasions, people gave things to children. In some cases, people tailored the clothes for Hari Raya or bought shoes for my nephews. Some people gave them bicycles, which made them very happy.

So many times, outsiders' views made me feel uneasy. While I was in school, close friends often visited each other's houses. They also visited my house, and they stayed overnight. However, not long after that, after the bad "incident" happened in my village, many of my friends didn't come to my house again. When asked why, they said their parents hadn't granted permission after learning that their children would "go to the house of a friend from Kuching Lepah Village." After the incident in which a female teacher, Chuling,[2] was killed, my friends and outsiders no longer dared to come to our village because of fear. When asked where I was from, I chose to keep silent because I didn't dare to tell the truth that I was from the village that they so feared.

I asked myself, "Is my village so fearsome, to the extent that it can kill

2. Chuling Pongkhanmoon was an assistant teacher in Kuching Lepah primary school, Chaloem Subdistrict, Rangae District, Narathiwat Province, who was held as a hostage and detained in the building of the prekindergarten in Kuching Lepah Village on 19 May 2006 and beaten until she lost consciousness. She died on 8 January 2007.—*Translator*

someone?" Indeed, our life and death are destined by Allah. Even if we are in a place that we think and believe is the safest place in the world, death can come to us.

Although at first our family didn't receive any remedy from the government according to its criteria, we firmly believed that the deaths of my mother and sister were not the result of personal disputes. My father and I were determined to demand justice. We contacted various government agencies, but our requests were denied each time. So we told civil society organizations that came to visit us of this matter. Many organizations listened to us. It was lucky that some government agencies helped us to solve our problems. Now we have received remedy money, even after a delay of many years. The amount of money paid to us was just 25 percent because only two parties acknowledged that the violent "incidents" were caused by insurgents.[3] Nevertheless, the amount of money helped our family face our difficulties.

I tried to review the lessons I had learned, why we didn't get remedy money while we tried to process the matter by ourselves. Was it because we didn't know how the government processes worked? Or how to approach them? Or because we didn't follow up the case closely enough, although the officers involved wouldn't tell us enough until much time had passed? Or was it because of the lack of understanding between the state officers and our family?

There were a lot of organizations, both from inside and outside the country, that contacted us to offer support for the education of our nephews. The condition was that they must go to a boarding school, and everything would be arranged without charge. They would be able to come home only once each month. At that time my grandmother was still alive. My grandfather and grandmother said that they were glad that there were agencies that had offered the scholarships. But, however poor our family was, they wanted to take care of their grandchildren by themselves as long as they were alive. So we declined the offer. But other agencies offered support scholarships of a different nature, and my nephews accepted them.

---

3. According to the Act for the Remedy of Those Who Are Affected by the Unrest in the Southern Border Provinces, B.E. 2548 (C.E. 2005), in order for someone to receive the full amount of remedy money (500,000 baht) from the state, he or she needs to be acknowledged as a person who is affected by an incident caused by the unrest by a committee of three parties, that is, the police, the military, and the civil administration. If only two parties acknowledge this, then the Remedy Effort Centre of a district would pay 25 percent of the amount, and the related documents would be sent to the provincial government to consider whether or not the additional 75 percent should be paid. — *Translator*

For me it was lucky that we had seminars between the state officers whose works were related to the Kuching Lepah village and the villagers. These were organized three times by the Civic Women's Network for Peace in the Southern Border Provinces at the Tanyong Hotel, Narathiwat Province, in 2015. I could explain the hardships faced by my family and what was on my mind regarding the deaths of my sister and mother, such as why there had been no remedy money allotted, or if it had been regarded as a personal dispute, why there was no progress in the case. I waited for someone to say something that might make me feel better. But time went by, and I felt disappointed. After I expressed what was on my mind during the seminar, a state officer said he would help with the matter of the remedy money and other things that could be addressed. Our family felt much better because we had waited for an answer for a long time. This assistance would be a guarantee that my nephews would have lives better than now.

Apart from what I could express to the state officials during the seminars, what stuck in my mind was that there were a lot of people who encouraged us and believed that our family members were not terrorists, as others had alleged. Our losses in the past would be remembered by my family. Those of us who had been bereft of my mother and sister still firmly believed in their innocence.

Today, although only a small number of people listened to the fact that justice hadn't been delivered to us, I feel as if a part of a big stone that had been stuck in my chest has been removed. I'm determined to continue until justice is delivered again to our family.

A Gray Memory

Saimah Che'nae with Khamnueng Chamnankij

Just the term "summon" could lead to my imprisonment, right at the time my child was two months old and still drank milk from his mother. While in prison, the scar from my caesarean section hurt, especially when the weather was cold. I also had to wash the toilet according to the work shift arranged by the prison. At night, we had to sleep squeezed close to each other. I couldn't even sleep on my back because there wasn't enough space. Imagine what my situation was like. Seven of us had to sleep in the width of six tiles on the floor. We could only sleep on our sides. Imagine how a person who had just gone through a caesarean section might feel. If you are not in prison, sleeping on your side is an ordinary thing that is relaxing. But for me, relaxing was a dream that would never come true.

After the "incident" in which a female teacher, Chuling Pongkhanmoon, was held as a hostage, Kuching Lepah Village, Rangae District, Narathiwat Province, was seen as a violent community by the outside world, and I was seen as a criminal, detained upon an arrest warrant according to the emergency decree and Criminal Procedure Code.

I had a happy family life with a decent income. I had nothing to worry about, and there was no ongoing dispute in the village. Children in the village were happy, and so, I think, was every villager. My husband was a rubber tapper, and I was a housewife, having no experience in anything else.

After the incident happened, I lost my freedom, immediately being detained in prison for fourteen days. These events caused hardship for everyone in the family in living our daily lives. My child was just two months old, and the task of raising it fell to my husband and my mother. My mother also had to cook food, and my husband would bring some food for me when he visited me in the prison.

Losing freedom by imprisonment was a painful experience. Even though security officers and prison wardens didn't understand me, Allah still understood us. I still had to continue my life as long as my breath continued.

On 19 May 2006, Chuling [the female teacher] came to a restaurant beside my house to eat a bow of rice noodles. When I heard a lot of sounds,

I opened the door to see what was going on. At that time, I didn't go out, as I had been sleeping with my child who was still very small. It was about one month after I had given birth. I raised my voice to ask someone in the rice noodle shop what had happened. He said some people took the teacher forcibly to a *tadika* school and detained her in a nursery. I only prayed that no horrible thing would happen. A few hours later I heard people saying that the teacher had passed away.[1]

Two days after the incident, about fifty police officers from Narathiwat and Yala searched houses of the villagers in Kuching Lepah. A helicopter was flying above the village, watching the operation.

This unexpected "incident" was a very severe test from Allah. Outsiders saw our community as a frightening place, as if it were a cursed community, and all the villagers were stigmatized. I prayed to Allah for our strength and safety. We must be patient. But unexpected events happened one after another. My husband was detained upon an arrest warrant based on the emergency decree on 21 May 2006. He was released on 17 June of the same year after twenty-eight days of detention. I thought everything was over, but a graver challenge was to come. After my husband stayed with us for only one night, on the next day it was my turn to go.

1. According to media reports, on 19 May, 2006, two female teachers, Chuling Pongkhanmoon and Sirinat Thawonsuk, came to a restaurant in front of the village mosque to have lunch. A group of villagers rushed into the restaurant and forcibly took them to a nursery building close to the mosque to detain them there. Villagers also scattered spikes on the roads and felled trees to prevent security officers from coming close. Later they knew the reason for the sudden change of attitude from the villagers, who had been friendly until then. In the morning of the same day, around one hundred military, police, and administrative officers raided and conducted a cordoned search in a village in Chaluem Subdistrict, Rangae District, Narathiwat Province. Two suspects were detained on a charge of being involved in a raid of the security checkpoint of a railway station in Lalo Village, Rueso District, Narathiwat Province, in which two navy personnel were killed. After this incident, sympathizers of the insurgency instigated villagers to demand the release of the suspects, exchanging them for the two teachers who had been captured as hostages. During the negotiation between the demonstrators and the authorities, a group of men got inside the place where the teachers were kept, and hit Chuling on her head, rendering her unconscious. She was brought to the district hospital, then to the Narathiwat Provincial Hospital. Finally, she was referred to the hospital of Prince of Songkla University in Hat Yai, Songkhla Province. She became a patronized patient of Queen Sirikit, lying in a hospital bed unconscious for eight months. The doctors reported that her brain was so seriously damaged that there was no hope for her to recover. On 8 January 2007 she passed away peacefully.—*Translator*

After the "incident" of Chuling on 18 June 2006, I was summoned to the local police station, detained there for two days, and imprisoned in the Narathiwat Prison for fourteen days. The pain from the operation scar hurt less than the pain of my heart, because my child was only two months old, and all the burdens fell upon my mother and husband. How my child would drink milk? It was a heavy grief for a mother of such a small child.

I asked myself a question: What was my offense? On the day of the incident I didn't go out, sleeping with my newborn child. I only asked questions of those who were passing in front of my house. So I asked my mother and husband to bail me out to fight the case outside the prison. We took the title deed worth two hundred thousand baht for the bail, and "Alhamdulillah" [thank God][2]. . . the court granted us a bail.

When I came home, I realized the difficulty my husband had faced while I had been in prison. He had to change his life completely to perform the tasks of a father and a mother at the same time. He had to live his life with a lot of difficulties. When he visited the prison, hearing my voice from the telephone [that was set on both sides of a transparent plastic board that separated inmates and visitors] could make him happy and cheer him up in every one of his visits. He liked to ask me, "Does your scar hurt you while you're inside?"

I couldn't tell him it was painful because I didn't want to upset him, but he understood from the look in my eyes. He said: "Be patient. No problem. Regard this as a test from Allah for our family. We have to be very patient."

He said he was sorry for our child who had nursed from its mother but now had to drink milk from a bottle.

After I came out of prison, my husband always said, apart from his heart that had been so badly hurt, he felt so sorry for me when I was in prison. He looked at his child. He had never imagined that a mother could be separated from her child. He had no idea when his child's mother would come home. Whenever my husband mentioned this, I always cried.

Twelve days after I was imprisoned, I went to court. I asked the court to grant bail, because the operation scar was so painful. Alhamdulillah [Thank God] . . . I was the first who was granted bail from the eighteen female suspects (among these suspects, fourteen of them were sued, including me).

Disappointment stalked before we had time to brace ourselves. On 24 June 2008, instead of happiness, our family had to face yet another thing that we didn't want to happen. It was so cruel that my mother fainted. Oh Allah, my

2. In the original text, the term used here, "Alhamdulillah," is explained as "God willing." This might be confused with "Insya Allah," which means "God willing." The change is made accordingly. — *Translator*

family had to be tested so severely! My younger brother was shot dead. The case wasn't acknowledged as a security case by the officers in charge of "remedy money" from the army, the police, and the administration.[3] Only Allah knows the truth. It took a long time before our family could accept this. Even my case wasn't finished yet.

At that time, Kuching Lepah Village was utterly chaotic. Hardly anyone smiled, as many villagers had to face a fate similar to mine. They felt scared when they had to go to the mountainous area for their work. I was always worried when my husband went to the estate to tap rubber. After the deputy village headman in charge of security, who was a relative of my husband, had been shot, my husband was always accompanied by his father whenever he had to go out. I wholeheartedly wanted this village to be peaceful, but what happened was the other way around. Troubles happened in our village all the time. The news of the "incident" was so widespread that it was as if the village had been cut off from the rest of society. Even people from neighboring villages were afraid of us—everyone in the village.

I had to fight for four years before my case was closed. On 12 September 2011, the court dismissed my case. Finally, justice was delivered to me. Butsaba Chimphlikanon, a lawyer from the Lawyers Council, helped with my case. For the four years I was fighting my case, there were a lot of costs to be paid, such as meals and transport to and from the court. Every time I went to court, I had to wait there from morning until the late afternoon. On such days I had no income, as it was inconvenient for my job. I was really worried. The only good thing was that I didn't have to pay the fee for the lawyer.

After the dismissal of my case, the court issued an order to release me, and I got an "innocent letter," an official document to show that the case had been closed. After that my friends and I went to the Southern Border Provinces Administrative Centre (SBPAC) to apply for "remedy money." Later I recovered twenty-four thousand baht as compensation for the time I spent in prison.

The remedy money only could alleviate pains in our heart at certain levels, but it was not the way to solve the problem of injustice. If someone had to be detained, it should be clearly stated why he or she was charged. By managing this way, the government didn't have to pay remedy money for those who had been so haphazardly arrested.

3. After a violent incident happens in the southern border provinces, victims or their families will be qualified to receive "remedy money" from the government if the case is acknowledged to be a security case related to insurgency (and not a personal matter) by the army, the police, and the administration (usually at the district level).—*Translator*

Being acquitted from the case didn't mean that we were acquitted from nightmares. I tried to think about how to spend my life afterward. In retrospect, I thought that losing something was not always bad. Allah would give it back to us in time. At least now I knew that friendship between human beings, whatever their religions might be, really exists.

Nowadays I volunteer to teach [how to recite] the Qur'an for those who do not have as much knowledge as they should. I teach in the daytime for four days and in the evenings for five days. In the evenings, I teach in my own village for three nights, and two evenings in other villages, in Pase Village and Lubok Kayoh Village in Chaluem Subdistrict, Rangae District, Narathiwat Province.

The rest of my life has been a bonus. I was glad that I had opportunities to join the activities with the Civic Women's Network for Peace in the Southern Border Provinces. Hosting a radio program called *Voices from Women in the Southern Border Provinces* was a big challenge, something that I had never done before. I trained to become a moderator of seminars in Pattani, and after a second training course, a seminar was held by the Civic Women's Network in Kuching Lepah Village.

The "seminar" I mentioned was a meeting between those villagers who had been affected and the security officers so that the villagers could give voice to the hardships they faced. By doing so, the officers could learn what kind of problems confronted the villagers, and it might help to solve these problems too. For instance, for those who had been arrested in the case of Chuling, even though their cases were over and each of them received an "innocent letter," their names still appeared on the list of the police for those who had been issued an arrest warrant according to the emergency decree. I knew that my name was on the list due to the warrant when I was stopped at immigration on my way to Malaysia. I had to call the Rangae Police Station to guarantee that my case was over. Major General Chawalit Rianchaeng, director of the Department for Law Enforcement and Human Rights, ISOC Region 4, was at the seminar, and he said he would contact departments concerned to rectify the problem.

Not long after that, the general, together with the working team of the Civic Women's Network led by Soraya Jamjuree, came to our village to see eighteen of us whose names were still on the blacklist. They took pictures of our identification cards and other legal documents from the courts. The general also brought with him officers in charge of warrants.

In September, he sent Khamnueng Chamnankij, a representative from the Civic Women's Network so that eighteen of us could see the commander of the Rangae Police Station, and the army officer in charge of the Bringing People Home Project, Colonel Sitthiporn Musikasin, vice president of the

Committee for the Ordination and Campaigning to End Violent Struggle in the Southern Border Provinces, ISOC Region 4, to hear the progress of the process to acquit the warrant after Major General Chawalit had contacted the police. Even if our cases had been over, if the police hadn't deleted our names from the blacklist, our freedom to travel was not guaranteed.

For me, the seminar enhanced understanding between the officers and those who were in the community, because each side could tell their truths from their respective points of view. It was the first step the people from the community could take in their effort to make the officers realize that Kuching Lepah Village was not as fearful a place as they had once thought. After the seminar, the officers gave us better cooperation.

Apart from this, I also became a panelist on a forum focused on vocational development. I learned of the problems in the community because sometimes, even though we lived in the same community, we didn't know the financial status of other families. Once I knew of these problems, I thanked God because a lot of civil society organizations came to help us in finding budgets for vocational trainings for those who had been affected in the community so that they could have a source of income. We also could build a good, friendly relationship with another community that had been affected, that was the Pho Ming community from Panare District, Pattani Province. We could learn how to build a group to support vocational development. We transformed ourselves from those who were affected into those who could help others who had been affected by security cases to return to their own communities.

It was as if I had entered a broader world, with new perceptions about surrounding society, and stood up again, because many people and government agencies came to encourage the community in Kuching Lepah.

The starting point of the village's development was the formation of a group of those who were affected to make herbed fish crackers of "Kuching." We meet two times each week to enhance our unity. If someone has a problem, we can discuss the matter to find a solution. We worked together, and finally we produced "edible peace" that connects agencies both inside and outside the community continuously.

Apart from these vocational activities, our group wanted to extend the range of our activities in the village. At first, we tried to establish a vocational group for the future of the community.

At this moment, I'm the president of the vocational group called Muslimah KL. I feel glad and proud that the Civic Women's Network came to support us and introduced us to the wider world so that we could be a part of society again. I am determined to sustain this work so that it will be able to last a long time.

Thank God, who has made me realize my own value again and enabled me to go through such horrible experiences. To this day I teach my children that in our life we have to face a lot of things, positive and negative, good or bad, happy or sad. We have to be patient. Allah said those who are patient shall be rewarded for their patience.

A Smile amid the Tears

KHLUEAN SANG-AMPHAI WITH RUSNEE KASENG

I tried to listen to the stories told by Khluean Sang-amphai, an old lady in her late seventies, with my full attention in order to remember every detail. She told her own life story and her own thoughts, which seemed to stream out from her pure soul. Listening to her stories, I couldn't help but shed tears, yet all the while smiling.

Khluean was born and grew up in Thiaraya Village, Take Subdistrict, Yaring District, Pattani Province. Her mother had passed away when she was born. She said her family without a mother was "like a broken raft." Her father brought her brother to Yala Province, while she was left with an old couple in the village.

In the past several decades, in Thiaraya Village, Buddhists and Muslims had lived together peacefully, understanding each other without even the slightest feeling of enmity. In the past, about 30 percent of the village's population were Buddhists. However, now most Buddhists had moved out of the village after violence had happened targeting several Buddhist families, even though this village was their beloved homeland.

I was surprised that she still could smile when she was telling of her experiences, which would be completely unacceptable for many. She said she could accept that, but she would never forget. To this day, every day when she awakens up, she can't help but think about her husband and son who had passed away. She felt victimized by her own fate. She had to go through hardship and struggle without stopping since she was very small even into her old age. She had to leave the place where she had worked, move to the town, and rent a house with her children and grandchildren for the safety of her family.

Khluean is one of those who have been repeatedly affected by the unrest in the southern border provinces. In 2004, she lost her son after he was shot dead by insurgents. Then three years later, her husband was beheaded, his body burnt within the flames of their newly built house.

Before these horrible murders, Khluean had been the leader of her family since her husband had become disabled due to a fall from a sugar palm tree. She had already lost one of her daughters while she was still young. Khluean faced terrible moments in her life, one after another. She expressed her frustration about her own fate: "Why have these things happened to me? Is it because of my lack of merit and my sins?"

I asked how she had dealt with these terrible incidents. She said: "We must heal our own hearts. I just try to think simple good things, like how much money I will get after I massage someone . . . ," and I smiled.

Khluean knows a lot about herbs and the skills involved with massage. She finds extra income by selling herbs and massaging. She said the service fees for her massages "depend on how much they give. I just take the amount they give. I'm reluctant to utter the price, because I'm already old and don't have much strength like young people do. They have much strength." From selling herbs she earns money that is just enough to make ends meet. Apart from selling herbs, she also cultivates plants in public places. "These days it's difficult to find certain species of herbs. I plant drumstick trees [*moringa oleifera*] in public places so that people can eat them. It's giving alms to trees, and I will get merit," she said, laughing.

"We must accept the realities of life so that we can go on living like other people, no matter how good or terrible some realities might be." Khluean had to accept reality. She gnashed her gums (she had no teeth) when thinking about the cruelties that had befallen her life, however difficult and stressful they may have been. Sometimes, she was so stressed that she used to bleed from her nose. Nevertheless, she still could deliver good acts of kindness to others all the time. However, even if her spirit was capable of continuing her struggle, her body had grown weaker with the passage of time, not undefeatable forever like her spirit.

"After I experienced these terrible moments, I got heart disease."

She complained about her high blood pressure and heart disease due to stress. She said she was so stressed that a cupful of blood came out of her nose when she was admitted to the Pattani Hospital. Doctors prescribed medicines for blood pressure and tranquilizers. She only took the medicines for blood pressure; she didn't want the tranquilizers because they would make her dazed, incapable of thinking anything. She worried that if she took the tranquilizers, she wouldn't be able to take care of her children and grandchildren. Doctors told her to take medicines, but she was very stubborn. Not knowing what to do, the doctors finally gave up.

"A human body is covered with soft skin, not with bricks which can resist shocks caused by hard objects. The older we become, the weaker our resistance will be. But an amazing thing is that a human being has a spirit that is like the 'master' of our body. It means that our spirit is the leader. So, if the spirit is strong, it will make us survive."

Khluean is an example of a human being who has a spirit that is stronger than her body. Although she is beset by various infirmities, she doesn't let her children and grandchildren fret over her. On the other hand, she is the one who takes care of them.

While we were talking, she saw my laptop computer.

"How much is this machine?" she asked. I was surprised by her question, wondering why she wanted to know the price, but I gave an answer.

"I bought my computer many years ago. It cost me 23,300 baht at that time."

"There are cheaper models, aren't there?"

"Yes. Some models are less than ten thousand." I asked her who she wanted to buy a computer for.

"I'd like to by one for my grandchildren. They can use it for their study. You have to have one, don't you?"

She had saved some money for her children and grandchildren, from the remedy money given by the government agencies, and from her own efforts. I admired her affection for her children and grandchildren. She repeatedly said that their education was her highest priority. She was ready to exchange her happiness for their better future.

Khluean had only finished her primary education at Form 4. At that time, she was regarded as an educated person.

Based on her knowledge and experiences, she always gave me simple answers, but they contained a philosophy of ordinary people that she had accumulated for several decades. When World War II broke out, she was around seven to eight years old. She still remembered how frightful the Japanese soldiers were. She also related that every time there were bombs dropped from the sky, they had to find places to escape to for safety. They had to sleep early, and it was prohibited to turn on the light in the evenings for fear of being spotted by Japanese soldiers. However, Khluean explained that the atmosphere like that was enjoyable for kids like her.

I asked her about the current situation in our village.

"Now they call it as a war. It is a war of money. Money is abundant, so they kill each other. This is scary. But we have to endure. We must help each other to save our country, our homeland, no matter if you are Buddhist, Muslim, Chinese, Cham or anything else. I want to see our place peaceful like the era of Phraya Niwo."

The answer she gave reflects her mindfulness clearly. She didn't express suspicions about who perpetrated the violence or resent them. She only differentiated between good people and bad people. She demanded that bad people should stop destroying the country, and good people, whatever their ethnicity or whatever their religion, should help each other to save the country so that it can return to the normal condition.

"All these bad things come from human beings. I don't know who did what. So be it. God will punish them." This remark convinced me that my observation of her wasn't wrong.

The burning of her house and husband had happened more than five years ago. It was the heaviest blow in her life. I respected her spirit in taking up the role of the family's leader. After the death of her husband, she had to take care of her family members, who were all women. I regard her role as the commander of the family.

I told her, "You are like a female commander."

She smiled broadly and said, "The commander of a mobile task force, right?" She explained that when she was small, she had to move around to relatives' houses. This is how she came to be called "Khluean" [meaning, mobile, moving around], because she always had to move around, never staying in one specific place.

I thought Khluean still could live her life as usual like many other people, without losing her mind over all the horrible "incidents" that had disturbed her life. The most important thing to see, she would say, is that our lives are based in reality. She encountered reality and she could accept that. She could live with such a cruel reality because she had great responsibility in her designated role as the leader of her family. Her morality prohibited her from seeking revenge, and this in turn liberated her mind from suffering.

Khluean doesn't want to visit the place where her husband died because it might revive the bitterness of memory. But her spiritual ties with her neighbors, old Buddhist and Muslim friends, have never faded away. For instance, my grandfather is from a different village in the same subdistrict. But Khluean always asked about those who spent their childhoods in that village during the time she was young.

I think our lives are like a spiral of happiness and suffering woven together into a unity. After experiencing grave suffering, some people are just stuck in it so they cannot see that happiness might somehow be mixed in with suffering. It is pity when we cannot glean happiness as a gift for our lives. If we can change our way of thinking, "When we have tears, we still can smile."

Happiness might come to find us, like what happened with Khluean.

Life after Liberation

Duangsuda Sang-amphai with Chitlada
(Neelapaijit) Phiriyasat

Exhausted . . . this is the term I always uttered for six to seven years after the sound of shooting and the smell of blood. I could move around as I liked, but I have lost my freedom after my father died.

I was always asking questions: Why did my father have to die? Who killed my father? Why did he [the perpetrator] have to kill him? Was it because he was a person who preferred to live alone and so his life had no [social] value? These are questions that stuck to my heart. I tried hard to find answers to these questions, but it was like walking with closed eyes.

In this world, there are so many questions that don't require answers!!!

My father's face was anxious after hearing the faint sounds of gunshots that were followed by a confusion of people's responses on the morning of 28 April 2004 in the Kru Se Mosque, a calamitous clash between two groups of people holding differing ideologies. It seemed as if he already knew of the confusion that would later ensue and was wondering how his children could lead normal lives after such a horrible incident. But his anxiety soon vanished during the morning of 17 May of the same year. His body was soaked in blood from bullets that had killed him. We didn't know who shot him, but it was a bad omen, a harbinger of more danger ahead.

Three years later, on the night of 9 September, 2007, a bright flame consumed the body of my grandfather until it was hardly recognizable as the body of human being. In the coming morning, we only could see some bones scattered along with ashes. The head was not discernible. No word could express our family's feeling at that time. That moment indicated just how low the consciousness of our people could be. Our situation only descended from bad to worse.

My vengeful feelings stayed with me like a yoke for four years. We knew the reason, but our pain didn't end like the sun that sets and rises again to shed bright sunlight. The "incident" narrowed my thought to the extent that

I didn't want to think about anything. Then it was followed by loneliness. People began to leave our village one by one.

Thiaraya Village, Take Subdistrict, Yaring District, Pattani Province is a community of around 110 households of both Buddhists and Muslims. About 30 percent of the population were Buddhists, and the rest were Thai Malays. We had lived together peacefully for generations. My grandmother said that the villagers lived together in harmony, keeping good relations and helping each other in planting and harvesting rice. Both Buddhists and Muslim villagers were tied together by local customs.

"We must move out for the sake of our lives." This was uttered in the trembling voice of a strong old woman, my grandmother [Khluean Sang-amphai]. She had never given in to the fate dealt to her, but this time she had to give in to her own countrymen. No matter how much she loved her own homeland, her life had no happiness. It was so difficult to live our lives now without a family leader, given that our bereft family members were now all women. Whatever might be happening, I thought this must be the limit of her ability to endure, even though people thought that women had the most endurance.

My grandmother was born in this village and got married here to my grandfather [Neay Sang-amphai]. She had a son and two daughters. One of her daughters passed away a long time ago. My grandmother was awarded the Exemplary Mother Prize for her work in environmental protection. She was the community leader who resisted the digging of a canal cutting through the village. She also fought for the preservation of a sand dune forest in the village so that the forest of many acres could be utilized by the villagers. But today she has had to face terrible losses repeatedly. She's now seventy-eight years old, and my father, who would have been able to take care of his old mother, has already died. She has to stay alone without friends. Her son was cruelly killed by her own countrymen. He was beheaded, and his body was burnt. Such inhumane atrocities deeply hurt those who are left behind. How many people can endure such a fate that forecloses on their happiness? But it was quite remarkable that the relationship between the communities in our villages was not affected by my father's ghastly murder. The meaning of death is but a starting point, one that doesn't actually require any explanation about what will happen thereafter.

While experiencing tragedy, the Sang-amphai family essentially had to live alone without any help. Yet both our Buddhist and Muslim friends were like a prop that prevented our family from a complete collapse after fate's assault. I was surrounded by the generosity of people from different religions in a time of difficulty. In any case, we knew that our lives must continue, and safety became our priority.

We, my grandmother and I, together with my six sisters, were all female. We packed our belongings in order to move into the busy life of a town. This was the beginning of our exhaustion, probably like many other families that had experienced the same fate. In fact, I didn't want to go, leaving my mother alone in "Thiaraya Village." But it was difficult to persuade her to go with us, because she didn't like the town lifestyle.

"You can go. I can stay here," she said with no facial expression to show what was on her mind. This is my mother's style. She always said forgiving someone was the greatest of alms. Her attitude was aligned with a Buddhist proverb that "those who give are those who are loved." But for me, I struggled to understand the meaning of all these things, and I was quick to lose my temper, though that doesn't mean that I was wicked by nature. With regard to the Muslims in the region, I understood that not everyone was wicked. We could see the good people, but we had to see with our hearts and not with our prejudices. I thought in this way because no one can live alone without depending on others. Everything and everyone are interdependent. This is how I understand life.

My life had changed, and I had to struggle in order to sustain our family's economic situation. Every morning I had to inhale the air that is mixed with exhaust from gasoline in Pattani city. My family will surely have to stay here for a long time. Our life in town is hard because we have to stay in a rented house and buy our meals. We don't have a piece of land to plant vegetables like we did in our village. Working from the morning until the evening is not enough. I'm doing everything I can to earn money as long as the jobs I take up are not illegal. I'm not ashamed of anyone. I see that my life is worse than it used to be. But yet, despite the difficulties, I also have more opportunities than others.

Even though our life is tough, I have never seen my grandmother despondent since my father and grandfather passed away. No one knows how she feels inside under her smiling face. She always speaks politely and works harder than a woman of her age should. She has never complained about her fate. Everyone who sees her might think she is patient. But she might say: "If I'm calm, I can stay at my home, but my heart is hot. I feel scared. Because of fear I had to move out from our village to stay in Pattani. I don't mind if people might think I'm a coward. Being poor is still better than death."

For my grandmother, life itself is the greatest value. She taught me to value my life. It doesn't only mean being afraid of death, but to make use of my life to do something valuable, because doing so has more value than just being alive. Her teachings have enabled me to go through the crisis and formed my consciousness and trust in my fellow creatures. I was relieved from the burden of negative thoughts against the society in which I live.

When my father died, I only could ask a question about why it must be he. My mind was confused, not knowing what might happen to my family and my village. But after my grandfather was cruelly killed, I began to feel vengeful, wondering why such things must happen to my family again and again. I looked at people from different religions in a negative way. I felt there must be something coming into my mind, and I had to deal with these feelings.

In our life, there could be something unexpected, sad, sorrowful, or even cruel. But our happiness depends on how well we can accept our role in order to move forward with greater awareness. My family has received help from many organizations, including the group of other families who have been affected by the unrest, and the Volunteer Coordination Centre for Peace led by Lamai Manakarn. The social development agency helped us to find jobs. We also received scholarships for my younger siblings to reduce our family's economic burden. Finally, my grandmother and I could compose ourselves to be happy.

After receiving these remedies, I got more opportunities, and it has changed my perception about society. The negative feelings I had toward people from different religions have also gradually faded. I used to think too much, punishing myself, always pondering the reasons for our afflictions and wondering if it was because we were Buddhists. Today, I've stopped doing that, because everyone who lives in the southern border provinces has been affected by the circumstances, either directly or indirectly.

After these experiences, I also thought that I just couldn't be a person who had been affected by the unrest, but I must do something for others. Whenever I visit those who are affected by the unrest, I can see their loss of life and the damage it does to human relationships in the community. I found providing remedy for others to be a remedy for myself.

For my community, Thiaraya Village, in the past we villagers had good relationships with each other. After the unrest broke out, I feel the relationships are even stronger than before because we have had to struggle against so many problems. Everyone feels that they must play a role in protecting the community.

When I worked with Civic Women's Network, I hosted a radio program called *Voices of Women from the Southern Border.* This program was intended as a mouthpiece for both Buddhists and Muslims, so that younger generations could remember what had happened before and after the outbreak of the unrest, in order to consider what they should do to live a good life. This program also attempted to help local people see the problem of relationships between people from different religions in order to reduce prejudice against each other. At least we can build our society in order to live together peacefully.

Still Smiling

LIAM CHAIBUN WITH DUANGSUDA SANGAMPHAI
AND THANYATHORN SAIPANYA

Climbing up a steep hill is much less exhausting than losing your beloved one, analogous to leaves falling from tree versus letting the tree die alone.

Now I'm not sure at all which child of mine I can rely on, because I'm afraid it might cause more problems for them. But if I get older than I am now, they will be more reluctant to take care of me.

Talking now about my life with my husband, it started after he moved to Khian Village, Bo Nam Subdistrict, Panare District, Pattani Province, to stay with his brother. When he met me he immediately liked me, and his elder representatives came to my house to ask for my hand for marriage. At that time, I was still very young and not very sure about him, because I didn't know him very well. But my mother persuaded me to accept his proposal. She said if we couldn't live together, then we could divorce.

After we got married, he moved to Bang Mu Village (in Nam Bo Subdistrict) so we could stay together. He worked in paddy fields and farmed for his family. At that time, we had to work by opening up forests and jungles in the hills and valleys to plant coconuts, bitter beans, jackfruits, etc., on hilltops because the soil was very rich.

When I was still a small girl, the village was in a thick forest. Elderly people said originally there were only two households of Buddhists in this village. In this area, there were so many wild boars that villagers couldn't plant anything because the boars ate all the plants. Wild boars also pushed around the poles of our clotheslines until our washed clothes were scattered about. I still remember that when I was a girl, I liked to hit the wild boars that came into our house. Talking about these memories brings back the happiness of my childhood.

However, as the population of the village increased, the number of wild boars decreased, probably because they were caught and eaten, or their habitats were disturbed. They gradually disappeared. After I grew up, I didn't see them any longer. This is probably because this village is called Bang Mu to this day.

Although this village was far behind in terms of development, I was happy with my work of planting vegetables and raising domestic animals to take care of my family. I lived a happy life as an ordinary person. In the past, it was very difficult to earn a living. In order to work on the plantation on the hill, I had to carry my small children and lead cows and buffalos there.

I had a small hut on the hill to stay overnight because climbing a steep hill is a tough business. When I climbed up the hill I might stay there for a week, or until the food I had prepared was finished. At that time, the relationships between Buddhists and Muslims were very good. We were generous with each other in every aspect. We regarded each other as brothers and sisters. Even though I worked in a thick forest, I felt no fear whatsoever.

Living together in a multicultural community is a beautiful memory. I still remember that when there was a wedding ceremony in the village, people from different religions came together to help, regardless of the religion of the bride and groom. They helped each other as much as they could while following their religious regulations. For instance, if there was food made of pork, a separate zone was prepared in order to show respect for each other. The atmosphere was really merry and enjoyable. In the season to plant rice, we also helped each other. One day we worked in the paddy field of a Buddhist, and the next day we worked in that of a Muslim. Sometimes Buddhists got drunk while working in the paddy fields. Planting rice in paddy fields was a joyful experience. We laughed all the time, and our smiles were reflected upon the water. But after the unrest happened in this region, that atmosphere began to disappear. Trust was replaced by fear. We began to feel afraid to go out of house to go anywhere.

Before the unrest began, I didn't feel worried when I had to go out of my house. But after the unrest began, the use of violence became rampant, and Buddhists were killed mercilessly. Even though Muslims and the Buddhists in the village still had as good relationship as in the past, I felt scared because the daily news reports of violent incidents alarmed me all the time. The news reports about hatred and suspicion of Buddhists against Muslims began to increase. My fear at that time was not as heavy as when I had to stay alone without my husband and my children.

Because their clocks of life stopped one by one. My husband, who died of cancer, was the first one to leave me. He was my partner throughout our life together. But he went back to the eternal world, which was a fact I had to accept. Even in the midst of sorrow, I still had some hope because all of my children were still alive.

Fifteen days after my husband died, my third child was involved in a traffic accident and died. My feelings became uncertain, and I felt worried about things—that I had to face more of the inevitable.

After that, two years later, my fourth child left me because of a chronic disease. I tried to rely on the dharmic principle that this was reality of life in order to heal my heart, but it was difficult to accept all these things immediately. These losses happened one after another and so close in time that I had no time to dry the tears that soaked my face.

Four years later, my fifth son, who I expected would take care of me, was shot dead in a violent "incident" of the unrest.

When my youngest son died, my heart was so utterly broken that I wanted to die with him. I had no appetite, and I ate rice mixed with my tears. At that time, I really couldn't compose myself. If I saw things he had used in his job, I shed my tears. Every time somebody asked about him, I couldn't help but cry because he was very hardworking and took care of me in every way. He had ploughed the paddy fields and prepared food for me. He could help me in every respect. So it was naturally difficult to compose myself in a short period of time.

Painful events rushed into my life repeatedly. It was as if before I could deal with the sorrow from the previous events, a new tragedy would happen to me again and again, until my heart was totally exhausted.

At that time, I felt tired of my life. What kind of big sins [karma] had I committed in my life that I had to face separation after separation? My neighbors came to visit me in order to soothe me. Principles in religious teachings also helped me to heal my horribly broken heart.

After a long period of time these painful experiences became a motivation for me to be rather hopeful about life in the world of reality.

Now I'm living with a grandson, a son of my third son, who died in a traffic accident. His mother already had a new family. I was sorry for him because he had no one to rely on. So I took him to stay with me for his comfort. At night, after I lay myself to sleep, I only could ponder about how to earn a living for our survival. Even though the government provided us with remedy money, it had to be saved for the education of my grandchildren, including a son of my fifth son, who had been shot dead in a violent incident of the unrest too. I had to be frugal to save money because the son who helped me in my work had already gone.

My children who are still alive are also suffering hardship, not so different from me. I'm too sorry for them to ask them for some help. At present, whenever I sit down and look at my children and grandchildren, I can't help thinking about the future because no one knows when this unrest might be over. Therefore, I have never judged anyone about the unrest. In the depth of my heart, I still hope that before the end of my life, a peace-loving society like in the past will come back again so that we can live without fear again.

Even if horrible things happen in our lives, we still can tell of our experiences to other people, and it is a good thing if they can learn something from our stories so they can go on with their struggles.

A Mother Seeking Justice

KHAMNUENG CHAMNANKIJ

I sold food on Rong-ang Street. My husband worked as a plumber. We had two children. The eldest was twenty-two years old and worked as a driver of garbage collection vehicles for the public health office. He worked from 5:00 a.m. until 7:00 p.m. The younger one was eleven years, seven months old, still in his third year of primary school.

My house had two stairs, and the front space was used to sell food. I sold *khao mok* [curried rice with chicken], sticky rice, rice porridge, *kuai tiao* [noodles], tea and coffee, *khao niao sangkhaya* [sticky rice with coconut custard], and sticky rice with shrimp. Our financial status was relatively good. My family didn't have to face economic hardship. Although my husband was suffering from asthma, I had just enough money to build a new house and to extend and renovate the shop to make it wider and look better.

But everything ended.

On 19 June 2007, at about 7:30 p.m., my husband was on his bronchodilator, and the younger child was sleeping upstairs after finishing his homework. The elder son was sitting in a hut behind the house located on the riverside. He had just come back from his work. All of a sudden, more than thirty police officers and soldiers, asserting the prerogative of martial law, cordoned off my house on Rong-ang Street, Muang District, Pattani Province.

I remember the incident very clearly to this day. The security officers called us, knocking on the door for us to open, and asked to search the house, as they had received a report that some illegal things were kept inside this house. I asked them what the number of the house to be searched was, and who was the owner of the house. The police officer said it was this house where foods were sold and asked me to open the door. I asked him if he had a warrant to search my house because it was an improper time already. Hearing my question, the police officer turned around to the soldiers standing outside the house. Then I immediately realized that they were appealing to martial law. We couldn't resist, and I opened the door so that the police officers could search inside the house.

Three hours later, at about 11:00 p.m., the officer who led the search told his subordinates to get the identity card and the signature of the house's owner on a document to state that the search had been conducted without finding anything illegal. My husband was sitting in front of the house. He stood up and signed the document. My children and I stood behind the house, because the officers were still moving around in front of the house.

About fifteen minutes later, one of the soldiers standing under a big tree on the riverside shouted, "What is this?" A senior soldier then told him, "Bring it here." He picked up a container of paint and called for a police officer to have a look at it. The police officer opened a plastic bag inside the container, and uttered, "Yes, that's it." Then he took the container and put it on the street in front of my house. Police officers, soldiers, my husband, and children were standing by to see. They began to take the stuff apart on the street. Around ten minutes later, handcuffs were put on my husband and son. The younger son rushed into the house to hold me and cried as his body trembled.

"They put handcuffs on father and brother!"

I went out to the front of the house and asked, "On what charge are you arresting them?"

A police officer said, "Don't you know that that is an improvised explosive device?"

I said, "If it's a real bomb, how can you be that audacious?"

"Hey, you are so clever, eh?," the police officer bawled at me.

I could utter nothing, but I couldn't help asking in my heart where the stuff had come from and how it could have ended up here. Who did that? I entered the house again and hugged my small child for two or three minutes. A police colonel said to his subordinates to take my elder son. Then the police officer said: "You better confess. Then I don't have to take your father with you. I know your father is a hardworking man."

I asked my son, "Whose is this, or was there anyone who left this here?"

"If I knew I would tell you. I would confess if the stuff was mine. Mom, I really don't know. You know that I just came back from my work."

After that they took my son to the police station. About ten minutes later they took my husband too. He told me: "Don't worry. Take care of your child well. I must go." I sank into a sitting position while tears ran down my face. What I could think in my heart was only about what I should do and how I could help my husband and son. I couldn't sleep in the evening. I performed a prayer of need and supplicated to Allah: "Show me the path on which I must go forward."

The next morning, I tied up the cow and took some food to be handed over to my husband and son. My younger son didn't want to go to school.

My younger son and I will have to face a difficult test from Allah, I thought.

At the same time, my Muslim friends who used to be good to us began to pretend not to know who we were, as if we were strangers to them. One of my father-in-law's siblings cut off relations with us and didn't allow us to come to his house. Those who passed by the front of my house began to stare at us. Even former customers of my business just looked at us without even stopping as they had done before.

I consulted a Buddhist friend of mine, and this person brought me to see a lawyer to be hired for the case. The lawyer demanded two hundred thousand baht. I agreed without negotiating anything, although at that time I only had twenty thousand baht because we just had finished building our house a few months ago. The lawyer said, "After I receive one hundred thousand baht I will begin to work."

I decided to sell the two cows we had and the fishing boat that my husband had used. I also pawned my car, but the amount of money I received for that was still less than one hundred thousand. Then I borrowed money from illegal usurers at an interest of 20 percent. That amount of money was spent to hire the lawyer and to bail out my husband and son. During this hard time, I still sold food, even though the number of my customers had declined because what had happened to us had been reported by the media. The community already had judged us even before the court delivered a verdict. I had to endure all these things in order to save money. The money should have been spent for the education of my younger son and not for fighting this case. The lawyer prepared a document to ask for a temporary release, to be sent to the SBPAC [Southern Border Provinces Administrative Centre], but he told me to submit the document by myself.

On the day I had to go to submit the document to the SBPAC, I wore a big hijab that covered my wrists. My face was sad. I heard the young officer sitting behind the counter whispering, "Do you understand what I'm saying?" I didn't answer, pretending as if I hadn't heard anything, and showed my identification card because on the card my name was still my Buddhist name as I had not changed it. I did it so that she would know that I understood Thai.

During this period of difficulties, I had to divide my time between earning a living and fighting the case to bail out my husband and son. My younger son went to school but didn't attend classes. Instead, he stayed in the ethical education room. I immediately noticed that he already was having some problems. He used to be an active student with good achievements, always getting grade 3 or 4. After that, things wouldn't be the same.

I tried to do my best in performing my duties. Not long after that, many among the local people in Rong-ang, both Buddhists and Muslims, gave me some money in support. They also gave me sweets every week so that I could bring these to my husband and son in prison. I sent letters asking for justice to every government agency I could think of. The lawyer did his duty in the courtroom. Two months later, the governor of Pattani Province, Phanu Uthirat, signed a document to bail out my husband for five hundred thousand baht. But it was only my husband who could be bailed out, whereas my son had to wait longer. Phanu said, "Security officers want to interrogate him and investigate the case more clearly."

On 12 September 2007, almost four months later, the public prosecutor decided not to file the case against my husband. But the case against my son was filed on the next day, the first day of the fasting month. But Allah blessed me. I could bail out my son, and I could fight the case outside the jail. After I bailed out my son, I also had to take up the burden of taking care of the family because both father and son had become jobless men.

Although the case wasn't over yet, I again sent letters asking for justice to every government agency in Bangkok, such as the Human Rights Protection Department, Ministry of Justice, the Ombudsman and the Lawyers Council. While in Pattani, I made petitions to the Fair Justice Centre [Dhamrong Thamma Centre], the provincial prosecutor, the governor, and the commander of Army Region 4. The Pattani Provincial Court examined the witnesses for the prosecution many times for almost two years.

In October 2009, I had to bring my son to the courts in Nakhon Ratchasima and Khon Kaen because some of the soldiers involved in the raid of my house had already been moved, and they refused to come to the Pattani Provincial Court for fear of their safety or due to their government duties. According to the new law, trials and examinations should be conducted in the presence of the defendant, according to Article 172 of the Criminal Procedure Code. Therefore, defendants should be brought to the place of the trials (and if they are in prison they should be transported by a car with their legs chained). Therefore, when an examination of witnesses is submitted to a court located in a different place, defendants like us also had to go every time. This had become a great difficulty that my son and I had to face.

I had to leave Pattani with my younger son on 18 October because in the afternoon of 19 October we had to be at the Nakhon Ratchasima Provincial Court. I took a bus and arrived at Bangkok in the morning of 19 October. Then I took a taxi to Mo Chit to take another bus to Nakhon Ratchasima. This was the longest trip in my life, and I couldn't find any Muslim restaurant during this trip. My younger son and I had no choice. We had to eat bread and drink water to quell our hunger.

As a mother of children who had never experienced difficulty, I knew immediately that my son was hungry. I took his hand said: "Be patient, my dear. A boy must be strong and endure."

In the afternoon of 19 October, my son and I were in the courtroom of the Nakhon Ratchasima Provincial Court. The examination of the witnesses finished at 6:00 p.m. We left the court and took a bus to Khon Kaen. We had to stay in a hotel there, and we only ate bread and drank water like in the previous night. In the morning of 20 October, we took a *tuk-tuk* from the hotel to the Khon Kaen Provincial Court. The examination was over after noon. We left the court and took a bus to Bangkok. When the bus arrived in Bangkok, it was 7:00 p.m., and there were no more busses to Pattani on that day. So, we had to stay in a hotel for one more night. The next day we came back to Pattani. Two weeks later, we had to go to another court for the examination of the witnesses for the defendant. After that, on 23 June 2010, the Pattani Provincial Court would deliver the verdict.

On the day of the judgment, the lower court dismissed the case. The verdict stated that the plaintiff's accusation was irrational because keeping explosives in one's own house without hiding it in any way was not the type of behavior indicative of a terrorist. It was true that the court had dismissed the case, but my son was to be kept in prison while awaiting an appeal. I bailed out my son again, and we waited for five months. Finally, the plaintiff didn't appeal, and my son's case was over. I went to the court to take back the title deed for our house and land that had been used for bail.

Even though the court issued a letter to state that the case had finished, I still had to struggle for my life because no one in my house had a permanent job, while our younger son was in the second year of his secondary education. The hardship I had to face was even tougher. I used to sell fried chicken from 6:00 until 9:00 a.m. and used around fifteen chickens, apart from coffee and rice porridges. But now, I could sell fried chicken from fewer than three chickens.

Looking back at that period of time in 2010, when I knew that I had to go the courts in other provinces, I mortgaged my house, the place I used to sell foods, to a bank, and I got four hundred thousand baht. Part of the money was used for expenses, and the rest for settling the debt, both the principal and the interest. But in the end, I couldn't sell my food as customers didn't come to my shop. I couldn't pay back the instalment of the debt from the bank. I also wasn't able to give to my younger son pocket money for his school. At that time my life was really affected. Some local people still came to my shop to buy food, but I couldn't expect them to do so every day because they might get bored with my food. I could sustain my business because my house is on a main street, and there were always some customers. When I couldn't pay the monthly instalment of debt to the bank, I had to sell the house because otherwise the bank would seize it, and I would be really penniless.

I told my younger son that I had to sell the house and asked him whether it would be alright for him to stop schooling for a while and continue his study in the Informal and Non-formal Education Centre [Kor Sor Nor]. He agreed. I could sell my house for a suitable price. A part of the money was used to redeem my car, and the rest was used to buy a piece of land in Pakaharang Subdistrict. The place was more than 10 kilometers away from our old house, located in the countryside. Most of the villagers worked in rice fields or raised cattle. There was no place suitable for business at all, so I had to change my job from a food seller to a farmer by planting vegetables and raising fish, ducks, and chickens. I had no choice other than to buy this piece of land because of our financial limitation. On top of that, I still needed one hundred thousand baht more in order to buy the land. Luckily the owner of the land gave me the title deed in advance. I mortgaged it to the bank in order to pay the rest of the amount to the land owner. I just needed a place where my family could stay. The area was flooded during the rainy season every year, but we had to endure when Allah tested us. But I became stronger after I survived what had happened to me and my family.

To this day I still have to pay back the debt to the bank every month. My husband had some jobs as a plumber, and my children helped him. My younger son still studies in the Informal and Non-formal Education Centre because he likes to study. He wants to extend his study, but I haven't earned enough money for that because I still do not have a job.

Now I'm a member of the Civic Women's Network, and the tasks allocated to me are helping those women who are affected, making scripts for the radio program *Women's Voices from the Southern Border Provinces,* acting as a liaison between security officers and those who are detained under the special law. I also attend trainings to become a paralegal. I have never formally studied law, but I resort to my actual experience of being involved in legal cases. I only had a high vocational certificate in accounting for marketing, and my job experience was as a food seller. I need to become aware of new types of knowledge, to study it and to apply it.

I asked for justice in the form of vocational help from government agencies as a part of a remedy effort, but I have never been successful. To this day I have never stopped voicing a demand for justice on every relevant occasion. Many government agencies and organizations help the families of those who have been killed and those who are injured from the violence, but hardly any agency or organization takes care of those whose lives have been damaged by illegitimate security cases. Although people like us have never committed any crimes, we are always treated as scapegoats. No one can see what kind of damages we have to bear and how difficult and tough is the life of families like ours.

Although our cases are over, I still feel that justice hasn't yet been delivered to us. While fighting these cases, I requested every agency to examine fingerprints. The result of such an examination in our cases showed that there were no fingerprints from my husband and son. The question remains about whose fingerprints were on the explosive device. Why haven't the security people further examined them to determine whose fingerprints they are? This is the agenda about which I seek justice to this day.

I would like to tell everyone that in order to get justice we have to make our own effort and ask help from Allah. Whether or not we will be successful depends on the mercy of Allah. As for human beings, when we have a lot of money, everyone loves and cares for us and wants to be friendly with us. But when we go bankrupt or become penniless, even best friends and relatives might leave us behind. Only Allah will not forget us and has mercy upon us, however we are. I wish our Muslim brothers perform *ibadah* [religious duties] and stick to *iman* [faith], *insya Allah* [if God wills].

I Am My Father's Blood

ARIDA SAMOH

I have unconditionally forgiven the killer of my father.

My story is about a young girl who has lost her beloved father. Every letter I typed was tough and bitter. Whenever I put my hand on the keyboard, concentrating on the story that reminded me of that horrible moment in my life, my hand had to go in another direction to wipe tears that streamed down my face. The image of my father lying on the ground after bullets were fired from the barrel of a gun is still very clear in my mind. I have flashbacks of this image again and again, as if it had happened right in front of me. I was standing by him lying on the ground, breathing feebly, until finally he left us. This is an image I made up by myself because I was actually the last person who came back home to see the soulless body of my father.

Dear readers,

I am Arida Samoh, the second child of Abdulloh Samoh. I am trying to revive him in my writing. He is the inspiration that made me decide to join a group of people who were searching for something called "peace," something that had vanished from this region since the war broke out in 2004 at the edge of this kingdom.

My mother's name is Parida Samoh. Now she has taken up the responsibilities of my father. My family used to have nine members, but now we only have eight, after my father passed away.

When I was a small girl, I cried very easily. At that time, we, I mean my family, were a big extended family. I still remember that my relatives called me a whimpering girl. They had to endure my loud crying voice. My grandmother soothed them by saying, "A child who cries a lot will be a wise person." That is what she said. However, after the passage of a long time, I felt the truth must be that a small child who cries a lot grows into an adult who cries a lot! To this day, I often have to endure things that hurt my feelings. Every time I have this kind of experience, I cry. I don't know how to grow into a wise person.

There is nothing outstanding about my appearance, but my mind has never stopped asking questions to compensate for my sense of loss, seeking something that might be able to explain why my father had to be shot.

The body of a dead person disintegrates and returns to soil, just like the very beginning of the creation of human beings. On the other hand, the death of a beloved one is the beginning of a very long period of remembering and missing that person, as if they were meant to live forever.

The unfair death of my father has certainly affected my life. What happened to my family has produced a very strong drive for me to be one of those people who is trying to change this land of killing into a happy, safe, and peaceful homeland for everyone, so that people in the war-torn area can also hope. It sounds naïve, but I made up my mind to build such a land together with those who have the same intentions.

"I was the last one in the family to know that my father had been shot, wasn't I?"

Six years have passed since 15 September 2006, the day my father left us forever, but my attention always comes back to what happened on that day. I still remember the sentences I uttered. I was angry with everyone because they didn't tell me the reason why my father had died. I was angry with everyone who let me believe that my father, lying on the floor, utterly motionless without responding to my cry to wake him up, died because of the chronic disease that he had suffered since I was very small. I was angry with everyone because they let me, who my father loved beyond anything else in the world, be the last person to learn that my father had died because of live bullets released from the darkness by someone: an "incident" witnessed by nobody.

My face was covered with tears. I jerked the hand of a close relative to ask, "My father was shot, wasn't he?" My question was followed by silence, then my sobbing. Finally, she only said: "It was the will of Allah. It was the time for him to leave us. Bullets were just the means of his death. You must brace yourself." After finishing what she had to say, she moved to the kitchen, where people were walking around busily, leaving me to shed my tears. It was the beginning of my bewilderment in life.

Eight hours prior to that, I clearly remember that on that day I was preparing myself in the dormitory behind the campus of Prince of Songkhla University for the final examination scheduled for the coming week. At that time, I was in the first semester of the second year. I was the student leader of my major, so I had to study hard in order to be so acknowledged by everyone.

After midnight, a familiar voice called my name in front of the dormitory. "Da, are you there?" The voice called my name three to four times, and stopped. I craned my neck out of a small window. It was one of my close relatives, standing in front of the door as if waiting for someone to open it. There were some other relatives too. I was surprised and rushed to the door to open it. I asked: "How did you know I stay here? Why do you come here at such an odd time?"

One of my relatives asked permission to come inside the dormitory to see my friends. Another relative said: "We came for holiday. We came here to pick you up to have dinner with us. Go and dress yourself up." I was surprised but did not ask more questions. I entered my room to dress myself up hurriedly, as I didn't want to make them wait for a long time.

There were five of us inside the car. After leaving Pattani city, the car followed the main road. The headlights of the car were the only light, and we only could vaguely see the roadsides. But it was not bright enough for me to know that it actually was just the main road that I had traveled many times when I came from and went back home.

We were inside the car for two hours. I felt cold and my face was pale, but no one cared. I was surprised because they didn't tell me where we were heading. I was intrigued because no one in the car had ever invited me to go anywhere before.

Questions popped up in my mind one after another, and I didn't know where to find the answers. I could only imagine: "There must be something that has happened to my family, and it must be my one of my brothers who is so naughty, since he listens to nobody."

When the car finally arrived at the village, one of my female relatives sitting next to me said: "Da, you can sense that something has happened, can't you? Whatever it is, you must accept it. This is something that inevitably will happen to us one day." When she finished what she had to say, the car arrived at my house. My body trembled, and I became stiff at finding many relatives from other villages gathered together. Some of them were waiting for me on the veranda in front of my house. I got out of the car, walking in bewilderment as if I was half-unconscious.

I noticed that many of my relatives were looking at me. A curtain was set in a part of my house. What I could remember was that it was the place where I had seen the body of my grandfather for the last time. Now the similar image appeared in front of me again. Straight legs came out of the curtain, wrapped in a piece of white cloth. I thought, "Is this my brother?" When I approached the curtain, one of my aunties dragged me by the arm and hugged me tightly, saying: "Your father passed away peacefully. Everything is destined by Allah." Another auntie tapped me on my shoulder and said: "Be patient. Everything happens according to Allah's will, and no one can do anything except Him. Be patient, my dear."

I was giddy for a few minutes. Tears were gushing out of my eyes because of the intense shock. My body shivering, I hugged my auntie and asked: "Why should it be my father? Why?"

A while later I went to see my father's body. I untied the white cloth from his feet. I bent down and saw my father's feet for the first and last time in my life. There would be no more chance to touch his body. He was leaving us forever. I opened up the cloth on his chest, then his face. I lowered my head to kiss his forehead. Finally, the white cloth wrapping his body was tied up again.

His other six children sat around this body with sorrowful faces. I was the last person among my siblings to learn this father of seven had passed away. While I was gazing upon his soulless body, I didn't stop shedding tears. A loud voice was echoing in my heart: "Why should this happen now? Why did my father have to die now?"

Exhausted from crying, I finally fell asleep beside my father's body, which was surrounded by powder to prevent ants from approaching. I asked to sleep beside my father for the last time in that night full of anguish. From the bottom of my heart, I wished that when I woke up, everything I had seen would turn out to have been a nightmare. During that night, I really wished that my father would be alive again when I awakened.

All my hopes of the previous night that my father would be alive again were dashed when I woke up.

The next morning, we waited for young men who would wash my father's body [before the burial]. I sat in the room with one of my sisters and two of my younger brothers. One of the younger brothers, the fourth child of my father, lamented: "Dad, you shouldn't have died! My dad is gone." I had never seen my brother crying like this out of sorrow before. I tried to soothe him and said: "Dad has gone. He can no longer make merit, but if we become a good people, do good things, he will be comfortable. But if we, his children, become bad, he will suffer in the graveyard. Understand?" All my siblings nodded as a sign of understanding, but I myself couldn't hide my tears from the others who were looking at my face.

It was about the time to wash my father's body, and the young villagers were ready. At that time, I approached the curtain to steal a glance at my father's body. I opened my eyes widely when one of the young guys said, "There are many bullets holes in his back, and on his chest too."

Did bullets have anything to do with my father's death? My father had died due to concretion and diabetes, hadn't he? Why were they talking about bullets?

At that moment, tears gushed from my eyes. What had happened became clearer in my mind. I jerked the hand of one of close relatives who happened to pass by me and asked, "My father was shot dead, wasn't he?" That was when all the memories I had with my father until the very last moment, when he lay motionless in this house, began to come back to me. In my mind, an old image arose of my father giving me a piggyback ride home when I had been a small girl. Then a scream came to my heart: "This is utterly unfair. My dad shouldn't have died in such a way. It's unfair for my father. How could they be this ruthless?"

One of the relatives jerked my arm and said: "No one, even you, could have prevented his death. No one could have made him die either. It was the destiny of Allah. The bullets are just one of the causes."

My relatives said my father was a victim. I don't believe that he became a victim due to more than one reason. As far as I can remember, my father, Abdulloh Samoh, was always involved with local politics, including the Volunteer Defence Corps [VDC or Or Sor], a deputy village headman in charge of the village's security; and finally, he became a village headman in 1999.

One of the credible reasons for his demise is the network of drug dealers. At that time the government tried to heavily suppress drug abuse. Orders were issued to the big drug dealers in the village to report themselves to the authorities. If they didn't report themselves to the state officers to declare that they would stop selling drugs, they would face severe consequences that might threaten their lives. There were no written documents, but everyone in the village understood. The result was that the drug dealers who had earned an enormous amount of money from drugs at that time reported themselves. All the other drug dealers, both big ones and small ones, didn't dare to do anything. Eventually, drug abuse really vanished from my village. Information about these drug dealers came from those who had been given the responsibility to prepare reports on their movements, such as village headmen. This assumption was surely in the minds of those who had lost their drug-dealing business.

Yet another hazard emerged during the last period of my father's term as the village headman. A few months before the election for the position, my father had decided to run for it again. It was well known that the rival in the election, who was one of my father's friends, was supported by those who had lost business from the government policy of suppressing drug dealers. My father was defeated in the election. Our family's life began to be tough. I was very stressed with what had happened in my life at that time.

After I finally came to accept the reality of my father's death, the first thing I blamed for his death was the fact that he always had worked for the state. Ever since I could remember, I saw him in his uniform, starting with the khaki uniform of a deputy village headman, then a village headman for one term, and also the uniform of the Volunteer Defence Corps and the Village Security Team, or Cho Ro Bo. Most importantly, my father had never imagined that when the situation in the southern border provinces worsened from 2005 to 2006, he would be one of the important targets of the opposite side, to the extent they would take his life away.

My Mother: "Da, your dad volunteered for Cho Ro Bo."

Me: "Did you want him to join Cho Ro Bo? Why did you let him?"

Mother: "Your dad said he had no job. There's nothing wrong with joining it."

When I thought about what caused my father to leave us for good, I remembered my mother's voice on the phone as if she was consulting with me. He joined Cho Ro Bo two years after he had lost the election against his old friend. During that time, he had no job. I have blamed myself to this day because if I had stated my objection more forcefully, my father would have listened to me because he loved me most among my siblings. This, however, could be just my imagination. My father might have made up his mind to join Cho Ro Bo after considering many other options. His task was to guard the village headman of a different village, who was our close relative. I had comforted myself by believing that my father would be safe with my relative.

For a week after his murder, we received visits from my father's friends who had heard the news of his death. They all spoke of their memories of my father when he had been still alive. I felt we had heard enough of the stories of the past. I decided to go back to university, where I wouldn't have to be hurt by these stories and could turn my attention to the future.

Before I returned to university, my mother mentioned documents to be submitted to the district office in order to prove my right as a legal heir. At that time there was no system in the university to aid those students who were affected by the unrest. I didn't know who I could rely on to ask about a scholarship. I was afraid that I might have to stop my education halfway. I was sure that it would take at least a few months before I finally could be granted remedy money from the state. My mother had to stay home, according to Islamic law. After the death of a husband, a wife had to stay in the house for three months and ten days. It was the law followed in our society. During that time, my family had no income. My mother became more religious than before. I saw her always with the Qur'an, in a prayer garment all the time. She was often up after midnight to perform additional prayers. This was what I witnessed before I returned to my university.

Several months later, I cried more than before when I learned that one of my brothers had mental health problems. He confined himself in his room for a month and didn't talk with anyone. The only chance to see his face was when he came out of his room to go to the bathroom. It had been like this for such a long time that finally my mother called me and asked: "What should we do? His condition seems serious."

I decided to go home again to see my brother. We began to experience what we might call the side effects of the "incident." He was seventeen years old. On the day of my father's murder, my brother was in the house. He was the first person to dash out of the house to find his father. My mother said: "Your brother tried to find his father's gun to fight back. The gun was on your father's waist, so he couldn't use it." This short explanation was enough for me to understand how he felt, to the extent he would close the door of his room to be with the extreme pain of the past. If I had been him, I might have gone mad.

I guess that it was because he saw the culprits, even in the shape of vague shadows. Nevertheless, they were the ones who killed our father. One of our relatives investigated the place where the culprits had been hiding. There were two more stray bullets. Otherwise my brother would have been the second victim, and my father's auntie, who dashed to the place immediately, would have been the third victim of the night. My brother must be feeling distressed because he couldn't help his father. It was a real possibility because they were standing right there immediately after the shooting. If I had been him, I would have thought like him. Had I been on the spot and found the gun in my father's waist, I would surely have exchanged bullets.

"Please do something!" I begged for help from those relatives who were more strong-minded than my mother. In a discussion on the following day, everyone agreed that we would have to conduct some rituals following our beliefs. One was a ritual to calm people down, as was the ritual practice performed by Buddhists; but in our case, we ask for blessings from Allah. I was interested in the process in which many relatives communicated with my brother, who really needed those who were ready to understand him. It worked. My brother began to talk with my mother. I also came home more often than before. Not long after that my brother surprised us again. This time he said, "Let me study religion somewhere."

After I had heard this, I told my mother to grant to his wish, whatever might happen in the future. This was a chance for us to bring him back to a proper path, that is, the path of our religion.

"As a son of our father, I only ask one thing. Behave yourself. We still can do good things, but our father can no longer. Don't let him get more retribution. If you do good things for yourself, the merit will go to our father too." I spoke this to him as a reminder, so that he wouldn't do anything troublesome again.

Our house was an old, dilapidated one. Everyone agreed that after we received an amount of remedy money, we would pay off our father's debt and repair the house to make it stronger. This was the first plan we had for the money we were going to receive. After that, for the further steps, my mother said, "I will send him to pilgrimage." Everyone agreed to hire someone to perform the *hajj* pilgrimage as father's surrogate. We thought it was the most valuable thing to do for someone who had had no chance to step his foot in the holy land. The merit from a surrogate *hajj* could go to him.

There is no answer in the classroom . . . thus. I have to go out to the outside world, a vast, round, global classroom . . .

After I came back to university, I felt differently. I began to ask more questions about what was being taught by the lecturers. I felt restless whenever what I was listening to didn't answer the questions popping up in my mind, such as what was going on in my country, what happened to my society, and what was going to happen to my family. As a result, my achievements clearly declined, and I often disappeared from the classroom. Instead, I became a new face who appeared in various forums. People began to know me, and they contacted and invited me to join these events. I also began to submit my short writings to them, and through this process I hoped to gradually develop my skills. I felt that as I accumulated experience, in the end there might be some changes in me.

I studied in the Faculty of Education and majored in general science. English was my favorite subject, though I thought that science was the most interesting subject that could connect our thinking process with all the things in the world. However, it wouldn't be able to make me understand the most complicated things in the world like the human mind. The more my view of the situation became abnormal, the more necessary it became to understand the human mind. Our society was surrounded by so many things that were difficult to understand. Under such circumstances, joining events and activities organized outside the university gave me the chance to see many new interesting things, especially those things that I thought would be able to make me approach genuine information related to the causes of this terrible conflict in our region and stories about the consequences of violence. These things motivated me to go out into the society to find the relations between causes.

Always interested in learning, I liked asking many questions. My character drove me to study even more. I joined activities organized by those adults who saw my importance and potential. They invited me to take part in such activities as academic seminars, research, discussions about the problems in the southern border provinces, capacity building, and so on. During these days, I mainly joined a lot of capacity-building activities for alternative communication channels. Through these experiences I came to understand myself more clearly, although I didn't understand the basic principles of communication. During the initial period of my joining in these activities, I was dissatisfied with those youths who didn't express their opinions during the activities, especially when they disagreed with what had been proposed by adults. Instead, they left the venue of discussion only to meet up outside to criticize what we had just finished discussing. I couldn't help asking myself: "Why do they have to form another discussion group like this? If they want to solve the problem or disagree, they have to face those who disagree with them. Forming their own group is not the way forward. If they are always doing this, how can their opinions can be heard by others, and how the problem ever be solved?" I felt sorry. It would be better if their constructive opinions had been heard by others.

Later I tried to observe discussions among young people, questioning why they were the way they were. Then I understood that their attitude had come from a mutual distrust between youth and adults. Some of my youthful friends told me that they began to feel that their voices had no value at all because some of the adults didn't heed their proposals. The adults took advantage of the youths as their tools instead. On the other hand, I also heard some adults complaining about the attitudes of young activists, who had short attention spans, were not serious, and were undisciplined. I agreed with this opinion because I also found such attitudes among them as well. Their tendency to isolate themselves and not mingle with others was particularly problematic because in peace-building we must be ready to work with others. This was the main principle of my involvement because we come up with new ideas though working across groups. However, I, too, didn't trust others so easily. Thus, I only chose to cooperate with those who I thought would be most beneficial for peace-building in the three southern border provinces. I didn't want to know about political or financial gains for myself. What I needed was those who could facilitate my journey, while what they might gain was out of my consideration.

I thought that I must extend my world gradually to include other countries. I became a traveler. Since my third year of university, the timetable of my life was different from that of other students. I showed up at the events organized by civil society organizations to discuss the problem of violence in three southern border provinces, and gradually I began to learn a lot from these experiences. One day I felt that just joining these events was not enough for learning. Therefore, I started joining activities organized by seniors in my university, such as visiting activities, that made my worldview even wider.

At that time, I began to realize that I was not the only person in the world who was seeking justice. When I visited families who had lost their beloved ones, I forgot that I was distressed by what had happened to my family, but my attention went to the tears shed by so many others whom I had chances to visit.

Sometimes I cried when I heard the stories told by those ladies who had lost their husbands and children from violence including indiscriminate shootings, stories of mysterious bullets that came from behind a house, with no one witnessing who fired them. But these deadly bullets impoverished the lives of their families for such a long time. I cried at these stories, and I asked myself, "How long should we let this situation go on like this?" It was not fair that the world was so unkind to us.

On another occasion, one week after an indiscriminate shooting against local villagers in Pattani Province, I followed a peace volunteer group led by Ms. Naree Charoenpiriya to visit the victims and their families. This time I also heard terrible stories of the shootings committed by those who didn't want to see peace in this region. As a consequence, the villagers had to live their lives in fear. I was depressed to hear these stories, but I tried to listen to their stories to the end.

There was one new thing I learned from these visits. After I had heard the stories, I tried to document and compose them into written stories. Then I sent these stories to alternative media in order to spread them to a wider audience. There were many alternative media interested, and the stories told by the villagers became known to the public. We were happy to help the villagers in bringing their stories to light through the media. Through these experiences I developed a new desire to be a writer so that I would be able to draw stories from frightened villagers and give them to the public. So I decided to practice my writing, and my first piece was published by Aman News Agency. I used my own name, Arida Samoh.

My stories came out from time to time because I needed time for my studies. But people began to talk about my writings, and they began to call me a journalist. This convinced me that this could be a possible future of mine, that is, becoming a journalist.

"I don't want to be a teacher now," I replied briefly to my mother when she asked why I hadn't applied for an exam for a teaching license like most of my friends. In fact, I wanted to tell my mother that I had already found a job that I much preferred, a civil society activist. I tried to describe my job to my mother, but to this day she has never understood what her daughter is up to. She also doesn't know whether her daughter gets any salary from her job or not. I heard my mother's reply when a relative asked about my job. She said: "I don't know. But she often goes to many places. I don't know in which part of earth she is now." Hearing her reply, I couldn't help finding it amusing because what my mother just said was true. I myself couldn't describe my work. So how could my mother explain that to others? But in the depth of my heart, I thought my mother was proud of having a daughter who was not similar to other villagers.

I hadn't imagined that my not applying for the exam for a teaching license was actually an opportunity for me to take a long journey for the first time in my life. The journey later became an important turning point in my life that caused me to be seriously involved in civil society activities. This was a trip to the Philippines at the end of 2011 in an exchange program with civil society organizations of that country.

During the eighty-four days I spent in Davao, Mindanao, the Philippines, I learned a lot about peace-building on the island, which had been through a conflict for more than sixty years. Finally, some of the tension could be reduced due to the active engagement of the civil society organizations there. I also visited war-torn cities, and witnessed hardship faced by the local people. At that moment, I asked myself: "My homeland will be like this if we do nothing to stop the conflict. My homeland isn't going to be like this, is it?"

I came back from Mindanao determined to do anything to raise awareness of the people about their own matters. At the end of the day, they might be able to determine the future of their own country. My friends and I only could be catalysts for local people to realize their own power.

So, I've chosen . . . to be like this. The horrible loss that happened to my family is not a personal matter, but it was a public matter of the three southern border provinces. Everyone in the southern border provinces should think about why so many killings have been happening. This is a war in disguise that disseminates the seeds of hatred that in turn exacerbate the war itself. The lives of my father, my uncle, and my cousins were sacrificed. I always say to myself: "It shouldn't be like this. There must be a way out. The vicious circle of violence must be stopped." I was interested in anything that could end the vicious circle of violence. We must stop all of this violence. But the question was how to do that.

For many years I have listened to others' stories. Some stories were more severe than mine, and others were less so. One thing I realized from these stories was that it was not just personal reasons that had caused someone to be violent. It was also the stirrings of hatred connected with prejudices accumulated for a long time that cause great frustration. This frustration must be ventilated, and some people had tried to release it by resorting to violence that deprives others of chances to live their lives on the Earth, like what had happened to my father.

With these types of learning experiences, I began to see that the root causes of the conflict were not to be found in just the violent incidents themselves. In order to claim justice for my father, what I have to do is to solve the feud so that justice can be created in the society of the southern border provinces, rather than hunting down the people who pulled the trigger on that fateful night. The big goal of our movement is to stop killing. We must try to establish mutual understanding between two groups of people who do not understand each other. We also help those who are frustrated to ventilate their frustration in proper ways.

I think these things are possible if there is good communication. Journalists in the conflict area must be far more patient than journalists in other places, able to understand and endure heartbreaking "incidents." We are now working to untie the knots of disputes accumulated for a long time in our society that in turn might create peace once again.

I think I can do that thing. And I believe everyone can be a part of creating peace.

Becoming a "Defendant" and Coming Back as a "Mr."

AL-KAHFI (PSEUDONYM) WITH ARIDA AWAEKACHI

I will tell my story wholeheartedly so that everyone can know about it.

How nice it would be if this were a happy memory in my life. Some incidents resonate in my memory so vividly that I feel as if they happened just a few hours ago. And if you haven't gone through these kinds of experiences, never say that you understand a human being like me.

In the late afternoon on a Sunday in 2005, life was normal like any other day. There was a small difference, though, because in the morning of that day I had visited my friend whose family had lost their beloved mother. Everything else was as usual. I went out for exercise every late afternoon. I was sitting to tie my running shoes. After tying one shoe, and while I was tying the other, I sensed some people standing in front of me, only a few steps away. I slowly looked up and found three strong-bodied men standing in front of me. I immediately knew they were police officers dressed as civilians, from the police station that was in charge of my village. One of them said, "Could you come with us to the police station to have a cup of coffee?"

Although he spoke politely, I could see that this was an invitation that couldn't be declined. In my heart I thought, "I'm innocent," so there would be no problem with going with them. But I felt quite worried because at that time there was no one in my house, and I couldn't find anybody to tell my family where I was going and with whom. So I negotiated with the three men.

"Let me tell my relatives first. Otherwise, my family will worry about me."

I didn't know what rights I had as a suspect. But even if I had known, I didn't dare to decline the invitation because they came as three, and I was alone. All I could do was to tell someone with whom I was going. Luckily, they allowed me to go to a house of a relative. When I saw him, I opened my mouth to say what was on my mind at that moment: "Brother, you know . . ." But before I could finish my sentence, he cut in and said, "No, no, I don't know," waving his hand. He looked aside and didn't meet my eyes. My face became pale, and I felt sapped of energy. I almost collapsed on the spot. I only could keep silent and turn around to keep from facing him. I walked, following the police officers with pain in my heart.

At first, I was brought to a hotel. In the hotel room there was no conversation whatsoever. After a while I was brought inside a van, and it drove around the province. They didn't tell me where they were taking me. Inside the car, I was alone with the three officers, and two sat on the both sides of me. I couldn't think anything but, "Am I going to survive?" Both sides of the road were covered by the darkness of night. I was sitting inside a car with people whom I didn't know, and my family had no idea of my whereabouts. Even if I died, surely no one would know. My silent inward conversation turned around like the rolling tires of the car. At that moment, even though I tried to sleep, I couldn't close my eyes because I was worried and scared about what they would do to me if I fell asleep.

Finally, I arrived at a place where I was sure that they had brought me for a serious purpose. It was a police station in front of a flat. They brought me into a room that looked like an ordinary place, but I was surprised because, behind the door, there was a bunch of journalists waiting for me, and I was showered with the dazzling flashlights. These flashlights hurt my eyes. After I recovered my sight, I saw high-ranking police officers already sitting inside the room. One of them told me to sit down to face the journalists. My task was just to sit in silence, as all the explanations were provided by the high-ranking police officer. I didn't know him, and I couldn't even hear what he was talking about.

What I thought at that moment was, "Have I become a criminal?"

Even before the court delivered a verdict, they had already judged that I was guilty. But at the bottom of my heart I felt glad that at least I was still alive for another day.

(Do you understand how I felt? I had a ringing in my ear, giddy, and bewildered . . . Don't say you understand me, because you have never gone through what I had to go through!)

I was in the mysterious room for eighteen hours until midnight. After that someone came to take me to a sedan. There were cars in front of and behind the car in which I was taken. Inside the car all seats except mine were occupied by fully armed uniformed officers. I thought in my heart, "I must be extraordinary." The images of my father, mother, sisters, and brothers, together with our old house, came into my head. I felt as though this was the last scene of my life. Finally, the car brought me to the Front Operation Centre of the police in Yala Province.

I spent nearly one month there. I was interrogated every day, facing the same questions in the mornings, afternoons, and evenings. I was there for almost one week before I could see my mother. My family didn't ask painful questions such as "What did you do?" They also didn't judge that I had done something wrong like the others had judged me. They only asked about my health. That was all.

After one month, my status was as a "suspect" according to a warrant issued by dint of the emergency decree. The officers gave me one white shirt to wear, along with a pair of sweatpants. There could have been others who were sharing the same fate as I, but I couldn't see many others because only three or four detainees were kept in one cell. I didn't know those who were detained with me. But because we had been strangers, I only asked about ordinary things, not daring to ask a lot of questions.

On the final day, after I had spent one full month as a suspect, I again pondered, "So what was the charge against me?" They brought me to a police bus and announced that they would take me back home. Inside the bus there were around twenty other detainees, with everyone's face clearly expressing a hope to go home, including mine. Everybody got into the bus with the same feeling. We expressed hope, mixed with a feeling of being utterly fed up with this place.

One of the officers told us to get out of the bus and said, "Sign these documents before you get off." Everyone on the bus signed several documents. I didn't know how others felt, but I wanted to finish everything as soon as possible. My destination was my house. I badly wanted to go home. I didn't think about anything when I saw the documents. The officer told me to sign here and there, and I followed his instructions. It was as if the officer knew that I didn't care what kind of documents I had to sign. He only showed me the parts of the documents to be signed. When I signed the last document, I felt, "Now everything is over." Then I got into the bus again with a rose that a police officer had given. Each detainee got one rose.

When the bus was heading for my hometown, I observed both sides of the road. When the bus was about to arrive at the police station in my region, the driver drove through the gate. In my heart I thought: "I came home. I have survived." But the driver completely disappointed me because he just made a U-turn and drove inside the precinct police station. Most of the detainees had already gotten off from the bus. There were only six of us remaining inside, and I was one of the six detainees. I didn't know where they were taking me now. We got out of the bus, and each one of us was brought to interrogation rooms. Inside my interrogation room, apart from two police officers, there was one other stranger too. One of the police officers introduced him as a lawyer. A police officer held the documents I had already signed. "This is your signature, isn't it?"

I realized then that the document was regarded as evidence that I had confessed for "joining a criminal society and being involved in terrorism."

After that day, the police brought me to the court. On that day, the judge called me by a new name with which I was not familiar, but the status was extraordinary.

"Defendant, do you have any objections?"

After the court granted permission to detain me, police officers attended me on both sides, with my hands handcuffed. I got on a police pickup truck to be brought to the police station in the area of my house.

My thoughts at that time were disturbing, not knowing what to do, not seeing and hearing anything. I just wanted to know where they were taking me. While I was standing and waiting, an officer opened up a new accommodation for me to spend the night. In front of me was a square room, behind two doors made of long, upright iron bars, separate from each other, just wide enough to pass a hand thorough. Ordinary people called this place a "lockup." The size was about four square meters. From the outside, I noticed that there was a man inside. He was wearing a shirt and a pair of short pants. He was lying on the floor. I said in my heart, "Do I have the same status as this guy?"

The first thing I did was to make friends with him. He said he was suspected for burning tires on the road, and no one in his family knew that he was being detained in this police station. Our conversation got to the point that I felt very bad about this place. This man wore a pair of short pants and a shirt all day long. There were no other clothes to change into. He wanted to perform a prayer, but his request hadn't been heeded by any officer. His request was to have clothes to change into so that he could perform a prayer. Imagine how he had to perform his prayer with a pair of pants and a shirt that smelled of his sweat after being worn all night. Muslims can understand how he felt in that situation.

On the first day when I was in the lockup, my father visited me and whispered to me, "Like Father, like son." He once had been arrested for his driving license. Therefore he understood what it was like to be inside a lockup. (I acknowledge that my father could understand my feeling at that moment because he had a similar experience.)

At that time my status was as a defendant, and the charge against me was being a member of a criminal society that caused terrorism. . . . On the first day that I was moved to a prison, I still remember that I was wearing a white shirt and a pair of sweatpants from the police station in Yala. I went through the first and second doors, and many more. The first thing a "new plaintiff" had to do was to change his clothes to the prisoner's brown. The worst thing was that I had to take off my clothes in the middle of an open field, surrounded by tens of officers. Then they checked every part of my body to make sure that nothing prohibited would be brought inside the prison walls. Then I was allowed to wear a new set of clothes. I felt that I had lost my dignity as a human being at that moment, being no different from an animal.

In my first night in prison, I had to sleep in a room that already been dwelt in by more than a hundred inmates. As a newcomer, I had to sleep among other prisoners. Originally, they only had a space as narrow as the distance between the elbow and the tip of the finger for each person. It was hardly wide enough even to wriggle. Now, with my presence, the space became even narrower. Maybe there is no need to explain how bad this situation was.

I liked watching movies, and I had seen countless prison scenes. I imagined my fate, thinking that if I showed my weakness to others, powerful longtime prisoners would bully me. But I knew that most of the inmates thought that I was a real insurgent who had been involved in grave offenses. Therefore, in order to protect myself, I decided to behave like a real insurgent. It was effective. No one dared to disturb my privacy, and they were afraid of me, as if I was a big local mafia figure. Apart from this, I didn't socialize with others, and I was always stern with a pale, irritated facial expression, as if I was always angry at somebody. Those who were close to me were all insurgents who had been charged with serious cases. So the other inmates didn't come close to me, believing that I was a real insurgent.

During the initial period of my prison life, my emotions were not stable, thinking about the same thing all the time: how I could be free. I wanted freedom.

Every morning after we woke up, we took a shower and stood in line to show respect for the national flag. Then we were divided into work parties. For the inmates of security cases, the only work party allowed was fishnet making. After the lunch break, we went back to work. We had a meal break at three o'clock, and then we went back to our rooms. At seven o'clock we stood in line to sing a song of praise to the monarchy, and then we went to bed. The next day, the same routine would be repeated. Every day went on in this way, again and again. Have you ever felt that certain events in your life repeat themselves exactly in the coming day? Don't ask me if I believe it or not, because I knew that it was true during this time.

Another thing I experienced in prison was that our life was always accompanied by music, especially when we had to go out to go to court. Both of our ankles were shackled, tied together with chains touching the ground. Every step produced a jingling sound, especially when many people walk together. The more prisoners walked, the louder the sound. I was there for only a few days, but the other prisoners and the prison guards must have been with this sound longer than me. If I tried to think in a positive way, the sound was like music, but in fact no one appreciated it because it came from something that made your movement much more difficult.

It took three years for the court to dismiss the charge in my first case. But I had no time to be glad because it was immediately followed by my second and third case, as if someone had already prepared these cases against me in advance. I already had a vague hope, but I was to be disappointed again. While I was fighting the charges in my second and third cases, the fourth and fifth cases followed. It took me six long years to finally prove my innocence.

In the final three months of the last year of my struggle, when my family and I were fighting the fifth case, I was confident that I would win. The court had to dismiss this case because the evidence against me was so weak, like in the previous cases. But in my heart, while waiting for the verdict during the last three months, I felt that this period was even longer than the two months that I had been originally detained in the interrogation center. I was like a computer memory bank that was already full. I could not receive, know, or listen to anything. The only thing I could think at that time was, "When will the day come?"

I was like a man in the middle of a desert, utterly thirsty, who can only think about a well and is completely uninterested in anything else, with giddy eyes focused only on a well. In my case, it was not a well but freedom.

Finally, the day had come. It was a Wednesday that I have never forgotten. I was standing in the courtroom in order to listen to the verdict for which I had been waiting for such a long time.

"The court dismisses the case." I felt like a madman.

At around seven o'clock in the evening of that day, I stepped out of the prison as an innocent person again. I remember that the first step was by my right foot. As I was taller, I had to bend myself a bit at the prison gate. When I went through the last door, I looked up to investigate the atmosphere outside the prison, which I hadn't felt for a long time. I hoped that a lot of my family members would be coming to celebrate and pick up me. But the scene in front of me dashed my gladness. It was replaced by the fear that the same vicious circle was about to start again when I saw a police pickup truck from the police station near my house. Some police officers approached me and said, "You have to come with us to the police station."

It was delight in vain. I could smile for merely a few seconds, and now I had to come to the police station, a place I didn't want to go again. But this time I was lucky because it was over in less than two hours. The police officers cleared the warrant and said, "Everything is OK." This time I thought I would surely be able to go home.

I still remember that on that day I hardly could remember the way to my own home. My father drove a car to our house. We passed through the roads that I had known since I was small, including the junction with the alley to get to my house. I didn't realize it was the junction with the alley, as if I were unconscious. The next thing I knew, I was already in my house.

A few days later I had a new identification card made. The photo of me on the card was the first one since I had been released. I could sense that the person in the picture was very different from me. I just noticed that I had changed a lot. My skin was darker. My hair was cut short because this was the compulsory hairstyle in prison. This picture reminded me of the time when I had been in prison. Even though my family and I had struggled to prove my innocence until the court believed us and dismissed my cases, the verdict from society that was delivered through people's eyes clearly indicated that, from their point of view, I was a real terrorist. Did I have to prove my innocence in the court of society too? Or should I just let things go on until they finally understood what actually had happened? Yet, what was most important for me was not other people in society but my family, who had given moral support and healed my wounded heart until it came back to the normal again . . . until I could come back and face society again.

According to ordinary people's perception, those accused of security cases were highly likely to have been educated in *pondok* schools or religious schools. However, my education was very different.

I studied in ordinary schools all the time. After I finished my secondary education in a provincial school, I studied in a vocational school. However, due to financial problems, I couldn't complete my course. After that I worked in the field that I studied in the vocational school. But I was arrested less than one year after I started working.

During my school days, when I was in the lower secondary school, I was strict about religious observance, never missing prayers. Teachers appointed me as the leader of prayers in the school. Most of the Muslim students were not very strict in performing religious duties. When I was in the vocational school, I was elected as the president of the student union, and I was in charge of the Muslim club too. However, when I had these positions, it was a time when a number of students were summoned by the security forces due to the suspicion that they had been involved in the insurgency. Apart from me, I later learned that those students who had been presidents of the Muslim club three years prior to me were all summoned and released later. But these "incidents" indicate that Muslim student leaders at that time were marked by the security forces, and my name was on their black list.

When I was fighting my cases, the Muslim Attorney Centre that helps defendants of security cases free of charge had not been established yet. I had a lawyer who had been appointed by the court. But I was not confident that a lawyer whom I hadn't chosen would be able to give me effective help. So, I read a lot of books to acquire legal knowledge while I was fighting my cases in the court. These books were available in the library of the prison.

I searched legal books and read diligently, especially those parts that were necessary for fighting a legal case. In whatever way, I just wanted to follow the game going on inside the courtroom. In the sessions inside the court, I was a defendant, standing in the center, and the referees of the game were the judges. There were two teams competing in providing information. On one side was the prosecutor, who wanted me to lose the case by means of their information. On the other side was the lawyer, who tried to have me win the case. Whether I won or lost depended on which side provided more convincing information. I always told myself, "Innocent, innocent, I'm not guilty." The information from my lawyers and their way of handling the case proved that the information provided by the prosecutor was not true. Finally, I could prove my innocence.

When the court believed in my innocence, that was the end of my being called as a "defendant." But if the court hadn't believed in it, "Mr." wouldn't be used in front of my name.

After going through this difficult time of my life, I became an "innocent man" again following the final court order. However, in the eyes of those who knew where I had been for almost six years, the verdict of the court had no effect on their understanding of me. I was still like a "defendant" to society.

I tried to restore myself and resisted just blaming my fate. I began to see who loved me and who was most important to me. It was my family, who had never let me down. My mother taught me to know myself, to know God and believe in what He had arranged. Whether you liked what happened in your life or not, these things had been arranged by God in order to test human beings. And my mother taught me: "We can't control other people's thoughts. If people see us negatively, what we can do is behave ourselves as best as we can, and ask for His mercy. Then after a while they will know what is true and what is not."

Society is not used to a man like me. They might have questions or suspicions, and they make their own judgments based only on whatever they know. But I want them to open their hearts and accept what I feel in the bottom of my heart. Imagine if this kind of fate happened to any one of your family members, and try to understand what is needed by him. Imagine how he might feel when everyone judges him as guilty, even though the court hasn't begun any investigation of his case. If his family and his community that he used to trust as the source of his motivation turn around and blame him, how can his life afterward be stable?

I tell this story for those who are trying to understand the feeling of "defendants" in the past, at present, and in the future, and how much their feelings are damaged. As to the question, "How can these people come back to society as a member in good standing?," I want everyone to consider this question seriously and find their own answers.

I Endure . . . This Is a Test

BURONG PUTEH (PSEUDONYM) WITH SUKKREEYAH
BAHE AND MUALLIMAH SATA

I want to vent about my burdensome feelings so that I don't have to be plagued by them anymore. If I talk about my life in the past, without curbing my thoughts, asking questions about why these things had to happen to me, then sorrow crawls into my heart and tears fall on the paper. Pieces of horribly painful memories link together, as if these things had just happened yesterday.

When the court delivered a verdict of capital punishment, my heart was utterly broken. I said to my *buya* [father] and *ummi* [mother], "*Jago diri teh nah*" [take care of yourselves]. But the meaning of this in the depth of my heart was: "Father, Mother, if I have to leave this world, you take care of yourselves. Don't worry about anything anymore." These thoughts went around and round in my heart, and I really couldn't stop shedding tears.

Let me talk about my childhood. I am the third child of six siblings. My family's status was middle class. My father was a *khatib*, or a member of the local mosque's committee, respected and having the confidence of the people in the village. He also worked in the paddy fields and did rubber-tapping, the main occupations of the villagers. My mother helped my father in rubber tapping. Both of them were hardworking. They went out for rubber-tapping at 3:00 a.m. and came home at 11:00 a.m.

When I was in a primary school in the village, most of my school uniforms were secondhand. I didn't have many occasions to wear a new outfit. My clothes were always the ones that had been already worn by my elder brother.

I had an auntie called "Mak Ngoh" who awakened me to take a bath and prepared breakfast every morning before I went to school. Every day she gave me three baht of pocket money to bring to school. At that time, I didn't understand what poverty was. At least my family had enough rice to eat and didn't have to buy it. Even though we didn't have a car, I was proud that my father still had an old Yamaha motorbike.

In the evenings, we sat together in a circle to have dinners. While having dinner, my father often asked: "How was today's study? Do you have homework to do? Don't sleep late." My achievements in school were not bad. I was among the three best students in class all the time. After I finished my primary education, my father sent me to a private Islamic school located in Yala city, where male and female students studied separately in different classes.

According to the school's system, we studied religious subjects in the mornings and academic subjects in the afternoons. Every morning I sat in front of my house, waiting for the school bus that was painted yellow. When I was in the first year of the secondary education for academic subjects, I was in the third level of religious subjects. In the religious teachings, if a student gets more than 85 percent in the examinations on all of the religious subjects, he or she will be promoted to a higher level. My achievement was at such a good level. When I finished the secondary education for the sixth year, I was in the tenth level of religious subjects. When I was in the fourth year, I began plans to take an exam for a scholarship so I could study until the tenth level, in order to have a chance to study in Egypt. It was surely a dream that wasn't too-farfetched.

But the dream that I had drawn vanished in an instant.

On 27 October 2005, one week before Hari Raya, the celebration after the fasting month of Ramadan, came a turning point that changed my life completely. I was riding a motorbike to buy some sweets for breakfast in the late evening. The basket in front of the motorbike was filled with sweets to be brought back home. Father, Mother, and Auntie were awaiting my return. When I was riding my motorbike, heading for my home on the road by an irrigation canal, the day was getting dark faster than usual. It was time to prepare foods for breaking the fast. There was no one coming out of our house . . . then I heard a sound that was unmistakably a gunshot. I lost my balance on the motorbike and fell to the road. I was so taken by surprise. I tried to find a hiding place away from the sound of bullets that continued to be fired. Feeling pain, I sank down on the ground. I knew then that my left leg had been shot and that the bone was broken. The injury wasn't too severe, and I still could move my toes. However, because I was shot on the upper part of my leg, I couldn't even crawl. I could think about nothing at that time. I just submitted my life to Allah with all of my faith.

Three police cars arrived at the scene. No villagers dared to come out of their houses. The police officers began to investigate. One of them aimed his flashlight at me and my motorbike on the roadside. What should I do? Did I have to say that I was not the culprit? Would they believe me? What they would do with me?

One of the police officers approached me and checked my pulse. I only knew that he tried to put me in their pickup truck. At that time, I felt extreme pain as my broken leg bent like the letter *V.* However painful it was, I couldn't say anything for fear of consequences. I didn't know where they wanted to take me. I regained my consciousness in a wheelchair that was pushed into the emergency room of a hospital. A nurse inserted a tube into my throat, and I choked and vomited. Then the nurse injected saline solution into my wrist and put on an oxygen mask. I lost my consciousness again and didn't regain it for the night.

When I woke up again, there was already a piece of iron planted in my leg so that the broken leg wouldn't pierce my muscle. Then I was sent to the Fort Ingkhayutthaborihan Hospital in Pattani Province. Sometimes there were soldiers coming inside the ward to talk with me, asking questions about the "incident" in the night. But they didn't believe me. Instead they bawled at me, "You are lying!" In the evenings, soldiers came again to interrogate me. I was so distressed that I told myself that this was a nightmare, and when I woke tomorrow I would go back to the real world. Sometimes I pinched myself and felt a pain, but I tried to believe that this was a pain I felt in my nightmare. In the evenings I tried to dream that I wasn't there but actually in my house, studying in school. I thought in this way every day that I was in the fort.

Several days after that, a police officer told me: "You can go home soon. The soldiers will release you." Then they told me to sign a document with many pages filled with letters. As I was so glad at the prospect of going home soon, I signed that document without even reading what was written inside. It turned out that I was to be sent to Pattani Prison, not home.

My case proceeded very slowly. It took almost two years before the first session, that is, the first appointment to examine the defendant in the court-room. While waiting for that, I had to live behind the high walls doing noth-ing. I was charged on two serious counts. About the second case, murder, the police had already closed the case, and I was waiting for the verdict. About the first case, possession of guns, the sessions were postponed many times, as the witnesses for the police often couldn't come to the court. It was one month before the verdict for murder would be delivered. I thought the case would be dismissed.

On the day of the verdict, when the judge opened the envelope to read out the verdict, my heart beat very fast. Finally, I heard the court's verdict delivered: capital punishment! I understood that the only possible option had been capital punishment. My heart was broken. I had lost my case. I turned back to face my parents, who shed tears without being able to stop. I couldn't say anything. My parents hugged me as their tears flowed. I also cried after I saw my parents' tears, because this might the last time with my parents for me.

"Be patient," said my father through tears while hugging me. It was a long hug. Everyone cried, including those who came to listen to the verdict. The court officer had to tell them to let me go so I could be taken to the prison. After that I didn't talk with anyone because I thought the only thing waiting for me in the future was capital punishment. The next day a friend told me that I still had two more chances to fight for my case, first in the appeals court, and if I didn't win then, the case could be brought to the Supreme Court.

Four weeks later, my mother came to visit me alone, and said, "Father was arrested. Now he is in Fort Ingkhayuth, but I can visit him." This made me think more seriously and worry again. I didn't know what was happening to my family. What I had to face was already heavy, and now my father was detained too. Not long after that, my father was released as he had committed no offense.

For my part, finally the court delivered the verdict of eleven years, six months for the gun possession case. A few days later, I was transferred to Songkhla Central Prison. I was there for one week before I was moved to Nakhon Si Thammarat Prison. Two months later, I was brought to Bang Khwang Prison in Nonthaburi Province. While waiting for the verdict of the appeals court, I spent my time in reading and in vocational training, such as interior arrangement, cooking, boy scouts' activities, household electricity wiring, and fishing net- making. I also practiced my English with foreign inmates. At least these activities helped to divert my attention from what was going on outside, and I could spend my time with some benefit.

I had to spend two years and three months before the verdict from the appeals court on my murder case was delivered. At last, the appeals court dismissed the case, but I was still detained to wait for the decision of the Supreme Court. More than one year after that, the appeals court delivered a verdict of eight years, six months imprisonment for the gun possession case. My lawyer made the final appeal to the Supreme Court. While waiting for the verdict of the Supreme Court, I didn't know what it would be, and whether or not it would change my life again. I didn't think about what was going on outside the high walls because thinking about these things caused a headache for no good reason. I only thought about how to spend each day, what to eat, and what to do. I also thought what I would do on the next day. I only made a timetable for two days and spent my life in that way. When the murder case was dismissed by the Supreme Court, it had been three years.

Suddenly the path forward for my life became bright, and I saw a hope to get out from those square walls. Finally, after so much more time, the

Supreme Court delivered the verdict in the gun raid case. It was ten years imprisonment! However, as I had already been in prison for seven years, after more than just two years I would be eligible to get out of prison. My parents visited me in Bang Khwang Prison twice a year. These trips were made possible by the International Committee of the Red Cross (ICRC). After that, when Police Colonel Thawee Sodsong was the secretary general of the Southern Border Provinces Administrative Centre [SBPAC], there was a project to transfer prisoners of security cases from the southern border provinces to their place of origin. I was lucky. I was moved from Bang Khwang Prison to Pattani Central Prison at the end of 2013.

After that, I applied for parole by submitting documents to the officers so that they could an conduct investigation. My hope was dashed again when I was told that another murder case had been filed against me. I was really stunned, because after eight years of imprisonment, there was still another case being brought against me. Did it mean that they didn't want me to live outside prison? I began to worry again because, according to the regulations for parole, a prisoner must be free from any charge against him. I caused more grief for my parents when they found out what kind of case I was being charged with now.

Amid all these bad things, there was still some good luck for me. One day the SBPAC organized a prison visit. I prepared a petition to be submitted to Police Colonel Thawee, but on that day he couldn't join the visit because of other business. So, I submitted the letter to Kitti Surakhamhaeng [director of the Justice Management Centre, SBPAC]. Within a week after that, he came to the prison and told me the good news that the case against me had already been withdrawn because it was the same case that I had previously fought. After that, the procedure for my parole would be conducted within six months.

I still remember the date of my release from prison. It was Friday, 8 August 2014. My parents didn't know that in advance. On my way home in a car, I noticed that the villages on the both side of the street had changed a lot. There were more houses, and dirt roads were now covered with asphalt. When I arrived at my home, I noticed that not many things had changed. Villagers visited me to express their gladness at my release. For my part, I was bewildered. How could I have spent nine years in prison? That was a very long time. From a boy of eighteen years old when I was imprisoned, I became a man of twenty-seven years old. I felt relieved that I finally had regained my freedom. I wouldn't have to worry about anything more.

However, I got a visitation on another night a mere week later. After I was released, the security forces cordoned off my house again, alleging that terrorists were hiding in my house. I felt uneasy again and really worried.

Six months after that, my house was searched again, but the officers couldn't find anything suspicious. Did this mean that I would have to live my life surrounded by worries and fears again?

Even though I had to lose a half of my freedom, I still believed that the law was there to protect good people. As I had to be in prison for nine long years, my life as a youth had vanished. I didn't have enough knowledge to keep up with the changing world. So I decided to extend my studies. I didn't care what other people had to say. I believed that learning would give me a way out for my life. However, I still couldn't help thinking and worrying about the rest of my life, even though I was innocent in every sense.

I'm a Muslim who firmly believes in Allah. This is a new test that is not more than I can accept. And for every test, Allah will reward us with better things every time. I have to continue my struggle without feeling any fear for my survival. When I have this strength, I'm prepared to face everything. Some people can't accept the difficulty of life inside a prison. Some of them commit suicide, and others go mad. I witnessed these many times. But for me, I was able to get through it safely probably because of my religious knowledge, which helped me to comfort my spirit. I could face all the difficulty in prison by resorting to my prayers. Firm faith in Allah relieved us from worries.

Wherever we are, Allah always protect us.

Every test has its way out.

I'm Fighting Because I've Done Nothing Wrong

SUBAIDAH DOLOH WITH ROHANI CUENARA

It's been more than ten years since I took up the position of a school director (which used to be known as a "headmaster") of this private Islamic school. This is a position that I never expected to assume. Moreover, I had never expected to be an administrator of a school in any capacity. Islam Burapha School, locally known as "Pondok Sapom" among the villagers, is located in Kaluwo Nuea Subdistrict, Muang District, Narathiwat Province, and is the first school that was closed down due to the violent unrest in the southern border provinces that erupted at the beginning of 2004.

I was always asking myself, "Why must I take up such a heavy burden?" I felt this way especially because I had many other unsolvable problems to face: being criticized or making mistakes in my job. But there were always people around me who offered encouragement: "It is common to make mistakes in our jobs. Regard this as a test from Allah." After hearing this, I could think that no one was perfect, and there was nobody who was good at everything.

Many people might wonder why I, as a woman, should be a leader among men who are senior to me and have more experience, and why these men have to have me as their leader, because in general in the southern border provinces, a female leader is not accepted well. Moreover, I'm not more learned than others in this school. For instance, a daughter of an administrator has a B.A. with good achievement, and more abilities than I.

However, the school administration board at that time knew that I could speak Thai fluently, which was useful in communicating with the authorities. I was seen as an active person with confidence in myself. Therefore, I was regarded as a suitable person to be an administrator for a new generation of challenges. In addition, I had studied education per se and had many years of teaching experience. One more reason was that my stepfather had been one of the five founders of this school.

I was selected as the headmaster of Islam Burapha School in 2002 with no monthly salary in recompense for the position. I only received a daily allowance of 150 baht per day. On days when I had no classes to teach, I had no income. I worked on these terms until I got a monthly salary of six thousand baht, for which I had to perform the tasks of an administrator, an office worker, and a teacher. I did my best to perform these tasks in order to live up to other people's expectations. Even though there were many obstacles, it was a normal situation for an administrator.

In the classroom the other teachers and I had tried to encourage our students to extend their studies to the university level. There were only three students from the first generation who had gone to university. The second generation had five to six students, and in the third generation the number increased to more than thirty students. For the fourth generation, as many as forty-nine students went to university, or around 80 percent of our sixth-year students. Almost every capable student went to university. Now many of them have become teachers, and some are even teaching in this school. I felt some pride that I could inspire my students to gain a good education. This is the intention of every good teacher.

At one time there was a group of students who didn't want to study at all. Some of them got the grade zero, and they were even reluctant to come to a makeup exam. I visited their homes to encourage them to come to the makeup exam, but they said, "Why do I have to study when there is a war going on in our country?" I was surprised to hear this reply.

I said: "Do you just want outsiders to come in here and teach our younger generations? How can we struggle without gaining knowledge?"

Two or three years later, this group of students came to my house and asked for the certificate certifying six years of secondary education so they could extend their studies. One of them said, "I regret that I wasn't serious in my study, letting my achievement scores go down." I still remember this very student who had applied for a job in a post office, but his application was turned down because his grade was too low, just 1.9. And yet he had a chance to study in a university, and he persevered until finally he did graduate. Now he works as a teacher in a government school in Tak Bai District. His success came because he developed an intention to study hard.

As for a being "female leader," our local culture does not really welcome this. Even if I had a brilliant idea, some senior administrators and experienced teachers wouldn't accept it. They just stuck to their own ideas in their decision-making. If I didn't attend a meeting, they didn't care, because I was younger and a woman. They had more experience than I. Therefore, they didn't trust me.

On 5 June 2007, Islam Burapha School was ordered closed. Security officers claimed that terrorists were embedded in our school. As the headmaster of the school, I was charged with the accusation that "as a holder of responsibility, [I, as] an administrator, a headmaster, or a teacher, [had] used or let others use, the school or the precinct of the school for teaching and training to support ideas that threaten national security or safety, or [ideas that are] against the democratic administration based on the constitution, or [have] acted against the law or threated national peace and order or damaged the school."

On 2 June 2007, security officers from the military, the police, and the civil administration descended on our school. They were accompanied by Dr. Pornthip Rojanasunand, deputy director of the Central Institute of Forensic Science, Ministry of Justice. He said terrorists were hiding inside our school. The security officers put up a blockade and searched the school in order to find a suspect named Manase Ya and his gang of followers.

On that day, the officers arrested six suspects who were actually outsiders to the school, hiding in an abandoned hut inside the school precinct close to a cemetery. These young men were neither students of my school nor relatives of any of our students. However, they were friends of a religious teacher (*ustaz*) who used to work in our school. The teacher no longer worked in this school, and the school hadn't known that the religious teacher had anything to do with the insurgents. There was also a student in our school, Torik Pirichi, who was detained as a suspect. In fact, the officers wanted to arrest another one of our students who they believed had been involved in the insurgency, but he had already escaped. So they arrested another student instead because he looked like the man they wanted.

I was shocked that I had to be a defendant in a security case together with two more administrators of the school, Soma Hama and Useng Purong. On the next day, the officers arrested one more of our administrators, Harong Bakok. I was fortunate because an anonymous person bailed me out.

I remember that it was almost at the end of the court's session when I requested bail on a day when I wasn't sure whether or not I could be granted bail. No one knew my fate but Allah, so the only thing I could do was to pray to Him: "*Don't let me be punished for something I didn't do. I know nothing about this offence. Oh Allah, don't test me with a burden which is more than I can take . . .*"

At four o'clock, the lawyer told me: "Congratulations. You are granted bail. A friend of my friend bailed you out." I was so relieved. At the same time, I wondered who could be the person who had bailed me out. I was grateful to Allah for sending such a good person to help me, and I badly wanted to thank him or her.

When I was fighting my case in order to gain justice, I was helped by Phongcharat Ruairam, a well-wishing lawyer who provided me with legal aid free of charge. He even paid for my lunch and didn't allow me to spend any of my money. But I had to pay for my transportation to court. Phongcharat was a skillful lawyer from Bangkok. He was a member of a human rights subcommittee of the National Human Rights Commission, a man with a love for justice. He saw that in my case the state had misused its power outside the principle of rule of law.

For this case, I believed that neither I nor the school was in the wrong. The only thing I had to do is to tell society that I wouldn't accept this false accusation. In any case, the order to close the school had many negative consequences. The state should file its cases on individual bases, as its order to close the entire school was not fair at all.

I already had heavy burdens, but after I was charged, I had to take up an even heavier burden. After the school was ordered closed, all our teachers and *ustaze*s were jobless. Their applications for new jobs were usually deemed unacceptable by other schools, and the fate of the religious teachers was even more serious because many of them didn't have a formal certificate to teach. A lot of the students also didn't continue their study by attending other schools.

For me, for more than one year, I did my best to have the school reopened by sending letters to many government agencies asking for justice. I also spoke publicly about our problem on many occasions, but my efforts were not successful. I felt exhausted, so I retreated and reconsidered ways in which to open the school again.

Apart from my own case, I also had to fight the case for the school. For this reason, I was the liaison between security officers and the school administrators, precisely because I could communicate fluently in Thai.

One year after the school was closed, my savings were running out. Fortunately, I have always struggled to face big problems in my life so I knew that I could face this big problem too.

I am originally from Nongchik District, Pattani Province. I have a sibling from the same parents, and eleven more siblings from a different mother or father. My father died when I was twelve years old, and I stayed with my maternal grandmother when I was a small girl. I finished my secondary education in Darunsat Witya Islamic High School, Saiburi District, Pattani Province, and extended my study in Yala Rajabhat University, majoring in science. But while I was studying at the university, I had to earn money from part-time jobs such as being a typist or a teaching assistant because my mother had to take care of the younger siblings.

When my money ran short, I had to think about how to earn a living. I invited two wives of the teachers who had been charged to open a restaurant in Kelantan, Malaysia. We stayed in a relative's house and found a cheap place for rent. We repaired and modified the place into a restaurant on our own to save money, including electricity wiring, painting, making tables, and setting up the kitchen. However, our business could only survive for three months because the wives of Ustaz Harong and Ustaz Soma had to visit their families. The wife of Harong, in particular, had to visit her husband in Narathiwat Prison every week.

When I returned home, my savings were almost gone. I had to start something new, so I recruited ten wives from the school's staff and established "Bunga Tamsao," or, in Malay, "Bunga Tembusu." At that time, we had no money, and I told our story to Metta Kuning, a lecturer from Prince of Songkla University, Pattani Campus. She kindly donated eight thousand baht for our group, which made us hopeful again.

I divided the money among our members. Some of them bought cloth to stitch into prayer clothes. I decided to make sweets to sell because at that time it was the fasting month of Ramadan. While I was selling sweets, it rained heavily, and no one came to buy my sweets. In my heart, I said: "I used to be a director of a school. Why do I have to be so impoverished as to sell sweets?" I cried in the middle of rainfall. But at the bottom of my heart, I knew I had to continue to struggle to earn money. I only hoped that any work I might do would be honest. However, in the end, this business wasn't successful.

After experiencing these failures, I realized that before investing money we must consider carefully how not to lose money. We must invest in things that wouldn't be ephemeral and could be used for a long time. So, this time I set up a group to stitch clothes. At that time, I received twenty thousand baht from Chalita Thacharoensak. I bought batik cloth to be sewn into bags, trousers, clothes, and pillow covers. Those who had sewing skills made these products, and they were sold at an event held at Prince of Songkla University, Pattani Campus. At the beginning of 2011, I got a loan for twenty-eight thousand baht from the SCG Foundation to extend the business. This business survives to this day.

By the end of 2009, I had a chance to work for the Hilal Amar Foundation as a liaison officer supporting the families who were victims of violence. Soraya Jamjuree, who was the project manager of the Civic Women's Network, had recommended me to the foundation. My task was to visit the families and encourage them. These visits, in turn, strengthened me, because these experiences made me realize that the problems I was facing were small ones. Others had lost their loved ones who were the breadwinners of their households. They also had to struggle to earn their livings as well.

Working with a civil society organization like the Hilal Amar Foundation enabled me to better network among civil society, and provided me with more opportunities to learn about the peace process and peaceful coexistence amid the conflict. I began to apply and disseminate this new knowledge to those who were around me and to communities in my region.

I resumed my struggle for the Islam Burapha School at the end of 2011. The other school administrators went to see the then secretary general of the Southern Border Provinces Administrative Centre [SBPAC], Police Colonel Thawee Sodsong, so that he could help the school to be opened again. I didn't join them. They submitted a letter to request a permission to reopen the school to the local educational office, but the person who had submitted the letter had no qualification to do so. Since by that time I was in the position of being president of the foundation, I became the person who submitted the letter.

The secretary general of SBPAC gave an interview in the radio program *Voices of Women from Southern Border Provinces* and talked about the reopening of the school. In that interview, the secretary general said, "Education shouldn't be affected by the conflict." So I contacted those who might be concerned, especially the Ministry of Education and security agencies, and told them that since the school had not committed any offense against the law, they should process our request to reopen the school. If the closing of the school was meant as a punishment, it was not a punishment aimed well, but a punishment of people who were not responsible.

I still remember that while asking for permission to reopen the school, circumstances were chaotic. It seemed that many people didn't want me to take part in this effort. But these same people were not qualified to submit the letter to apply for permission either. But finally, they had to come to me so that I would go on with my effort, because I was the only person who was qualified to do so. I was glad because at least they recognized my value.

When everyone came to a meeting to discuss the matter of the school's reopening, I only could sit quietly. I wanted everyone who came to ask for my forgiveness. In the past, I had to negotiate the legal case, and many people were critical in saying that the school couldn't be reopened because I had been charged earlier; and if I were the one to ask permission from the authority, it wouldn't be granted. But finally, Allah accepted my prayer, and everyone apologized to me. I also apologized to them because sometimes I had tried not to be concerned about the problem.

I, as the proprietor of the Addirosat Al Islamiyyah Foundation [Islam Burapha School] asked for the permission to reopen the school. It wasn't until after more than twenty days that the local education office granted permission to reopen the school on 26 December 2011, which made me and the community happy and delighted. However, I still worried because the legal cases against the school and me hadn't yet concluded.

After the school reopened, an officer from ISOC Region 4 came to the school and said in a suspicious way, "How is it possible to reopen this school while you still lack a school administrator?" In fact, this was his misunderstanding because at that time we already had all of our administrators in place. Military officers often came to our school because they were suspicious about why the school had been reopened while the relevant cases were still in the court.

One time a military officer suspiciously asked questions like these: "Do you have permission to open the school? Are there students coming to learn? Are these students old ones or new ones? Do the teachers have a bachelor degree?"

After listening to these questions, I promptly picked up the notification of permission to show to him, together with the list of our 160 students' names and addresses. After that he visited the school less frequently.

But then, within the month, soldiers from the Narathiwat Special Task Force came to the school and ask for detailed information about the school staff: names, addresses, their parents' and children's names, their children's schools, the colors of their cars, etc. But we also understood that it was the duty of the security officers to know this information. So we willingly cooperated with them.

On 2 October 2012, an officer came to talk to us about an incident on 31 August 2012, the Independence Day of Malaysia. In the three southern border provinces, more than four hundred Malaysian flags had been hung, and the officer insinuated that our school was somehow involved in the incident. He said: "You should stop doing such a thing. It's better to develop your country."

We were being suspected because, on 30 August 2012, a journalist from Thai PBS had come to the school to make a news report about the flags. The Malaysian flags were hung all over in various other locations throughout the three provinces, but the film footage taken at our school was used during the news report of the incident as a whole. Even though the reporter hadn't said that our school was involved in the incident, I felt uneasy.

Apart from security officers, there were nongovernment organizations, both national and international, that visited the school to ask about the recent development, but the purpose of their visits was actually more to encourage us.

The problems and obstacles I had to face were so heavy, but with my faith, I thought all of it was a test from Allah. My case hadn't yet finished, but I was confident about my innocence because I was involved in nothing. I must thank a lot of important people from government agencies who love justice and were ready to be witnesses in court, which was very helpful. Surasee Kosonnawin, a former member of the National Human Rights Commission,

and high-ranking officers from ISOC demonstrated that even security officers saw the situation in the same way as I.

Even though I was appointed as the director of the school for a second
time and the school received permission to reopen, it doesn't make my life
much happier because this is not the position I wanted. I feel rather distressed, and sometimes I just want to resign to find another job. But in my
heart, I thought I must endure this, being in a position to meet the responsibilities invested in this position.

Although my job has never been smooth, my family life is happy now. I
got married three months before the permission to reopen the school was
granted. Now I have a partner with whom to think things through, a person
whom I can rely on, who encourages me all the time, and I have become
more patient and calm. I used to be impatient and reacted rather sponta-
neously, but now I consider everything before I do anything. Love within my
family supports my soul so that I can stand up to continue my struggle for
the religious principles of rectitude and justice.

I'm fighting for justice so that children in our community can study in
their own way.

In the Middle of a Happy Forest

PHONG TAE-IAU WITH MARISA SAMAHAE
AND THANYATHORN SAIPANYA

Try to imagine me. Whichever direction you face, north, south, east, or west, my house is surrounded by many trees. Most of them are coconut but also neem, white *thingan, tembusu,* and many other small trees.

My name is Phong Tae-iau. My house is located on the side of the irrigation canal between Nat Pa Thung Village, Saiburi District, and Nam Po Village, Panare District of Pattani Province. Through my village you can get to the Halal Industry Area. There is also an exemplary or model farm established as a royal project. People from villages nearby are hired to work on this farm. In the near future, this region will develop economically, and it will also make my village well-known.

My own village is called "Nai Nuea," and Muslims call it "Nae No." It's located in Tambon Ban Nam Bo, Nanare District, two kilometers away from the main road. If you are coming from Pho Ming Village, you turn right to come to my village.

In the past there were only nine houses in my village, and the population was just twenty-five people. All of them were Buddhists. The land was barren. We only had small paths to walk on foot. If we wanted to go out of the village to buy things, we had to walk on ridges between paddy fields and cross small bridges to the main road that led to Bo Nam Village or Poming Village. If we wanted to go to the market in Palas, we had to go through Poming Village, Khok Krabuea, Tha Nam, and Khuan Villages. The trip took many hours. It was only twenty years ago that a road was built. Although movement at that time was difficult, we were happy because we didn't have to be alarmed by anyone. If we had business anywhere, we could go out at any time, even in the evening.

This was a nice and safe village. I had many Muslim friends. I could stop at their houses to drink water. If I was tired, I took a rest at roadside pavilions. But unrest started in 2004,[1] and it caused many changes in Nai Nuea Village. Some families had to move out to other subdistricts such as Khok Krabuea and Don because of the sense of fear caused by violent incidents. But my family and I had never thought to move because we were very attached to this village.

Now in this village there are only four Buddhist households, with a population of only twelve people. After an incident in which a Buddhist temple was burned and monks were shot in Panare in 2007, the government sent a military force to be placed in the village. That convinced the remaining villagers to stay. Since then, the village has been free from drug and violent incidents. The villagers live happily.

Originally my grandfather was from Khok Krabuea, but he came to Nai Nuea to earn a living. At that time, no one owned a piece of any land, and there was no selling and buying. Anyone who was industrious could become the owner. For this reason, my grandfather came to this place. Among my relatives there were Muslims too. My grandfather married a Muslim woman, and they had a daughter called Mek So. He divorced this Muslim woman and married again with a Buddhist woman. Later they had a son called "Thong Kaew," my father.

Later, my father, Thong Kaew, married Mae Nim. They both had lived in this village since they had been born. Later my father had another Muslim wife from Bo Nam Village whose name was Che Song. This Muslim woman spent her life in the village with my father, and they had three children. The family stayed in the village until my father died. Then they moved out of the village. We still regard each other as siblings. Apart from my stepmother and half siblings, I also had many Muslim relatives, and we are on good terms.

When I was a child, my life was very happy. I studied in Ban Khian Primary School in Poming Subdistrict until I finished four years of primary education. After that I didn't continue my study, but I helped my mother doing household chores. I had never worked hard and just stayed inside the house. I was not good at doing anything because my family was wealthy. I got married when I was seventeen years old. I helped in the family business. At that time my main work was to produce sugar from sugar palms. It sold very well. Merchants from other places came to my house to buy the sugar. It sold so well that production was always lower than demand. Therefore, my family could save money. We had three children. The eldest one is a daughter, who

1. In the original it is written as "(B.E.) 2548" (C.E. 2005), but in the translation this has been changed to 2004, when the unrest actually started.—*Translator*

lived near my house. The second one is a son, and now he lives in Pattani. The last one is another son, who was shot dead.

When I was seven years old, a group of insurgents from PULO, led by Seng Tha Nam,[2] who was one of the leaders of PULO, regularly stayed in my house as a hideout. They often stayed for months. Seng Tha Nam was very close to my family. They came and went again and again for months on end, but they had never caused any trouble for my family. About twenty years ago I heard that Seng Tha Nam passed away a few years after he surrendered.

At this point in my life, I lived happily in this village with cordial neighbors. We relied on each other. I worked to earn a living for my family. There were many jobs to do, but the thing I loved most was planting vegetables and fruits, such as watermelons, cucumbers, long beans, corn, cassavas, etc. I planted them without feeling exhausted, and felt happy whenever I harvested them because it meant that I would earn some money. All the fruits and vegetables could be sold in nearby villages, both Buddhist and Muslim. As a seller of fruits and vegetables, I came to know a lot of people. Muslims in such villages as Poming, Nam Bo, Thasu, Na Chak, and others all knew me. I took fruits and vegetables to be sold in these villages. We built good relations between us.

I took my fruit and vegetables to be sold in Nam Bo Village, and on my way home I bought *budu* [a type of fish sauce] in Khok Krabuea Village. Before arriving at Khok Krabuea Village, I stopped at Poming Village to sell fruits and vegetables. I spent my life in this way all the time. I made a lot of Muslim friends from selling fruits and vegetables. Importantly, I spoke Malay very fluently because I was always with my Muslim brothers.

I was happy when people came to visit me. I gave them fruits or vegetables such as cassavas, watermelons, corns, limes, etc. These were available all year. It was a life full of happiness, attachment, and sufficiency—a kind of happiness that you cannot buy anywhere.

In 2009 my younger son applied to be a Ranger. He was placed in a base in Bango Yuering, Buere Subdistrict, Saiburi District, Pattani Province, for two years and got to know a girl from Prachuapkhirikhan. They become intimate

2. Seng Tha Nam was one of the guerrilla force leaders of PULO (Patani United Liberation Organization), from the same generation with Haji Sama-ae Tha Nam and Haji Da-oh Tha Nam. "Tha Nam" is not their family name but the name of their place of origin, that is, Tha Nam Village, Panare District, Pattani Province. This place is seen to this day as a red zone where insurgents are still active. There was a news report that Seng Tha Nam was cruelly killed by a group of people in 1976. At the same time other leaders were detained and charged with separatism in 1997.—*Translator*

and agreed to marry. My son resigned from the Rangers to live with his wife in Prachuapkhirikhan. He worked there to earn a living for his family, and they lived together happily.

In September 2009 my husband became sick with liver disease, and I asked my son to come back home. My husband told our son to take care of his mother in case something happened to him. Not long after that, my husband passed away. My son decided to move back from Prachuapkhirikhan to live with me. He found a new job at a duck farm, and his part-time job was to catch butterfly lizards in coconut farms nearby.

My son worked for three months after my husband died. I still remember the date, 14 February 2012, Valentine's Day. My son and his wife went out to catch butterfly lizards. On that day I fainted as if I was going to die when the *kamnan* [the head of a subdistrict] told me that my son and daughter-in-law had been shot dead. When I recovered consciousness, I went to the scene to claim their bodies. I asked help from villagers to bring them to Panare Hospital. In the hospital I fainted again, and by the time I regained consciousness, doctors there had already processed the bodies. I took them back to the Khok Krabuea Temple. Rituals were conducted for three days before their bodies were cremated.

On the day of cremation my heart was so broken that I wanted to die with my son. I cried and screamed so that they wouldn't take my son's body for cremation. I didn't know how I could live without him. I fell on the coffin and cried until I lost consciousness again.

Now I can tell you that it took quite a long period of time before I could accept the fact. I cried again and again, as it was the most heartbreaking experience of my life. I couldn't sleep well and hardly ate anything. I was delusional and confused. Every night young soldiers came to my house and stayed with me. On some occasions, I went out at night to the street, talking to myself, or sometimes talking to vegetables. My neighbors thought I had gone mad. Before my sorrow would disappear, I had gone to many temples to ask for a blessing from monks. I also had to summon much patience before I could be as strong as I used to be. I can't explain the extent of the suffering I had to go through at that time. If you don't experience it yourself, you can't know how horribly painful it is to lose someone you have loved.

Now I can say I feel composed and comfortable, strong enough to go on with my life again. After I came to know the Civic Women's Network, I felt comforted because the network helped me to know those who have shared the same fate as I. We could talk together, share our experiences, take part in activities, and join public forums. From these indelible experiences, I could see things more openly and learned more about how we can live together with Muslims. Most importantly, the Civic Women's Network provided me with opportunities to talk about my own life experiences, so that those who have been affected by the unrest would be inspired and encouraged to go on with their struggles in life.

Finally, I would like to thank the Civic Women's Network for Peace in the Southern Border Provinces. Because of their encouragement, I could come out of the nightmare to live an ordinary life again, going everywhere at any time as I had done in the past.

Living with Memory

THITINOB KOMALNIMI

The father was standing in front of the door for a long time, waiting for us to come out of the room. He wanted to show us something that had never appeared in news reports: "This is a piece of cloth woven by Chui's mother when she was still small. At that time, I worked as a guard and a construction worker in Bangkok to earn money for my daughter's schooling. After growing up, Chui took the cloth woven by her mother and drew flowers on it." He showed us the cloth with flowers drawn on it, which now hung on a frame hung on the wall. It was more eye-catching than the other pictures. This was the first picture the father showed us.

"These are the pictures of the king drawn by Chui when she was in high school, and they were exhibited in her school too." The father stood still, gazing at the set of five or six pictures of King Rama IX. Some of them were drawn with pencil, and some were oil-painted. These pictures were put in beautiful wooden frames and proudly displayed on the wall. While the father was telling us about these pictures, he put his palms together and raised his hand high above his head to show respect.

We noticed that the father didn't guide us to the pictures according to the route set by the designer of the gallery. But he brought us to see the pictures following the life of Chuling Pongkhanmoon: a pencil drawing of tools inside the house, a funny cartoon for the anti-*ya maa*[1] campaign that was drawn when she was in Chiang Rai Vocational College. There was a relief of a funny character, crying in a sad face, kept in a black wooden frame. Upon the character's cap, pieces of gold leaf were attached. We were looking at them with wonder.

"I took these gold leaves from many temples, praying for the recovery of Chui. I missed her, and waited [with hope] until she would stand up and laugh with us. But she didn't stand up again." The father, Soon Pongkhanmoon, looked away from the sculpture and looked at the window. The

---

1. The direct translation of the term is "horse drug," a kind of drug containing methamphetamine that has been rampant in Thailand. — *Translator*

sunlight of the winter surely cast warmth, but the bodies of the listeners [to the father's story] were very cold. Every picture in the gallery was a space to keep memories of his only daughter while she had been still alive. The tools for painting, colors, a designing table—everything used by Chuling was displayed here in good order. It was an image that reflected the life of the Pongkhanmoon family at one time in the past.

The pictures and things described the imagination of peaceful coexistence between people from different religions and cultures.[2]

"Let's go to my house. My wife has prepared some foods for us."

After extending his invitation, he closed the windows, turned off the lights, and closed the door of the "Khru Chuling Pongkhanmoon Gallery" and led us out. It was a two-storied building that contained the biography and pictures of Chuling. The drawings in the gallery were drawn by her from the time she was in a kindergarten until university, and while she worked as a teacher in the Ban Kuching Lepah School, Chaloem Subdistrict, Rangae District, Narathiwat Province. Inside the gallery there was a figure of Chuling dressed in the formal attire of a teacher.[3] The gallery is open to the people and students to visit, located in the Doiluangwitthaya Kindergarten, Chiang Rai Province. This is where she was born, and her name is remembered as a teacher who sacrificed her life.

The two-storied house painted in light blue was located in Pongnoi Subdistrict, Doiluang District, Chiang Rai Province. In front of the house was a large wooden table to receive guests all the time. The mother, Khammee Pongkhanmoon, was a small woman, wearing a *sinh* [a traditional northern Thai–style loincloth], a hand-woven cotton shirt, and a long-sleeved silk shirt to protect her from the cold weather. She had gray hair and looked thinner than in the photos we had seen in the media ten years ago. She welcomed us with a friendly smile. She brought drinking water for us, the representatives of the Civic Women's Network for Peace in the Southern Border Provinces, who had traveled almost two thousand kilometers from Patani to Chiang Rai. We felt our fatigue vanish with her friendly attitude, and all the concerns we had brought with us disappeared too. Our group had two Muslim women who wore hijabs, and we were looked at with curiosity, suspicion, and distrust all the way to the northernmost part of the country.

After introducing ourselves, Mrs. Khammee invited us inside the newly

2. The literal translation of this sentence is as follows: "The pictures and various things were playing their role in drawing the imagination of people learning to live together between different religions and in a multi-culture."—*Translator*

3. A picture of the figure can be seen here: http://www.cots.go.th/travelview/detail.php ?id=263.—*Translator*

built drawing room: "We sold our rice fields and added this part of the house to receive guests. We are too old to work in the rice fields."

Looking at the pictures surrounding us, we shivered and got goose bumps. There were pictures of her happy childhood, her graduation ceremonies, and of her receiving various awards. The pictures that had been used for her government officer identification card were enlarged. And there were painful pictures of the news reports of her lying unconscious in the hospital bed, and the big funeral held for Chuling in this district. These pictures were framed and hung on the wall of every side of the drawing room's wall, except the one side that had a glass door. Some pictures were put around the telephone. There was hardly any vacant space left on the wall. When either of the parents sat in the rocking chair in front of the television, did they see the pictures on the TV screen as something that happened at that moment, or did they only see the pictures of their only daughter's memories who had left them? And this was the picture of this family's memory.

"For the last ten years, people have always visited us. Some of them came in a group or on a tour bus. So, we had to receive them and told them stories of Chui. So, we had to have a drawing room like this."

Thai society has never forgotten the incident in which Chuling was harmed, and this attitude of not forgetting also causes distress to both of her parents—they were also suffering. The words we had prepared to address the mother stuck in our throats. We dialogued through silence, showing our respect to the deceased for nearly one hour. Mrs. Khammee led us to walk through the exhibition of Chuling's life, and finally she invited us to have a simple lunch she had prepared.

"Chui once brought me to the village during school holidays. I stayed with her for a few days, and I understood why she taught in a school in Narathiwat. It had good air, a beautiful village surrounded by nature. The trip took four days. In order to get there, it took two days and two nights. We took a train from Chiang Rai to Bangkok. We got off the train at Hua Lamphong Station and took another train to the south. We got off at Tanyongmat Station. After that we had to take public transport several times before we finally arrived at the village. Chui accompanied me on the return trip for two days and two nights too.

"'Don't worry mother. The incidents there have nothing to do with us.'

"She said there was nothing to be scared about. All the students were lovely. That year she would teach her students at a quick pace. The students of fourth or fifth degree of primary school were still illiterate, unable to spell their own names. Some students had to bring their younger siblings to the school too." She told plenty of happy stories about her daughter, while her hand was peeling the skins of oranges to give to us.

"She left this house on 15 May. . . . On 19 May 2006 she was assaulted. The images still stick to my memory. Before returning to the village, she stayed in our house for only two days. It was the last two nights that I could stay with her. She took the school's work with her, occupied with making a tool to encourage the students to plant trees. I remember that she put the tool that had been newly made and some pieces of clothes into her knapsack and took it upon her shoulder, and said, 'I'm going.' These were the last words from her. Then she left our house with the sack."

The stories about the daughter were not told in a chronological order, but they came out following a timeline of the memories. "After she was attacked, she lay unconscious on the hospital bed. I attended her in the Prince of Songkla University Hospital for eight months and eleven days. During that time, I went to every merit-making ritual, hoping for a miracle for my daughter . . ."

While the mother was still talking, the father looked up and cut in to invite us to see the hall where things were kept. We saw a motorbike, a stereo set, a television, a computer and a printer on a ready-made desk covered with a plastic sheet to prevent dust, and a closet. The things Chuling used in her daily life had been moved from the teacher's accommodation in Kuching Lepah to here. The room was a replica of her daily life. Although a long time had passed, everything was kept in just as it used to be.

"Her friend, who was a soldier, helped us to bring the stuff in 2008, after her body was cremated. I went there to pick up the things myself and held a ceremony in the nursery of the village where she had been attacked, so that her soul would rest in peace.

"I'm not sure if this is my wild imagination, but I thought she was planning to get married. But she didn't tell me about that . . ." And her voice faded away.

The father then showed us a lot of documents. The parents had received the exemplary parents award, and the mother received the exemplary mother award, on important days of the country from the king and the queen. One of the documents was a letter from Her Majesty, the queen, dated 7 April 2010, that said: "It has been three years since Chuling left us, but I have never forgotten Chuling and her good service to the children in the southern border provinces. Today, every time I see the news of southern bandits killing people ruthlessly, I always think about Chuling with worry. I hope that you two, Mr. Soon and Mrs. Khammee, take good care of yourselves so that Chuling does not have to worry about your health. However, if you have any health problems, you can tell me immediately. I'm ready to help at any time."

"Chui is no longer with us, but she has made us proud. Now we get good care from the local villagers and government agencies." The father told us that after the funeral, this area that used to be a minor-district subordinate to Mae Chan District had been upgraded as Doiluang District in 2007. The bridge upon the Kok River that had collapsed was rebuilt so that it could be used for transport again. Not long ago, the Doiluang Subdistrict Hospital was built.

The father showed us an old calendar made by a shop in the district in which pictures of Chuling showed how she was paid homage to by the local people. The mother told us that they were invited to give blessings or to celebrate newly wedded couples "because the local people see our family as always ready to help other people. We became an exemplary family of this community."

We continued our talk, listening to each other. The mother asked about the village headman, Arng Yusoh, who had helped out Chuling from the site of the incident and brought her to the hospital. So we told her that the village headman had been shot dead many years ago. He had driven his car to take a family of a victim of violence to the local police station to give testimony. On their way home, the car was surrounded by bandits who fired bullets. A girl and a pregnant woman inside the car survived the incident, but the village headman was killed. After listening to this horrible story, the mother put her hand on her chest and said in a distressed way, "He should have been granted the exemplary village headman award." This was the starting point of our talk about the current situation in Kuching Lepah.

Our group told some stories that had never appeared on media. In the incident in which two female teachers, Chuling and Sirinat Thawonsuk, had been detained as hostages, several men from outside the village and some local women from the village were involved. After that as many as twenty-three women from the village were arrested and charged for detaining the two female teachers that led to the serious injury and death of Chuling. The cases of most of the women were dismissed by the court, but five women were sentenced to imprisonment of three to six years. Some of them were released from prison after being granted amnesty, but they had to struggle to regain ordinary lives.

Apart from this, there were altogether thirteen people [from the village] who had been killed, including four women, and among them were a mother and her daughter who had been shot dead in a rubber plantation. One soldier was shot dead in the village too. The villagers were suspected by the security forces, and detained for interrogation according to martial law and the emergency decree. More than one hundred villagers were affected by security cases. As many as fifty-seven villagers were issued arrest warrants according to the emergency decree. Most of the villagers believed that these incidents and their aftermath, especially at the initial stage, were connected with the incident of Chuling, either directly or indirectly. The village would be never peaceful again. It was always painfully affected, suspected by the state officers and left out of development schemes. Even people from neighboring villages were afraid. The villagers couldn't go out of the village to earn a living in nearby villages.

"Most of the women were either arrested or summoned. The men had to take up the burden of caring for the family, or they even had to go to Malaysia to find a job, leaving their children to be raised by elderly people. Grown-up children had to go to schools in cities far away from the village. They were told not to tell others that they were from the village. If they couldn't find a place outside, they would be stuck in the village, and it would be difficult for them to earn a living. Those villagers who had nothing to do with the incident were directly affected in various ways."

The mother listened to us and sighed. We, as the representatives of the Civic Women's Network, told her about the project with which we were engaged, that is, a women's empowerment project to enhance democratic peace.[4] The purpose is to restore some communities that had been affected by violent incidents so that the people would be able to recover their ordinary lives again. Kuching Lepah Village was one of these communities. Forums at a community level between villagers and state officers were arranged to rebuild mutual trust by opening up a space where they could talk about their problems and exchange their agendas on what was going on in these communities. A vocational group focused on those women who had been released from the prison and these women in the village were trying to produce herbed fish crackers. We brought the crackers for the mother to taste. There was a training program for them to write a book in order to tell of the lessons they had taken from the violent incidents, and we wanted to include the story of the father and mother inside *Behind the Smile* too.

We explained that these forums at the community level were a continuous process to bring about a reduction of conflict between individuals and communities. It started with a meeting between those who had been affected by violent incidents and their families, and those who had been affected by security cases of the same religion. Then, for the second meeting, those who had been affected from different religions were brought together to learn from each other. In the third meeting we brought state officers from the administration, the army, and the police and the officers in charge of remedy efforts from the Southern Border Provinces Administrative Centre to talk

---

4. Funded by the United Nations Democracy Fund (UNDEF). — *Translator*

with those of both religions who had been affected. The fourth meeting was to restore the life of those who had been affected and to find a way out of the problems for them, by inviting those who were concerned.

And for the case of Kuching Lepah, it was more than those who had been affected and who had suffered inside the village. No one forgot about the distress of the Pongkhanmoon family. We couldn't organize forums without listening to those who had been behind Chuling and her friend, and as the representative of the village, to show our respect and apologize on behalf of the perpetrators. But even after a lot of attempts, we couldn't contact Sirinat Thawonsuk, another female teacher who had been involved in the violent incident.

"We haven't been contacted by Sirinat either. She just disappeared. I always remember her.[5] I know she testified that many of the women from the village hadn't assaulted the teachers, and had tried to protect them. They were attacked by men. I don't know what kind of remedies Sirinat was given. But the experience must be a horrible nightmare for her, extremely difficult to forget, like it is to me."

The Civic Women's Network understood the suffering of the people. The violent situation has continued for twelve years, and every number [in the statistics] was a person's life. We also explained the overall picture of the peace dialogue that had been started between the representatives of the Thai government and those who had different opinions from the state in February 2013, with the Malaysian government as the facilitator. The process was going on step by step at the initial stage. Some people agreed with this way to find a solution, and others disagreed. Sometimes the situation seemed to become more violent. However, as it was always villagers who would be most affected, we had to speed up our assistance so that they could gain access to remedy efforts. We couldn't afford to wait for the result of the peace negotiations between the conflicting parties.

We paused to listen to what the mother thought about that: "I agree with this. It's a good idea. Doing things in this way is good. The situation in Kuching Lepah will be better. I miss everyone too. I sometimes see the news too. When I hear news about the village, I shed my tears."

Then we asked the mother to taste the fish crackers given to us by the women's group in Kuching Lepah: "This fish cracker tastes good. I hope they continue producing stuff like this, and their business develops. I really want to encourage them."

"Are you still angry with those who attacked Chuling?"

5. Spoken by the mother. She used the word "mother" as first personal pronoun.—*Translator*

"No, I'm not. I don't feel vengeful against anyone. I always forgive them. The circle of retribution is endless. I don't want to have retribution upon anyone. I only want them to be good people, change their minds. Then I will be glad about that. I don't want them to use violence against each other. Don't do any harm to each other. That's enough of it."

"What kind of future do you want to see in the southern border provinces?"

"I want to give my moral support to everyone who is working in the region. I hope they work for the society, not only teachers, but the police, the army; these also work for society. I hope every teacher there is safe. My moral support goes to them. I hope everyone can live together."

"If Chui were still alive, she would think in this way too. This is why she went to Narathiwat to teach. I hope everyone can live together." This is what was asserted by the Pongkhanmoon family.

An interesting question here is, "What kind of memory might enable everyone to live together?"

Recovering Kuching Lepah

YAKARIYA SAPAE-ING WITH SORAYA
JAMJUREE AND AISHAH TIMUNG

"Di atas ada amanah;

  Di bawah ada ummah."

[Above is responsibility (between us and God); below is *ummah* (between human beings)].

When life follows this, heavy burdens are cast upon my shoulder: my responsibility to God and to the community [in this context, to those who are my own community—*Translator*]. What's more, I am *khatib*,[1] and therefore my responsibilities are heavier than ordinary people's. My village is also not an ordinary place like other villages.

Kuching Lepah, my village, located in Chaluem Subdistrict, Rangae District, Narathiwat Province, is a hidden place near Motae Mountain, isolated and very far from the city.

Extraordinary events befell the village, including me and my family, in 2006.

When the name of Kuching Lepah Village is mentioned, most people remember the incident in which Chuling Pongkhanmoon was detained and attacked on 19 May 2006. About eight months later, she passed away. Since then all the people in the village were seen by many as terrorists, or those who didn't even try to help the teacher out of the predicament, letting her be assaulted until she had to die.

After Chuling's demise, everything changed for me and my family, and the entire village in the following way. . . .

I was arrested. My wife was arrested. Many villagers were arrested, most of them women. As many as twenty-one women were charged, and the court dismissed the charges against seventeen of them. Not long after that, my case was dismissed too. But sadly, four women from the village were sentenced to four to six years (after that, one more woman was sentenced to imprison-

---

1. A position of a religious leader in the community, next to an *imam.—Translator*

ment, and another woman's case is still in the Supreme Court) for the charge of detaining the teacher. What was sadder still for me was that one of the four women who was imprisoned was my wife.

I don't deny that on that day my wife was in the place where the teacher was detained. The incident happened after she, holding our small child, brought lunch for another child who was in the preschool class in the Ban Kuching Lepah School. I was inside the mosque, counting the amount of money donated by congregates after the Friday prayer.

I felt sorry about the death of Chuling. No one imagined that such a thing could happen. About my wife's imprisonment, allow me not to speak of it further. The court has already delivered its verdict. In fact, our family knew Chuling. She came to my house to pick up my child who studied in the pre-school class. At that time, four of my children studied in Ban Kuching Lepah School. She once told me that my children studied well and encouraged me so that they would be able to get higher education.

My family gave priority to our children's education. When my wife wasn't there to send them to school because she was in prison, I had to take on the additional tasks of a housewife. I realized that it was an extraordinary burden.

My daily routine began before the dawn, at about 5:00 a.m. After *subuh* prayer [the first prayer of a day, at dawn], I went to the kitchen to heat left-overs from the previous day to feed my children around 6:30. After that, I had to ride a motorbike to take two of my children to Yingo District, where they would catch a school bus to their school in Saiburi District, Pattani Province. Then I had to hurry back to my home to take three more children to Ban Kuching Lepah School. After that, I rode my motorbike to Sisakhorn District, Narathiwat Province, where I worked as a construction worker. At around 3:00 p.m., I hurried home again to prepare meals for my children.

Once a week I visited my wife in the prison. I would leave work early because the prison closed at 3:00 pm. Sometimes she cried, worrying about and missing her children. I would say: "There is nothing to worry about. I do everything for them so that everything is okay."

In the late evenings, my life would be hectic again. I had to go and pick up my children. Those children who studied in the village school would come back on foot, but picking up the children who studied in a school far from our house was my duty. At about 5:00 p.m., I rode my motorbike to pick up my children in Yingo. The school bus often arrived late, and we would arrive home after the sky was dark. We performed *maghrib* prayer [the prayer after the sunset] in a mosque on our way home.

In the evenings, I washed my children's school uniforms. It wasn't only that. I had other duties as a *khatib* too. Every evening I taught the recitation of the Qur'an to the village children. On Saturdays and Sundays, I taught religion in the *tadika* school. I repeated this routine time and again for two years, four months, and twenty-seven days until my wife was released from the prison on 3 April 2013. In fact, she had been sentenced to four years, but after being granted amnesty she was released earlier.

It was a tough period of my life, but I thought everything was a test from Allah. I struggled with determination and endured everything that happened in my life with a smile on my face. I have never felt hopeless in my life. Today I feel very satisfied because three of my children are at the university.

I'm just a poor construction worker, with no property to leave my children except for education. I also wanted to have good education and tried to do so during my life amid the poverty of my family. So I made up my mind that when I had children I would make as much as effort as possible so that they could study according to their wishes. I hoped that we would be a good example for other families, because in our village most parents didn't give much priority to their children's education. It was one of the obstacles that had hindered the development of the village.

The village changed. . . . After Chuling's "incident," Kuching Lepah locked down because outsiders didn't dare to come and insiders didn't dare to go out. Various fruits such as langsats, durians, and mangosteens were left rotting in orchards. No fruit brokers dared to come to the village to buy fruits. The villagers were too afraid to take care of their orchards or plantations because at that time a lot of soldiers were always patrolling in the forests and the hills. There was an orchard of ten *rais*[2] commonly shared by the villagers. Fruits from the orchard were sold and the profit donated to the mosque and the *tadika* school, but now it was abandoned.

Villagers didn't dare to leave the village except for very urgent business. They were afraid of so many checkpoints. They were also worried that a violent incident might happen on the way. At that time many villagers and people from nearby villages were shot on the roads.

When we went out of the village, we were often seen as terrorists and asked hostile and painful questions: "So, you are from the place where Chuling was attacked? Why did you do that?"

Our village was isolated and stigmatized, cut off from the outside world after the "incident." The only group of outsiders that came into and out of the village every day was soldiers. They came in tens of military cars to patrol. The evenings were the most frightful. Villagers couldn't sleep well, listening to sounds and watching soldiers from holes in the walls of their houses.

At that time every single square inch of Kuching Lepah was monitored

2. One *rai* is about 1,600 square meters.

by soldiers. They used GT 200. At that time, the officers were very confident about this device, but later it was discarded after it was proved that it was not credible. However, many villagers were affected by this device. Every corner of the village was searched to find suspicious objects such as bombs or weapons. Thereby, Kuching Lepah was full of holes dug after GT 200 indicated that there were weapons hidden underground. Many villagers were detained because of GT 200 indications too.

Social and religious activities that used to be performed were stopped because the security officers suspected that we were going to stage violence if we assembled. Even if someone died, villagers were still scared to join in prayer out of respect for the deceased. Relatives who lived outside were also too afraid to come, especially the relatives of those families whose members were charged with security cases. Those families whose members were accused were cut off from society, sometimes from our friends, or even from relatives too.

After the death of Chuling, I think there is one more important thing that has been unknown to the outside society. As many as thirteen villagers had been killed in violent incidents in the village, including four women. Among them were a mother and daughter who had been shot dead at the same time in a rubber plantation. There is one soldier who died here too. Apart from this, the villagers were detained for interrogation following martial law and the emergency decree. Some of them were released, but others were charged, imprisoned, and released, like what happened to my wife. In our village, about 157 people got arrested based on the emergency decree. Villagers believed that the aftermath of violent "incidents" had something to do with the "incident" of Chuling either directly or indirectly. After the "incident" of Chuling, the village was never peaceful again, having been painfully affected by the loss of lives and freedom. The villagers' lives teemed with fear. What's more, this village was endlessly stigmatized by the security officers and the outside society.

In April 2014, this silently isolated village accepted outsiders. They were from the Civic Women's Network for Peace in the Southern Border Provinces. They opened the door to the outside world again.

In fact, this women's group had already known those families who were affected by the security cases after the Chuling incident. At that time the leaders of the network, together with peace activists and human right activists from Bangkok, came to visit the families of the women who had been arrested for security cases, and connected us with the National Human Rights Commission to help bail out these women. There was a female lawyer from the Lawyers Council who volunteered to help us, and we didn't have to pay for this. When I think back on these things, I could see the kindness of the outsiders who came to help us, even though we hadn't known them before and some of them were from a different religion. They were not afraid, although we were defendants in the horrible case.

Later I learned that the Civic Women's Network (at that time it was called "Friend of Victims' Family") also visited Chuling when she was treated in the Prince of Songkla University Hospital in Hat Yai. I also learned that the Civic Women's Network helped many groups of those who had been affected so that they could access the remedy efforts [of the government], including Buddhists. When the Women's Network came to visit us, some Buddhist women joined the activities too.

In an important activity organized by the Civic Women's Network, I and the villagers had formed a group of people to meet with state officers from the army, the police, and the administration. Usually when villagers like us had met state officers, we always felt that we were seen as terrorists or suspects.

In the meeting, we felt relaxed in seeing the officers wear civilian attire, ready to listen to us. So I didn't feel stigmatized, although we still had mutual suspicion. But we began to feel friendship and humanity. Apart from the stories from my friends about the losses they had faced, we also listened to the officers who had been affected while performing their duties. The officers listened to our stories of loss, including the negative impact of their operations on the villagers that had been caused by their suspicion that we were terrorists or their supporters. Some problems had been caused by the misunderstanding of the officers about our religion and culture. After hearing their views, we also adjusted our practices so as not to cause more misunderstandings.

In the meeting there was a state officer who had a deeply rooted prejudice against us, regarding us as a bunch of terrorists and openly expressing his prejudice. I was so embarrassed that I walked out of the venue, and this caused a leader of the Civic Women's Network who performed the task of moderator to cry. But I also saw the goodness of some officers who also came out and hugged me. One had said: "I'm sorry. It shouldn't be like this." He apologized to me.

"I'm alright. Don't worry. I'm strong," I said to a young state officer who had come to appease me. I felt good that there were still some officers who understood me and the villagers. At least this man had known us, coming to Kuching Lepah where he was in charge. Before Raya [the day to celebrate the end of fasting] he ordered a piece of cloth to be worn on the celebration day too.

I joined the meetings and activities organized by the Civic Women's Network regularly. I also have to face the soldiers who often come to my home to see me as a religious leader. Today I know that I have to adjust myself and how to behave myself in front of state officers. I have learned how to communicate and negotiate with them. These are important things, because these are the things I and the villagers have to face in our real life unavoidably.

As a leader of the village, I would say once again that we are sorry for the death of Chuling and the injury experienced by Sririnat. We are also sorry for every loss of life that happened in the village, including those of the teacher, the state officer, and more than ten villagers. Our village was heavily wounded, so heavily affected. We don't want anybody to lose their lives. We don't want to live our lives with fear and suspicion anymore. We want to be accepted as human beings with dignity, not seen with hatred, fear, and suspicion.

What's important is that we don't want to escape anywhere because this is our home. We hope Kuching Lepah develops, and all the children in the village get education, including me, my family, and everyone in the village. (Now I'm studying in the Informal and Non-formal Education Centre to obtain a high school certificate.) I have built a school to teach the way of reciting the Qur'an. There are 150 students from the village and ten teachers. In the evenings we study how to recite the Qur'an, and in the daytime, from Monday to Friday, it functions as a primary school. On Saturdays and Sundays, it becomes a *tadika* school. The children can acquire both religious and academic knowledge.

It has been not easy for Kuching Lepah to recover after it became almost dead following the death of Chuling. But it has revived again today. I and many other villagers are ready to work together. For me, this is my religious duty to my community. It connects me to this world and the next world too.

Suffering Has a Starting Point.
I'm Waiting for Its End.

Saniyah (Pseudonym) with Khamnueng Chamnankij

When I woke up on the morning of 5 June 2014, I prepared a meal and performed the *fajar* prayer at dawn. Then I went out for rubber-tapping in the plantation behind my house. After finishing rubber-tapping, I went to see a doctor to check my blood pressure and diabetes. My husband went out to sell rubber. After coming back, he cleared weeds in the plantation until about noon. A man from the village came to ask if we had dead rubber trees or those trees that didn't produce rubber anymore. He wanted to take these trees to furniture factories. We had a chat until noon so I invited him to have lunch with us. He declined the invitation, but he drank a cup of coffee out of courtesy. Then he left our house.

We used to have a chat after lunch in front of my house, which was surrounded by shady trees. My husband came back at about one o'clock. When he was performing his prayer, three strange men came into the place where my relatives who live nearby and I were sitting. One of the strangers approached us.

"What are you doing?"

"We are chatting," I answered. I was about to go into the house.

The other two strangers who were in front of my house asked, "Where are you going?"

"I'm going home."

"Which is your house?"

I was followed by these two strangers without knowing it. When I opened the door, they jumped into my house. After that they seized my shoulder.

"Sit down here and don't go anywhere!"

They said they would wait until my husband finished his prayer. I was surprised and confused about what was happening. After my husband finished his prayer, they held the two of us and told us to wait in front of the house. A number of officers then came into my house. Some of them held my relatives and neighbors in front of my house too. After about twenty minutes, the officers detained a stranger and brought him before us.

"You know this guy?"

"No."

"Who is he?"

"Why do you have to arrest him?" I really didn't understand what was going on, so there were many questions in my heart.

After that, other officers took another man. "Then, do you know this man?"

"I know him. He's from this village. I've known him since he was small."

This was the man who had come to my house to ask about rubber trees at noon. Later he was charged as "defendant number 1." The stranger was accused as "defendant number 2," and my husband was "defendant number 3."

The officers took the two other men into my house for about thirty minutes. My husband and I also were detained. Things inside my house were scattered on the floor after their search.

"What are these things?" one officer asked. I said I didn't know. The officers said this was a walkie-talkie used to assemble a bomb.

"These two guys were assembling a bomb inside the house."

I was surprised and confused. How that could be possible? After that, the officers took four of us with the others who had been detained. Altogether there were thirteen of us—four women, eight men, and one boy. They took DNA samples from inside our cheeks. I, my husband, and the two men who had been arrested in my house were detained in the Yala Police Station, while the remaining eight people were sent to Task Force Post 41 in Wangphaya Village, Yala Province.

The police in charge of our interrogation told us to confess so that our punishment would be lighter. If I were imprisoned, how would my children live, and who would take care of them? But I kept silent, and so did my husband. Later the police took our pictures and our fingerprints and then prints from our feet. At midnight, soldiers took us to Task Force Post 41 too. When I arrived there, I fainted because I was so stressed. On top of that, I had high blood pressure and diabetes. Two female soldiers took care of me and watched me all night. During the night, I wasn't interrogated while the others were grilled.

The soldier who interrogated me was a local commander who had been in charge of my village three years ago. We could remember each other's faces. He said that I should cooperate with him and tell him the truth. He asked about the circumstances of the "incident" on that day, so I gave him a detailed explanation.

In the morning of 7 June 2014, the soldiers interrogated my husband, and I helped them as an interpreter because he didn't speak Thai well. After lunch, I was brought to see the commander. He said that I, my husband, and the rest of us could go home, except two men who were from outside. He reprimanded us to lock the door carefully so that this kind of thing might not happen again. We were brought to the police station, where we waited for our relatives to come to pick up us.

On 9 June 2014, five of us were summoned again to be interrogated at the Yala Police Station. The police said we would be detained as witnesses. While we were detained, I felt confused, bewildered, and scared. I was afraid that my husband and I would be harmed. I was worried that if we were charged and imprisoned, what might happen to my children. I was so stressed that I wanted to cry out. But I regarded this as a test from Allah. I had to be very patient.

The story wasn't over yet. In the next month, thirteen police officers in civilian attire took my husband to the Yala Police Station again. They said it wouldn't take long. He would be released after everything was over. I wanted to go with him, but they didn't allow me to do so. After my husband was detained, I cried loudly. My husband had to go alone. At that time, I couldn't concentrate on anything. How could he break the fasting? [During Ramadan Muslims have to fast, not taking water or food during the daytime until the sunset. — *Translator*] After I could brace myself, I called the village headman. I hoped that he would visit my husband, but he said it would be alright, and he would be released soon. After I hung up, I cried very loudly like someone who had lost her mind. My auntie saw me in distress and suggested I ask a distant relative who was a village headman to visit my husband. This village headman visited my husband and brought him some food to break the fast.

In the evening, I broke my fast with water. My mind was too preoccupied to eat or to sleep. The only thing in my mind was what I should do if my husband was imprisoned.

The next morning, I went to visit my husband at the police station. The image of him inside and locked up made me feel sad and sorry for him. The police allowed me to come into the interrogation room. I sat by him. We saw each other's faces without uttering a word. He was handcuffed during the interrogation. During the interrogation he said nothing. The police told me to speak on his behalf. Before leaving the police station, I told the police officer to detain me instead of my husband.

"Are you not afraid of being detained?"

"There's nothing to fear or to lose."

The police officer asked me who would take care of my family if I were arrested. When I calmed down, I thought this was just the starting point of our struggle. There's no time to be disheartened because this was a test from Allah.

My life had changed completely. I had to take up all the burdens, working twice as hard as I had done before in order to earn a living and pay my children's school fees. I also had to pay the expenses related to the case, such as the transport to the court or to the Muslim Attorney Centre to consult about my husband's case. On top of that, I had to take care of my husband's aged mother too. My income was smaller than the necessary expenses, so I had to borrow money from my relatives.

When my husband was detained, in the first visit, we couldn't exchange words. I only could cry. Even my cry didn't come out of my mouth. I only could sob in front of him.

"You have to be calm and very patient. This is a test from Allah. His slaves must have faith in Him, and endure. Others have to endure much tougher things, but they can face their fates. You always have to remember who is behind you. You have our children, your mother, and me waiting for you. We must have hope. We must fight." The only thing he could do was nod.

On the second day, he smiled at me. His smile made me feel much better.

"How did you get here?"

"I drove a car myself."

He was surprised because prior to this I couldn't drive a car. I was determined that I must be able to drive a car. If not, who would drive a car for me? When he was detained, he didn't want me to come every day because he was worried. I wanted to visit him every day in order to support him.

On some occasions, he talked as if he was considering committing suicide and said that if he died everything would be over. I was surprised and distressed that he was thinking in such a way. So I tried to persuade him by resorting to our religion as a Muslim. In our religion, suicide is prohibited; it is a big sin. Perhaps we had done something wrong to Him without knowing. Allah is just, and we have to perform our religious duties regularly by refraining from forbidden things and by doing things determined by Allah. We have to make our supplications and ask for forgiveness from Him.

Afraid that he would really commit suicide, I tried to bail him out. An officer of the court said that I had to prepare title deeds worth six hundred thousand baht. I felt like I was in the middle of darkness, not knowing how to find title deeds. I had no money to borrow them too. I was so stressed and got such a severe headache that I couldn't sleep. I woke up at midnight to perform a prayer to ask for help from Allah so that He would show me the way out. During the next morning, one of my relatives in the village submitted his title deed to me in order to bail out my husband. We submitted the request, but the court said the police objected to the request. We submitted our request five times. After eighty-four days of detention, the court still didn't allow bail. What was worse was that my husband was also charged for being a member of a criminal society and being involved in terrorism.

When I felt weak, hopeless, or distressed, I always remembered my sister-in-law. Her patience always encouraged me. My brother was an *imam,* and he had been arrested. We tried to find his whereabouts to no avail. After a month, we came to know that he had been sent to a prison in Khlong Prem, Bangkok. My sister-in-law took care of her family alone. She had to send her five children to school and take care of her smallest child, who was three months old. My brother fought his case for twenty months, and finally the court dismissed it. But he had to be bailed out with one million baht. It was a huge amount of money for my family. It took another three months before we could collect title deeds worth one million baht and he was released. He only could stay with his family for three months because he passed away due to his disease. My sister-in-law had to take care of her children alone, but she was able to negotiate this hardship in her life. I thought I must be able to face my hardship like her.

Apart from my sister-in-law, there were other women who had similar experiences. Help for those women who were victims of the conflict and violence came from the Civic Women's Network. They came to visit my house to encourage me. They also gave advice about how to contact the related government agencies to get remedies and how to deal with the cases. They gave me a book, *Voices of Hope,* that related the stories of women with similar fates to mine. These women had experienced a lot of damage and hardships, but they still could persevere in their lives. These stories lifted my morale to face the obstacles in my own life.

The most frightening day in my life came when I had to stand in the courtroom as a witness for my husband. I was worried about what I might be asked, not sure if I could answer the questions or not. If I couldn't answer the questions, would my husband be imprisoned? The night before I had thought about these questions constantly until my mind was filled with them. No one could help me except Allah. So, I performed the prayer of hope and asked Allah to provide protection from all the charges made against my husband. After the prayer I felt better. Whatever our fate, it must happen. I would answer all the questions smoothly.

The day of the judgment arrived on 10 August 2014. The court of the first instance dismissed the cases against my husband and the other defendants, but an order was issued to continue their detention pending an appeal. However, the court granted bail. We were so glad that we cried with joy. I tried to gather title deeds worth five hundred thousand baht. Finally, my husband was released on 20 August 2014.

At first, after he came home, he was often absent-minded. He was afraid every time a stranger appeared in front of our house and was particularly frightened when soldiers visited him. I was really worried about him. Whenever I went out, I invited him to go along because I didn't want to let him stay home alone. I told him that if soldiers came to our house, he shouldn't try to run away because they might misunderstand him again. Although we could live together again, we still felt uneasy because my husband was still out on bail.

Members of the Civic Women's Network invited me to join a forum organized for those who were affected by violence in Yupo Subdistrict, Muang District, Yala Province, on 8 May 2015. I said I would join the event. However, the night before the event, I felt reluctant and couldn't sleep well. "What are they up to? Why did I agree to join the event?" I began to feel afraid, but I thought that I wouldn't know if I didn't go.

The participants of the first forum were those Muslims who had been affected by violence. We introduced ourselves, told stories of the violent incidents that happened to us, and exchanged ideas. This was the first time I learned that we were not the only ones who had to go through hardships; people from other villages also endured difficult circumstances.

The second forum was held on 31 May 2015. It was a forum between Buddhists and Muslims who had been affected by violence. On that day we cried and laughed together. This was the second time I picked up a microphone to tell my story to others. I felt brave to express my own thoughts and ask questions. This activity was very beneficial for us. It was an opportunity to listen to other people's hardships. Some women had lost their husbands, children, or the leaders of their families. I was luckier than others because at least my husband got back his freedom, and he could stay together with us.

The third forum was held on 12 December 2015 between security officers [the police and the army] and those who had been affected, both Buddhists and Muslims. This time I was determined to bring along my husband so that he would be able to overcome his fear of the officers. This time I was very excited: "Will I be brave enough to speak? Can I talk like in the previous events?" The experience of the house search and the detention had made me frightened to face security officers. However, when I got to the event venue I felt better because the officers were dressed in civilian attire that reduced our fear and made it more comfortable to talk. We spoke about the problem of the lack of understanding between security officers and the villagers. We also mentioned problems we had to face because of the operation of the security officers.

I said: "Every time there was a violent "incident," either inside the city or outside, why did the officers have to come to cordon off our house and search inside? These operations made my husband very scared because he thought that the police had come to arrest him again. If you have to search our house, could you bring some community leaders, like the village headman, or *kamnan*, or at least a deputy village headman? This would reduce our stress."

The officers said all the requests from the villagers would be considered in their operations.

The fourth forum, "Remedy to Restore Life and Community," took place on 25 January 2016. Those who had been affected and community leaders reflected on the problems, the need for remedies and the efforts to restore the community in Yupo Village by government agencies, including officers in charge of remedy from district offices, SBPAC, ISOC, the Provincial Justice Office, and the Office for Protection of Human Rights and Freedom in Songkhla.

I and those who had been affected very much benefited from these forums. In the past, I didn't dare to speak and negotiate with state officers. Whenever I met with the officers, I didn't dare to ask questions. But this time I dared to ask questions and talk with them. When a bomb "incident" happened inside our village on the morning of 13 December 2014, the police cordoned off my house in the afternoon. I asked them: "Which agency are you from? What is your business? Do you have a warrant [to conduct the house search]? If so, bring the village headman with you."

He said they were from the Yala Police Station, Muang District, Yala Province: "I'm sorry that we didn't inform the village headman in advance. But you must understand us too. We have to perform our duty. Today I would like to ask permission from you to go inside your house to search. Do you agree?"

"Why do you want to get into my house? What is the problem?"

"There could be terrorists hiding inside. If you are innocent, you don't have to be afraid."

"You may enter. I will open the door for you, but please take off your shoes. And I will allow only two of you to come inside because there are only two of us inside the house too." The police did what I requested. Before going back, he said, "If there is anything, I will come again."

"You don't have to come that often."

Today I can stand up and confront the horrible experiences in my life, overcoming obstacles and facing problems. I always think that this is a test from Allah. My husband's case was finally concluded on 30 December 2016 in the appeals court; it was not brought to the Supreme Court.

I believed in my husband's innocence and the justice system. And what I believed in has been proved.

Every day after the five prayers, I ask Allah to protect our family and everyone in the village.

From the Standpoint of a Believer

Hasana Chelae with Amini Saidi

Many years ago, my husband taught me how to drive a car. He thought it was a necessary life skill. When we had to go somewhere urgently, if we knew how to drive a car, we wouldn't have to wait for someone else. Now I know that the driving skill is really useful. I can drive to anywhere, something I had never done in my life before. It's as if my husband knew that when he was no longer with us, I still could do everything by myself.

Friday 11 Ramadan, 1426 Hijriyah [13 October 2005] was the day that changed my life. At around 19:45, my husband and our small daughter of seven years dressed themselves with clean clothes to attend *tarawih* prayer[1] in a mosque near our house. I didn't join them as in the previous nights because I felt dizzy. My husband started his motorbike. I walked to the pile of washed clothes on the floor to fold them and put them into the wardrobe.

About one and a half hours later, I heard the sound of five to six gunshots in succession. I stopped, and a question popped up into my mind: "Am I going to have bad news?" Soon a neighbor came to my house. Looking upset, the neighbor told me that my husband had been shot. I was dumbfounded for a while. At that moment my heart beat very fast and my hands shivered, but I neither cried nor fainted. I braced myself and asked a question in a quivering voice: "Did he die on the spot?"

While waiting for the answer, I could think only one thing. "I must be strong, I must be OK, I must fight, I must be patient, and I must go out to help my husband and daughter." According to the neighbor, my husband was shot while he was riding the motorbike. No one dared to approach them for fear of stray bullets. Immediately after that, my neighbor and I drove to the spot. We saw nobody while driving. When we drove into an adjacent village, I found my husband's motorbike tipped over on the roadside. A group of villagers said they had already sent him and my daughter to the Panare District Hospital.

---

1. Prayers performed during the nights of Ramadan (the fasting month of Muslims).—*Translator*

I headed for the hospital, about 8 kilometers away, to see my husband and daughter. Arriving at the hospital, I went to the emergency room, where he was being treated. The scene still sticks in my mind. He was lying on the bed, surrounded by relatives and close friends. I wanted to cry but I couldn't because I didn't want others to see my tears. The doctor told me to wait outside of the emergency room. I felt suffocated and tightness in my chest, probably because I had tried to hold back my tears. After a while the doctor said that my husband had lost a lot of blood, and it was necessary to treat him in the Pattani Hospital, which was about 35 kilometers from there.

I don't know how to explain how scared I was while the medical staff were moving my husband into the ambulance. I only knew that he was about to depart from this world, leaving me and my children behind. I got into the ambulance with a close friend of his. At that time my husband was still conscious.

He opened his eyes and looked for his friend. I thought he must be the one who my husband had wanted to visit. He held his friend's hand and asked him to take care of his family. Hearing that, I felt sad as well as inspired. Even though he was about to leave us, he still bore responsibility for us and worried about his family. The doctor told him not to speak too much as it might cause more bleeding. I told him to remember Allah all the time.

In about half an hour we arrived at the Pattani Hospital. They moved him to the emergency room. My children and I followed them and waited in front of the emergency room. Before the door was closed, my husband held my arm. I shed tears, feeling anxious, afraid, sad, and sorry for him. Then the doctor closed the door. I waited until well after the midnight. The doctor came out with a sorrowful expression and tersely told me that my husband had passed away.

Later my daughter told me that after the prayer was over, her father had gone to visit a friend who lived in a nearby village about 1 kilometer away. She sat behind her father on the motorbike as usual and laid her legs on his lap as she always did. He was shot by someone on the road while he was heading to his friend's. She heard his painful groan, but he still managed to control his motorbike. Then it fell down after it was trapped in a hole on the road near a bridge. Her father collapsed unconscious. She embraced his body on a pool of blood. She cried in the darkness. The villagers heard her cry and came to help, then sent them to the district hospital.

I sat down in my home and pondered the reason my husband had been shot and who the perpetrator could be. In fact, there had been violence in our village previously when one of our own villagers had been shot dead. But I had never imagined that my husband could be the next victim because he never had an enemy or had a dispute with anyone. He always helped others, even if they were not his relatives. He always offered his help to anybody who had problems.

Saree, my husband, was a teacher in Watnatham Islam School, locally known as Pondok Pombing. He worked there for more than ten years. When he died, he was only about forty years old. He wanted to work there due to his strong affection for the school. It was also not far from his home. I finished my secondary education in the school too. My husband taught social studies, and his students called him *cikgu* [teacher, in Malay]. After finishing his work in the school, he worked in the watermelon field near our house. He hardly had any time to rest.

Pondok Pombing was famous because it was the only *pondok* school in Pombing Village, Panare District, Pattani Province. Every villager sent their children to the school. Students also came from other provinces such as Narathiwat, Yala, Songkhla, Satun, Phukhet, Pang-nga, Krabi, and so on.

However, since the situation [in the southern border provinces] has worsened, people from outside and the state began to see the *pondok* school in a negative way. It was regarded as a place to train terrorists by indoctrinating students. Recently the security forces had begun to raid the school more frequently than before. This caused people from outside to be wary of the school. In turn, suspicions arose between local Muslims and Buddhists. The ties between them frayed. Nonetheless, everyone in our village tried to live as normally as possible. I want to state that all the teachers in the school taught their students to be good people. All alumni had good jobs such as teachers, traders, other business pursuits, etc.

After my husband died, journalists came to interview me for their news reports. Various organizations also visited my family, including the group of women who had been affected by the unrest in the southern border provinces [a group of victims' widows] which later changed its name to the Civic Women's Network for Peace. They had heard the news of my husband and came to help us. According to them, government officers had understood that my husband's death was caused by personal disputes and not by the political unrest. As a consequence, my family wasn't offered any compensation from the state to meet the ordinary costs of living, or scholarships for children and so on.

I found this unfair, and I felt disappointed because I was being denied any help from the state. But I didn't know what to do. I had neither knowledge about the law nor enough money to fight in court. In addition, I felt ashamed because some villagers had labeled me as the wife of a separatist who had tried to defend the wrongdoings of her husband. Accordingly, I couldn't demand justice for my husband. The only thing I could do was to brace myself. Finally, I learned that the state officers couldn't explain any details about the cause of my husband's death, nor were they able to identify and punish the perpetrator.

Since then, my life totally changed. In the past, although I wasn't rich, I could live comfortably without any hardship. I used to stay in my house as a housewife and take care of my children. My husband was always with us. But after he was no longer with us, I had to take care of my aged mother and three school-age children by myself. I had to be the leader of the family. For the first six months [after my husband died], I only stayed in my house, not going anywhere for fear of being gossiped about. I only left my house when I sent my children to school in the morning and picked them up in the afternoon.

I lived with my seventy-year-old old mother and three of my children, but I felt like as if I were living alone, having no one to rely on. I couldn't help feeling dispirited, sorry for my family who had to live with the fear that someone might do even more harm to us. As I had no permanent job, my savings dwindled day by day, and I also began to accumulate hundreds of thousands of baht in debt. I had to spend as frugally as possible. From time to time I sold valuable things in my house, such as a motorbike and a water pump. I also sold cows, and my family's land was pawned to obtain some money. At night, I couldn't sleep well, worrying about so many things. In such moments, I often cried alone. I couldn't imagine how I would be able to take care of my children or send them to school or how I would earn money now that my husband had gone. It was almost beyond my endurance to think about all these things alone, having no one to consult with.

It was the hardest period of my life. When I felt downhearted, every time after prayer I made a supplication to Allah that I could live long enough to take care of my family and find the best way out of the current circumstances. I always remembered Allah, confident that He would help me. I thought it was time for me to get beyond my sorrow. All of this was a challenge from Him, and I had to go on with my struggle. I must find a job and things to do.

At that time, fortunately, the Pombing Pondok School offered me an opportunity to work because they saw me as the wife of a teacher who had contributed a lot to the school. The school provided me with a space inside to sell food. I could earn extra income, but it was still not enough for the school fees of my children. I sold paddy once a year and coconuts every three months. The income was not big, but it was enough to sustain our life. At that time, I was thoroughly exhausted. I had to wake up early in the morning to prepare breakfast, and after working during the daytime, I came home in the evening with no time at all for myself. Whenever I didn't sell food in the school, our family had no income on that day.

My life has been like this for seven years now. It doesn't mean that I have more savings. Indeed, expenses have increased due to the school fees of my children. My eldest daughter is twenty-one years old now, in the second year of university; the second one is seventeen years old, in a high school; and the youngest one is in a junior high school. I still can sustain our life because the selling of food in the school is increasing, thanks to the mercy of God. I have to work hard, but on school holidays my children help me, and that reduces my burden a bit. My life is still tough, but it is not as tough as during the first period.

In the past I had never worked outside my house, and I was rather slow in doing everything, but now I do things quickly because at present I have to do everything by myself. I felt like a frog that came out from under a coconut shell.[2] I didn't know many people, apart from my neighbors and close relatives. Now I know a lot of people, from villagers to senior government officers. Becoming a member of the Civic Women's Network for Peace has provided me with a lot of opportunities in many respects.

The Civic Women's Network often visits widows and families [of those who were affected by the unrest]. I got to know many new friends, and they have soothed me. At the same time, I also could help them in dealing with their hardships by giving them advice, hugging them and soothing them so that they would be able to overcome their challenges. At times there are chances to discuss and exchange stories of our past experiences. Although I still feel sad every time I relate my stories of the past, I feel stronger than before.

Not long ago I was invited by the Civic Women's Network to join a radio program called *Voices of Women in the Southern Border Provinces* for both Thai- and Malay-language audiences. We told the stories about what had happened to our families. I was also asked to talk about the villagers' way of life in Pombing Village, both Muslims and Buddhists. Having those who were affected by the unrest on the radio program contributes to peacebuilding in the region.

Apart from this, I have been a village healthcare volunteer now for several years. I will go on with this task of taking care of elderly people in the area I'm responsible for, and preparing health reports of the villagers. These tasks have opened up my worldview a lot too.

Thinking back on what had happened to me, everything is not lost when you lose [someone important in your life]. There are also some good things that have come into my life as well. At least now I know friendship with others really exists, regardless of their religion, even though we didn't know each

2. Based on a Thai proverb, a frog under a coconut shell, to describe someone who doesn't know the world outside. — *Translator*

other before. I was also helped by a remedy group that assists children who were orphaned due to the unrest, and the Ministry of Social Development and Human Security.

Thank God for making me realize my own value and giving me strength to go through horrible things in my life. I always teach my children that even though we have to face many difficulties in our lives, we must live as normally as possible. We must be patient, we must fight, we must be frugal, and we must be sensible all the time. We can't just hold out our hands to receive alms from others; we also have to offer our help to others. Most importantly, we shouldn't forget God. In my life, I don't expect much. If my children become good people, finish their university educations, and acquire decent jobs, that is enough for me.

GLOSSARY

budu	A kind of fish sauce produced in the southern border provinces of Thailand, as well as the northeast states of Malaysia, especially Kelantan.
buya	Father.
Cho Ro Bo	Thai abbreviation for "village security team."
cikgu	A Malay word for "teacher." In the local context, this term is used to refer to teachers of *tadika* schools.
doa	Act of invocation, supplication, or request, or asking assistance from Allah.
fajar	The prayer performed by Muslims before dawn, also known as *subuh*.
ibadah	Religious duties for Muslims.
imam	A person who leads compulsory prayers in a mosque. In the context of the southern border provinces, an imam is also regarded as a spiritual leader of the community.
iman	Faith.
	Jawi The Arabic script adopted to write Malay with some additional letters.
kafir	Non-Muslims, or infidels.
kamnan	A head of a subdistrict or a *tambon*.
khao niao sangkhaya	Sticky rice with coconut custard.
khao mok	Curried rice with chicken.
khao yam	A kind of local dish of cooked rice, fresh vegetable, fish sauce, etc. mixed together.
khatib	A person whose task is to read out the preaching during Friday prayers. In Thailand, a *khatib* is one of the assistants of an *imam*.
kitab	Literally means "a book." In the local context of the southern border provinces of Thailand, this term refers to religious textbooks written in the Jawi script.
kuai tiao	Rice noodle.
maghrib	The prayer performed by Muslims after the sunset.
Maulid	The celebration of the Prophet Muhammad's birthday according to the Islamic calendar.
nahu saraf	Arabic grammar taught in *pondok* schools.
Pattani or Patani	"Pattani" with two *t*'s refers to the name of a province located in southern Thailand; whereas "Patani" with only one *t* is used to describe the entire region of the conflict area, which is almost the same as the area governed by the Patani Kingdom in the past.

pondok	A religious school traditionally run by a headmaster who is an Islamic intellectual. The lectures are mostly delivered in Malay by using *kitabs*. In the context of the southern border provinces of Thailand, Islamic private schools with academic subjects taught in Thai (*madrasah*) are also still called as *pondok*.
Rayo Poso	The celebration after the fasting month of Ramadan. Also known as Aidilfitri.
salat al-hajjah	The prayer of need.
subuh	See *fajar*.
tadika	A religious school attached to a mosque for primary school children, where they learn Malay and basics of religious duties.
takdir	Destiny.
tambon	A subdistrict that consists of several villages. The head of a *tambon* is called *kamnan*.
thanawi	A religious curriculum for advanced students in *pondok* schools.
tarawih	Additional prayers performed by Muslims after *isyak* prayers (the evening prayer) during the fasting month of Ramadan.
ummi	Mother.
ustaz	A teacher of religious subjects in a *pondok* school.

ABOUT THE CIVIC
WOMEN'S NETWORK

Soraya Jamjuree established the Civic Women's Network, originally named "Friend of Victimized Families Group," during the outbreak of extreme violence in the southern border provinces of Thailand in 2004. Hundreds of men had been killed, and others had been "forcibly disappeared," leaving many women as widows and children as orphans. Tragedies at the Kru Se Mosque and Tak Bai had just occurred. She was joined in her efforts by female students of Prince of Songkla University in Pattani. At that time, there were no remedy efforts provided by the state. (Remedy efforts provided by the state, including compensation, began much later.) Family members of these victims suffered enormously, especially those mothers who had to care for their now fatherless children. At the same time, people were afraid, intimidated by the rising tide of violence committed by both sides of the conflict. Engulfed in suspicion by others, without having any clue as to the causes of these incidents, most women were so frightened that they were extremely reluctant to be involved in any kind of social activities, out of fear for their own and their family's security. By being involved in any type of public activities, they might be marked by the state's security officers, or they could become the target of the insurgents.

"Friend" began by visiting the houses of those families directly affected by violence, providing humanitarian assistance, such as scholarships for children and vocational training for women. It also acted as a liaison between these bereft families and aid agencies, both inside the region and out. Initially, "Friend" collaborated closely with another civil society organization in Bangkok, the Family Network Foundation, which had been established by Sophon Suphapong (a government senator at that time, and a member of the National Reconciliation Commission). Mr Suphapong's devotion in bringing aid to the affected earned him national acclaim in empathetic quarters. He raised millions of Thai baht from well-wishing people from all over the country. The money was distributed among children whose fathers had been killed in the Kru Se Mosque massacre. Early on, "Friend" was also supported by the Canada Fund, which was the first foreign organization that provided assistance.

In 2010, "Friend" became Civic Women's Network for Peace in the Southern Border Provinces of Thailand. The work of providing help to those who were affected by violence continued, but now there was an emphasis on the empowerment of victims, to help turn them into victors in order that they could support one another. Civic Women encouraged them to team up and to develop their skills collaboratively. The aim was also to help them acquire vocational skills to augment their incomes. Civic Women used media outlets as much as possible, so that those who were affected by violence could make their voices heard through radio and TV programs (such as *Citizen Journalists of Thai PBS*). Their voices had not been heard before, but now they could become agents of change in the peace-building process.

The first activity conducted under the name of Civic Women was focused on enhanced food security, jointly organized with the Office of Academic Extension and Services, Prince of Songkla University. This project was financially supported by Oxfam and the European Union. Most of the activities organized by Civic Women have been supported by foreign funding sources. Apart from the organizations mentioned above, other activities have been supported by three different UN agencies for women and USAID. In some cases, Civic Women has also received some funding from Thai government agencies, such as the Southern Border Provinces Administrative Centre, revived after its disestablishment by the Thaksin Shinwatra government.

Civic Women has encountered significant obstacles over the years. The first continues to be security arising from traveling in the so-called "red zones" designated by the military as areas where continuing violence occurs. Random roadside killings still occur unpredictably. Second, Civic Women has also come under suspicion from state security agencies. Some associates have had their houses searched or have been called in "for a cup of coffee" by the police or military. This problem has abated somewhat as Civic Women's work has gained public notice. Third, local traditional Muslim perception does not encourage women to assume leading roles in public affairs. Finally, Civic Women faces financial obstacles. It is a small organization able to conduct its projects only by writing successful grant proposals to various agencies, both in and outside the country. Even when Civic Women does not receive any support, it continues its activities on voluntary bases, but there are limitations. Recently, international organizations supporting local CSOs are being closely monitored by state security agencies in the region. This has made it difficult for local CSOs to access funding sources, and working in the region has become less free.

BIBLIOGRAPHY

Albritton, R. B. "The Muslim South in the Context of the Thai Nation." *Journal of East Asian Studies* 10 (2010): 61–90.

Andaya, Barbara. "Gates, Elephants, Cannon and Drums: Symbols and Sounds in the Creation of a Patani Identity." In *The Ghosts of the Past in Southern Thailand: Essays on the History and Historiography of Patani,* edited by Patrick Jory, 31–52. Singapore: National University of Singapore Press, 2012.

Aphornsuvan, T. *Origins of Malay-Muslim "Separatism" in Southern Thailand.* Singapore: National University of Singapore Press, 2004.

Aree, Srawat, and Christopher M. Joll. "The Religious Geography of Thailand's Malay Southern Provinces: Revisiting the Impact of South Asian and Middle Eastern Transnational Islamic Movements." *Sojourn: Journal of Social Issues in Southeast Asia* 35 (2020): 343–63.

Arin, S. "Women in Rural, Southern Thailand: A Study of Roles, Attitudes, and Ethno-Religious Differences." *Southeast Asian Journal of Social Science* 21 (1993): 81–97.

Barter, S. J. "Strong State, Smothered Society: Explaining Terrorist Violence in Thailand's Deep South." *Terrorism and Political Violence* 23 (2011): 213–32.

Benharoon, S. Y., and S. Binsaleh. "News Coverage on Feminist Issues in Thailand's Southern Unrest." *Procedia-Social and Behavioral Sciences* 91 (2013): 532–38.

Braam, E. H. "Malay Muslims and the Thai-Buddhist State: Confrontation, Accommodation and Disengagement." In *Encountering Islam: The Politics of Religious Identities in Southeast Asia,* edited by Hui Yew-Foong, 271–312. Singapore: Institute of Southeast Asian Studies, 2013.

Bradley, F. R. *Forging Islamic Power and Place: The Legacy of Shaykh Daud al-Fatani in Mecca and Southeast Asia.* Honolulu: University of Hawai'i Press, 2015.

Buranajaroenkij, Duanghathai. *Women in the Peace Process in the Deep South of Thailand.* Pattani: Peace Resource Collaborative, Center for Conflict Studies and Cultural Diversity, Prince of Songkla University, 2018.

Burr, A. "Buddhism, Islam and Spirit Beliefs and Practices and Their Social Correlates in Two Southern Thai Coastal Fishing Villages." Ph.D. diss., University of London, 2018.

Chachavapongoun, Pavin, ed. *Routledge Handbook of Contemporary Thailand.* London: Routledge, 2020.

Chongsuvivatwong, Virasakdi, Louisa Chan Boegli, and Supat Hasuwannakit, eds. *Healing under Fire: The Case of Southern Thailand.* Bangkok: Deep South Relief and Reconciliation Foundation and the Rugiagli Initiative, 2014.

Engvall, Anders, and Magnus Andersson. "The Southern Conflict." In *Routledge Handbook of Contemporary Thailand,* edited by Pavin Chachavalpongpun, 291–304. London: Routledge, 2019.

Frydenlund, Iselin, and Michael Jerryson, eds. *Buddhist-Muslim Relations in a Theravada World.* Singapore: Palgrave Macmillan, 2020.

Glassman, Jim. "Class, Race and Uneven Development in Thailand." In *Routledge Handbook of Contemporary Thailand,* edited by Pavin Chachavalpongpun. London: Routledge, 2019.

Grabowsky, Volker, ed. *Regions and National Integration in Thailand 1892–1992.* Wiesbaden, Germany: Harrassowitz, 1995.

Harish, S. P. "Ethnic or Religious Cleavage? Investigating the Nature of the Conflict in Southern Thailand." *Contemporary Southeast Asia* 28 (2006): 48–69.

Holt, John Clifford, ed. *Buddhist Extremists and Muslim Minorities: Religious Conflict in Contemporary Sri Lanka.* Honolulu: University of Hawai'i Press, 2016.

———. *Myanmar's Buddhist-Muslim Crisis: Rohingya, Arakanese and Burmese Narratives of Siege and Fear.* Honolulu: University of Hawai'i Press, 2019.

———. *Spirits of the Place: Buddhism and Lao Religious Culture.* Honolulu: University of Hawai'i Press, 2009.

Horstmann, Alexander. "Ethnohistorical Perspectives on Buddhist-Muslim Relations and Coexistence in Southern Thailand: From Shared Cosmos to the Emergence of Hatred?" SOJOURN: *Journal of Social Issues in Southeast Asia* 19 (2004): 76–99.

———. "Living Together: The Transformation of Multi-Religious Coexistence in Southern Thailand." *Journal of Southeast Asian Studies* 41 (2011): 487–510.

Jerryson, Michael K. *Buddhist Fury: Religion and Violence in Southern Thailand.* New York: Oxford University Press, 2011.

Johnson, Irving Chan. *The Buddha on Mecca's Verandah: Encounters, Mobilities, and Histories along the Malaysian-Thai Border.* Seattle: University of Washington Press, 2012.

Joll, Christopher M. "Religion and Conflict in Southern Thailand: Beyond Rounding up the Usual Suspects." *Contemporary Southeast Asia* 32 (2010): 258–79.

Jory, Patrick, ed. *The Ghosts of the Past in Southern Thailand: Essays on the History and Historiography of Patani.* Singapore: National University of Singapore Press, 2012.

Keyes, Charles F. "Muslim "Others" in Buddhist Thailand." *Thammasat Review* 13 (2008/9): 19–42.

———. *Thailand: Buddhist Kingdom as Modern State.* Boulder, CO: Westview, 1987.

Larsson, Tomas. "Secularisation, Secularism, and the State." In *Routledge Handbook of Contemporary Thailand,* edited by Pavin Chachavalpongpun, 278–90. London: Routledge, 2019.

Manickam, Mira Lee. *Just Enough: A Journey into Thailand's Troubled South.* Chiang Mai: Silkworm, 2013.

Marddent, A. "Buddhist Perceptions of Muslims in the Thai South." ศิลปศาสตร์สำนึก, 7 (2007): 47–63.

McCargo, D. J. *Fighting for Virtue: Justice and Politics in Thailand.* Ithaca, NY: Cornell University Press, 2020.

———. *Mapping National Anxieties: Thailand's Southern Conflict.* Copenhagen: NIAS Press, 2012.

———, ed. *Rethinking Thailand's Southern Violence.* Singapore: National University of Singapore Press, 2007.

———. *Tearing apart the Land: Islam and Legitimacy in Southern Thailand.* Ithaca, NY: Cornell University Press, 2009.

———. "Thai Buddhists and the Southern Conflict." *Journal of Southeast Asian Studies* 40 (2009): 1–10.

Mohamad, Muhammad Arafat Bin. "Be-longing: Fatanis in Makkah and Jawi." Ph.D. diss., Department of Anthropology, Harvard University, 2013.

———. "Memories of Martyrdom and Landscapes of Fear: Fear and Resistance among the Malays of Southern Thailand." Master's thesis, Department of Southeast Asian Studies, National University of Singapore, 2007.

Nilsen, M. "Military Temples and Saffron-Robed Soldiers: Legitimacy and the Securing of Buddhism in Southern Thailand." In *Buddhism and Violence: Militarism and Buddhism in Modern Asia,* edited by V. Tikhonov and T. Brekke, 37–53. London: Routledge, 2013.

———. "Negotiating Thainess: Religious & National Identities in Thailand's Southern Conflict." Ph.D. diss., Lund University, Sweden, 2012.

Nishii, R. "Coexistence of Religions: Muslim and Buddhist Relationship on the West Coast of Southern Thailand." *Japanese Anthropologists and Tai Culture* 4 (1999): 77–92.

Ockey, James. "Individual Imaginings: The Religio-Nationalist Pilgrimages of Haji Sulong Abdulkadir al-Fatani." *Journal of Southeast Asian Studies* 42 (2011): 89–119.

Putthongchai, S. "What Is It Like to Be Muslim in Thailand? A Case Study of Thailand through Muslim Professionals' Perspectives." Ph.D. diss., University of Exeter, UK, 2013.

Saleh, R. "'New' Relations: Buddhists and Muslims in the Three Southernmost Provinces." *Imagined Land? The State and Southern Violence in Thailand,* edited by Chiawat Satha-Anand, 1–16. Tokyo: Institute for Language and Cultures of Asia and Africa, 2009.

Satha-Anand, C. "Buddhist Democracies in Thai Society: A Religious Critique." *Religion and Democracy in Thailand,* edited by Imtiyaz Yusuf and C. Atiligan, 103–15. Bangkok: Konrad-Adenauer-Stiftung, 2008.

Scupin, R. "South Thailand: Politics, Identity, and Culture." *Journal of Asian Studies* 72 (2013): 423–32.

Terweil, B. J. *Thailand's Political History: From the Fall of Ayutthaya to Recent Times.* Bangkok: River Books, 2005.

Tsuneda, Michiko. "Navigating Life on the Border: Gender, Migration and Identity in Malay Muslim Communities in Southern Thailand." Ph.D. diss., Department of Anthropology, University of Wisconsin, 2009.

Wheeler, Matt. "People's Patron or Patronizing People? The Southern Border Provinces Administrative Centre in Perspective." *Contemporary Southeast Asia* 32 (2010): 208–33.

Yusuf, Imtiyaz, ed. *ASEAN Religious Pluralism: The Challenges of Building a Socio-Cultural Community.* Bangkok: Konrad Adenauer Stiftung, 2014.

———. "Religious Diversity in a Buddhist Majority Country: The Case of Islam in Thailand." *International Journal of Buddhist Thought & Culture* 3 (2003): 131–43.

INDEX

Aidilfitri (festival marking end of
Ramadan fast and the tenth day of the
eleventh lunar month), 10, 41n1
Al-Kahfi (pseudonym), 83–90
Allah, xxv, xlixn40, 23, 99; blessings from,
67; not enlisted for political ends,
xl–xli; plan for the world to be just, xl;
prayers to, 29, 65, 70, 102, 127–28, 129,
130; test from, xl, 26, 31, 46, 47–48, 65,
69, 74, 92, 96, 97, 103, 126–27, 130–31,
134; trust in, xl, 5, 48, 51, 73, 90, 92, 95,
129, 133, 134
Ananda, King (Rama VIII), xxvi–xxvii
Anglo-Siamese Agreement of 1909, xxv
anicca (impermanence), xli
Aree, Srawut, xxix–xxx
Attaturk, Kamal, xxvi
Ayutthaya (early modern capital), xxiii

Bangkok, ix, xxii, xxv, xxxii, 7, 8, 67, 100,
121; Bangkok declaration of human
rights in 1993, xlvin4; Bangkok Remand
Prison, 29; as pivot of the *mandala*,
xxii–xiii; Thai media as sycophantic, xxi
Barisan Revolusi Nasional (BRN), ix,
xxviii
Behind the Smile, xiii, xvin1, 115
Bodu Bala Sena ("Army of Buddhist
Power" in Sri Lanka), xxxvi
British, colonial presence in Burma and
Malaya, xxv
Buddhism: Buddhist victims of insurgent
violence, 52–63, 108; mindfulness, 54;
sangha, xxxviii; shared practices and
peaceful living with Muslims, xl–xli,
xlvin3, xlixn41, 52, 57, 61, 77, 105–6;
understanding of theodicy, xl, 62;
Western and modernist understandings
of, xix, xlv–xlvin1
Buddhist militancy, xvii–xviii; conflicts
with Muslims in Sri Lanka, Myanmar,

and Thailand, xlvii; fears about Muslim
insurgents, xlix, 61–62, 106; militancy in
Sri Lanka and Myanmar, xxxvi; militant
monks, xxi; *sangha* cooperation with
Thai military, xlvin6
Burmanization, compared to Thainess,
xxxvii

Chaibun, Liam, 60–63
Chakri dynasty, xxii
Chapakia, Ismael Lufti, xxviii–xxix
Chamnankij, Khamnueng, 64–70
Charoenphiriya, Nari, Centre for Peace
Study and Development, Mahidol
University, 21, 80
Chelae, Hasana, 132–37
Che'nae, Saimah, 45–51
Cheuma, Masta, 27–31
Chiang Rai, xxxv
Cho Ro Bo (uniformed village security
team), 75–76
Chulalongkorn, King (Rama V), xxv;
modernizing reforms of, xxii
cikgu ("teacher"), 134
Civic Women's Network, 22, 24, 36–37, 44,
49–50, 59, 69, 108–9, 115, 122, 129, 134,
136; about, xiii–xiv, 141–42

Dao, Roshida, 1–9
Deep South conflict: victims of, xiii, 5,
52–59, 108; violent deaths attributed
to, x, xiii. *See also* Kru Se Mosque;
Pongkhanmoon, Chuling; Tak Bai
Dhammakaya (modern Buddhist sect),
aggressive presence in Deep South, xli
doa (supplication to Allah,) 5
Doloh, Subaidah, 97–104
drug dealers, 74
dukkha (suffering, unsatisfactoriness), xl

European Union, xv

147

CPSIA information can be obtained
at www.ICGtesting.com
Printed in the USA
LVHW102324070123
736642LV00004B/519